HUMAN RIGHTS

A Wholistic Revision of the U.N. International Covenants

ABOUT THE AUTHOR

Dr. James Vadackumchery, Criminologist & Advocate, M.A. (Crim.), D.Ph., LL.B., Ph.D., First rank holder for B.A. (Crim.) of Karnatak University and M.A. (Crim.) of Saugor University, 2nd rank holder for LL.B. (Law) and D.Ph. examinations; Ph.D. in Criminal Justice (Kerala University), Gold Medalist and National Merit Scholarship Winner (twice).

An author of more than 70 authoritative research books in the special areas of Police, Crime and Justice and 1000 articles— research and popular—in professional journals, newspapers and periodical publications of repute.

Member of many professional organizations; Visiting Professor in universities and institutions of higher learning, research and training including Reserve Bank of India, National Judicial Academy etc.; Member, Board of Studies in Criminology of Karnatak Saugor and Calicut Universities and State Advisory Board on Correctional Administration, Member, State Prison Review Committee (Kerala), Consultant to Police Welfare Commission, Public Speaker and Human Rights Activist, Broadcaster over AIR and Telecaster in Indian and International T.V. networks and a constant Consultant to the media (print and electronic) on criminological and human rights issues, Criminologist on the Faculty of the State Police Training College, Thiruvananthapuram for nearly three decades, now a practising lawyer.

Examiner in Universities, Service Commissions and Public Undertakings, Evaluator of research works and theses and supervising teacher for Ph.D. degree in Kerala and Mahatma Gandhi Universities.

A name in the International Dictionary of Biographies of the IBC, Cambridge, the recipient of the Distinguished International Scholar Award for Life time Achievements-2003 of the American Society of Criminology, a name listed in the Limca Book of Records-2006 for authoring most books in crime, police and justice and a personality honoured by the University of Calcutta with Suprabha Deb Gold Medal-2007. Recipient of the Award of Excellence by the Archdiocese of Changanassery, 2007 and a PROFILE viewed by 5 per cent of 200 million people in Linked in during 2012.

HUMAN RIGHTS

[A Wholistic Revision of the U.N. International Covenants] ICCPR & ICESCR

Dr. James Vadackumchery
Criminologist & Advocate

CONCEPT PUBLISHING COMPANY PVT. LTD.
NEW DELHI-110059

ISBN-13: 978-93-88937-28-3

First Published 2019

Published and Printed by:

Concept Since 1974

Concept Publishing Company Pvt. Ltd.
A/15-16, Commercial Block, Mohan Garden,
New Delhi-110059 (INDIA)
T : 25351460, 25351794
E : publishing@conceptpub.com, *W* : www.conceptpub.com

Cataloging in Publication Data--Courtesy: D.K. Agencies (P) Ltd. <docinfo@dkagencies.com>

Vadackumchery, James, author.
Human rights : a wholistic revision of the U.N. International Covenants : ICCPR & ICESCR / Dr. James Vadackumchery.
pages cm
Includes bibliographical references and index.
ISBN 9789388937283

1. International Covenant on Civil and Political Rights. (1966 December 16). 2. International Covenant on Economic, Social, and Cultural Rights. (1966 December 16). 3. Human rights. I. Title.

LCC K3240.V33 2019 | DDC 341.48 232323

To
My Parents
My Wife
My Daughters

Foreword

It's great to be great, but it's greater to be human—These words of W. Rogers came to **my** mind when I started to write an **Introduction** to this book. I know that the human rights are not humanitarian rights, but in many cases, they can be one and the same. 'Humanitarian rights' emerge from the ***Essence of Man,*** while 'Human Rights' hail from the ***'Existence of Man'.*** Yes, 'No person should be denied equal rights because of the colour, smoothness or beauty of his/her skin. Human rights are the rights to life, equality, liberty and dignity.'

Right to life: 'Every man's life is a plan of God'—Horace Bushnell felt so even before the Universal Declaration of Human Rights came into existence on 10th December, 1948. Every man is born to live and no one can deny life to another. This is what the Principle of Human Rights always says. **Right to liberty** is a human right. Mahatma Gandhi said: "No man loses his freedom except through his own weakness" and the human rights laws endorse the same. **Right to Equality** and that is what is seen in Rigveda 2, 13-2: "All who can walk are equally entitled to the use of paths and road".

According to Swami Ram Tirath:

> "If we look through all the earth, Men, we see, have equal birth. Made in one great brotherhood; Equal in the sight of God, The Good. Food or castle or place of birth cannot alter human worth".

The concept of human right existed ever since the man is born in the world. He had several rights, but they were not known as 'human rights' then. Right to Dignity is a human right and, Aristotle (384-322 B.C.), in the long past, believed in the dignity of man. He said: 'Dignity consists not in possessing honours but in the consciousness that we deserve them.' Massinger added: "True dignity is never gained by place, and never lost when honours are withdrawn."

U.N. Universal Declaration of Human Rights has been in existence for the last 7 decades and I feel that during the long period (since 1948) of its existence, the movement of human rights has been spreading all over the world. I think that –

Human rights speak in tender voice;
But are heard in spite of the noise.
Human Rights see simple beauty;
And find everyone worthy.

There are Declarations, Covenants, Conventions, Principles and Rules to ensure human rights to all.

Human Rights' ways are true and kind;
Anyone can easily understand them;
Human Rights break ties and fetters
Of Castes, Colour, Creed and Letters.

I say so always whenever I give lectures on Human Rights. In my considered view-

Human rights are the sharpest weapon
with which any heart can open; can be cut.
Human Rights are like the blazing sun
that gives light to every nation.
-Yesterday, today and always the same –

With these thoughts, I want to revise the two International Covenants on Human Rights. Human Rights Justice must be administered though the world may perish as a result—is my view on the subject. For, ***'Of all the virtues, justice is the best'*** and ***'Human Rights Justice is nothing but truth in action'.***

Preface

A Covenant is just an agreement. In common parlance, it is usually a formal agreement between two or more persons to do or not to do something specified. The **Covenant** with Noah, the Patriarch who built a vessel in which he, his family and animals of every species survived the flood (Genesis, 5-9, Old Testament) was, perhaps, the first and the oldest Covenant in human history. It contained the promises made to man by God, as revealed in the Sacred Scripture. To quote:

"God spoke to Noah and his sons. See, I establish my Covenant with you, with your descendants after you; also with every living creature to be found with you, birds, cattle and every wild beast with you; everything that came out of the ark, everything that lives on the earth. I establish my Covenant with you: nothing of flesh shall be swept away again by the waters of the flood. There shall be no flood to destroy the earth again."

Further God said:

> *"Here is the sign of the Covenant I make between myself and you and every living creature with you for all generations. I set my bow in the clouds and it shall be a sign of the Covenant between me and the earth."*

These words in the Old Testament (Sacred Scripture) had in later years got acceptance in law to mean 'a formal agreement of legal validity esp. one under seal.' This legal term—i.e., the **Covenant** has very special and specific meaning—both in the **(1)** ***International Covenant on Civil and Political Rights (ICCPR); (2) International Covenant on Economic, Social and Cultural Rights (ICESCR).***

If the commitment was then between God and Noah and every living creature with him for all generations in the Sacred Scripture, the Covenant here—i.e., ICESCR—commits its parties to work toward the granting of economic, social and cultural rights —i.e., ESCR to its parties as well as to the Non-Self-Governing and Trust Territories and individuals including labour rights and the right to health, the right to education and the right to an adequate standard of living. As of 2015, the Covenant has 164 parties. A further six countries, including the United States of America have signed, but not ratified the Covenant. Again, if the commitment in the Old Testament was between God and Noah, every living creature with him, the Covenant here—i.e., ICCPR—makes its commitment to the parties to respect the right to life, freedom of religion, freedom of speech, freedom of assembly, electoral rights and rights to due process and a fair trial. As of February, 2017, this Covenant has 169 parties and six more signatories without ratification. India signed the Covenants on 27th day of March, 1979 with certain amendments made therein.

Today we have the **UDHR, ICCPR and ICESCR.** The UDHR, otherwise known as the Universal Declaration of Human Rights is a Declaration adopted by the General Assembly of the United Nations on 10, December, 1948 at the Palais de Chaillot in Paris, France. The Declaration arose straightly and directly from the experience of the World War II, and represents the first universal expression and global consensus of what most people believed to be the inalienable birth rights to which all human beings are inherently entitled. The full text is given as Appendix-1. Nearly 70 years are over now and I found that the 1948 UDHR needed a thorough revision. I contacted the United Nations asking them to make a total revision of the Declaration to suit to the changed and changing situations for a new world order. But, I did not get any response from the U.N. and therefore, I revised the Declaration at my level and the draft prepared by me was published under the title **U.N. Universal Declaration of Human Rights and Criminal Justice: The Total Revision** (ISBN: 13-978-81-8069-912-2) in 2012.

The book received incredible appreciation from various quarters through **Linked In** and I felt that I did a good work for the cause of a new world order. Following the total revision of the UDHR—i.e., the new draft has 56 Articles instead of 30 in the 1948 Declaration—I wanted to make a complete revision of the two Covenants immediately. For, I knew that a Declaration on the essential Rights of man had been proposed at the 1945 San Francisco Conference which led to the founding of the United Nations. Subsequently the Economic and Social Council was given the task of drafting the above stated Declaration on the Essential Rights of Man. Accordingly, the above document was split into a Declaration stating the general principles of human rights and a Convention/Covenant containing binding commitments. As we know, the former evolved into Universal Declaration of Human Rights and it was adopted, as said above, on 10th, December 1948. A total revision of the same has been published by me now for international debate and discussion.

The drafting continued on the Convention/Covenant, but there remained significant differences and different opinions among the members of the United Nations on the relative importance of negative civil and political versus positive economic, social and cultural rights. In fact these eventually caused the Convention to be split into two separate Covenants—namely, one to contain civil and political rights and the other to contain economic, social and cultural rights.

When I saw the appreciation for my total revision of the UDHR, I thought that I must devote my whole time and full energy for revising as many UN Conventions, Principles and Rules before I bring out a complete revision a ICESCR and ICCPR. Thus the revised documents by me are:

In volume I—

(i) Convention against Torture and other Cruel, Inhuman or Degrading Treatment or Punishment,

(ii) Principles on the Effective Investigation and Documentation of Torture and other Cruel Inhuman or Degrading Treatment or Punishment,

(iii) Principles on the Effective Prevention and Investigation of Extra-legal, Arbitrary and Summary Executions, and

(iv) U.N. Code of Conduct for Law Enforcement Officials.

About the above volume I, it has been written by me that the antique, dilapidated or rusted Conventions, Declarations, Rules, Principles, Codes etc. of the United Nations need periodic amendments, revision, alterations, deletions and repeallings. Sometimes, they must be replaced by another. Most unfortunately that does not take place. An academic assessment of the existing U.N. documents on human rights and their relevance and validity in the changing and changed scenario must be periodically done to update the contents. In my considered opinion an appraisal of the U.N. documents is the need of the hour.

In volume II, one sees the revision of —

- **(v) Principles for Protection of All Persons under Any Form of Detention or Imprisonment,**
- **(vi) Declaration of Basic Principles of Justice for Victims of Crime and Abuse of Power,**
- **(vii) U.N. Blue Book for Law Enforcement Officials,**
- **(viii) Basic Principles on the Role of Lawyers, and**
- **(ix) Principles of Medical Ethics.**

About this volume II, I wrote: "Human Rights of Detainees and those housed in a Centre for Personality Development (Prisons), Victims of Crime, Abuse of Power, Misuse of Authority or Non-use of Power and/or Authority etc. need periodical revision and amendment. United Nations, it is alleged, do not do it once they have adopted a resolution. An appraisal of the above mentioned U.N. documents will be of great value for all who wish for a new world order.

When I was doing my masters degree in Criminology (1973-'75), I studied the Standard Minimum Rules for the Treatment of Prisoners. At that time, I had a feeling that the Rules were more western-oriented. The prisons, prison atmosphere, prison administration are, to some extent, different in Asian, African or Arab countries. As such, I wanted to give a complete revision of the Rules and a book titled **United Nations and Prison Justice: The Complete Revision of the Standard Minimum Rules for the Treatment of Prisoners** (ISBN: 13: 978-81-8069-961-0) was first published in 2014. About the book, I wrote: "The U.N. Standard Minimum Rules for the Treatment of Prisoners had nearly a century of history behind. It was indeed humanitarian in approach to prisoners. Nearly 60 years have elapsed since the Rules were accepted by the United Nations. Certainly, the Rules need a revision now because of (i) a long lapse of six decades, and (ii) developments in the field of correction, reformation, resocialization, rehabilitation and reintegration of the inmates in a Centre of Personality Development (as the prisons are now called by me in the revision) to society back. The book contains a complete revision of the existing UNSMR for the Treatment of Prisoners. From 1970, international debates (discussions) are going on the subject. The book will be of great interest for anyone concerned with the protection of human dignity, to exclude cruelty, neglect and degradation to the inmates in a Centre of Personality Development and in particular, to minimize, the effect and impact of isolation or segregation from the community, whatever be the offence committed.

Thus after revising altogether 11 U.N. documents which no one has so far done individually, I am now making an attempt to fulfill my dream project by revising the remaining two International Covenants on human rights. For, the International Bill of the Human Rights comprised of them too. They elaborated on the rights on the basis of the principles set for in the UDHR-1948. ICESCR entered into force on January 3, 1976 and the ICCPR on 23, March 1976. The **Preamble** of both the Covenants are the same and so is the case with Articles 1, 3 and 5. Nevertheless, the two international Covenants have come for very sharp criticisms by many throughout the world. One of the main criticisms was that the human rights, by their very nature could not be universal because of the simple reason that there existed a lot of differences from region to region—from State to State in view of the economic, social, cultural, civil and political conditions of the people living there. That is the precise reason why the States adopt regional Conventions of Human Rights. The European Convention on Human Rights, American Convention of Human Rights, African Charter on Human and Peoples' Rights and the Arab Charter on Human Rights etc. are instances in point. They are discussed in this book along with Asian Human Rights Charter. All of them are given in the Appendices to this book. Whatever may be the criticisms against the UDHR, International Covenants, the truth may be accepted that the International Bill of Human Rights has given a unique and singular service for the promotion and protection of human rights throughout the world. Many States (more than 75% of the States) have already ratified the Covenants, nevertheless there are demands from various quarters to effect necessary changes periodically to suit to the needs of the time. The two Covenants are very much criticized for their omissions of certain rights—say, those relating to property, rights which everyone seeks and enjoys in other countries' asylum from persecution etc. What is seen today may be of interest for those who are concerned with the enforcement of human rights. It may be noted that a formidable hurdle in the effective implementation of the two Covenants on Human Rights is that even those States which have signed and ratified them, have not specifically adopted them via their legislative enactments for application in the internal or State level. Even in India, only the provisions of the International Covenants which are consistent with part III of the Constitution containing fundamental rights are enforceable or are enforced. Section 2(d) of the Protection of Human Rights Act-1993 defines human rights as "rights relating to life, liberty, equality and dignity of the Individual guaranteed by the Constitution or embodied in the International Covenants and enforceable by Courts in India"

When I look at the Covenants from India—with the eye of a criminologist and a jurist from my culture and beliefs, I find that they need a through revision. In my view, the Covenants should understand the language of the people in developing countries too with their problems and difficulties. My opinion is that a thorough overhauling of the Covenants with amendments, alterations, deletions etc. is a must today. The Covenants have almost outlived their utility and purpose now. Human rights seen in the Covenants are very much the natural rights of man and some of such rights were not fully identified by the makers of the Covenants at the time they were adopted. The natural rights which were not identified then must be added whenever they are identified subsequently. This is not seen in the case of United Nations and I advocate firmly that the proposal must be accepted/recognized by the United Nations urgently.

Human rights were in existence before the United Nations came into being. They were the rights of mankind and the international law accepted them as fundamental rights even before World War II. Such rights were guaranteed to individuals both at home and abroad and whether they were the nationals of a State or were Stateless. Such rights of mankind then comprised of the right to life, liberty, freedom of religion and conscience and the like. When the United Nations was formed, the rights identified to be fundamental rights, i.e., the rights of mankind till then, were reaffirmed and more rights were added to them. I too urge the United Nations to add more and more rights of mankind (here, human rights) to the existing ones taking into account the ground realities seen in various parts of the world. Such an approach is taken throughout the history of man. Actually, it is found that the Greeks gave birth to natural laws. Sophocles (495?-406? B.C.) and Aristotle (384-322 B.C.) engaged themselves in this sphere. Indian mysticism is full of such natural rights. Romans elaborated the concepts of natural rights of mankind. They had the ***Jus Civil*** to begin with and later they developed another legal system called ***Jus Gentium*** which was considered to be the law of universal application. In the republican era of Rome, the ***Jus Gentium*** was reinforced by natural law which is otherwise called ***Jus Natural*** as was generally known. The natural law embodied the principles of justice which were the dictate of right reason. John Locke (1632-1704), the English Philosopher said that the human beings existed in a state of nature where men and women were in a state of freedom. They were able to decide their actions. In such a state of equality—in such a state of nature, no one was subjected to the will or authority of another. According to John Locke, people entered into a contract in order to avoid certain hazards and inconvenience of the state of nature, i.e., some sort of social contract whereby men and women mutually agreed to from a community and set up a body politic. Here, they retained certain natural rights—say right to life, liberty and property. It was the duty of the Governments to recognize, respect and protect the natural rights of its subjects. However, the concepts of natural law, natural rights etc. underwent many changes in different periods in accordance with time, situations and needs. This is what is argued when I say that the United Nations' International Covenants should undergo a thorough revision at this changed circumstances. Positivism, Marxism, man's dignity, equality, respect, enlightenment, morality, ethics, spirituality, victimology, equal justice, holistic justice etc. have a say in these days when human rights are recognized. My attempt here is to give due importance to all these aspects when the Covenants are revised and I think that I have done full justice to what I feel is just and fair.

This book takes into account –

(i) U.N. Universal Declaration of Human Rights (UDHR).
(ii) U.N. International Covenant on Economic, Social and Cultural Rights (ICESCR).
(iii) U.N. International Covenant on Civil and Political Rights (ICCPR).
(iv) European Convention on Human Rights (ECHR).
(v) African Charter on Human and People's Rights (BANJUL CHARTER).
(vi) Arab Charter on Human Rights (ACHR).
(vii) ASEAN Human Rights Declaration (AHRD).
(viii) Asian Human Rights Charter (AHRC).
(ix) American Convention on Human Rights (PACT of San Jose).

Just go through the Preamble and the rights guaranteed by the above instruments. One may see then that-

(a) Some rights are global and they are for all people anywhere in the world.
(b) Some rights are global only if and if only some changes, amendments, restrictions, conditions etc. are put. As such, they are not universal as they are treated now.
(3) Some are regional which means that the people in that sector or area do consider them as inalienable birth rights for them. They cannot live without them. Such rights are seen in Regional Conventions/Charters/Declarations.

Necessarily it follows that the instruments require periodical amendments. There is the immediate need to revise the two International Covenants as they are older than half a century now. They were drafted by experts who, mostly, belonged to a particular hemisphere and they did not necessarily know fully well what was happening in the other hemisphere. Mere knowledge is not enough. What is required is the direct experience of the denial of human rights. Doubtlessly, experience is the best teacher and my humble attempt is to make amendments to the existing International Covenants by adding, deleting and effecting some changes to the presently existing instruments. I know that it is not that easy for the United Nations to revise the instruments as an attempt will take a lot of time and labour. U.N., being a world body, needs the help and ratification from the Member States and it is indeed a herculian task to bring the Nations together for revising the International Covenants. I found the same difficulties and problems when I revised the UDHR, Standard Minimum Rules for the Treatment of Prisoners and other nine U.N. documents enumerated above.

Every instrument of human rights has a retrospect—a history and background. The background would have certainly influenced the framers of the instrument to think in a special way and form the concepts in a specified manner. The UDHR and the two International Covenants have a background. The former, as stated above, came into being in 1948 and the latter in 1966. Certainly many decades have elapsed since they came into existence. 70 year old UDHR was, as pointed out earlier, revised by me and the draft was put up for international debate and discussions. I have been engaging myself at the heavy task of revising the two International Covenants for decades and I feel satisfied today when I see the revised draft for public discussion.

Ever since the UDHR and the two International Covenants were adopted, there were regional criticisms everywhere. Thus came into being the **ECHR, Banjul Charter, ACHR, Pact of San Jose and AHRD.** For example, the Asian struggle for human rights and fundamental freedoms has deep historical roots—in the fight against oppression in civil society. There was the political oppression of colonialism and later democracy was established or restored. Precisely therefore, there arose the need for new enactments. There have been rapid changes everywhere and such changes affected the social structures, political institutions and their economy. New technologies came and resultingly political authorities, economic organizations were forced to manage the changes causing new forms of developments. The marketization and globalization of economics caused changes between the private and the public, the State and the International community. As a result, one sees the worsening of the situations of the poor, disadvantaged and the economically handicapped. The traditional values were threatened. Consequently, there came the dehumanizing effects of technology. One finds here (i) material orientation of the market, (ii) destruction of the community, (iii) people having decreasing control over their lives and environment, (iv) lack of protection even against eviction from their traditional homes and grounds. The workers are exploited in a massive way—they are given wages that are frequently inadequate even for meeting their bare needs. The safety standards are found to be low and there is the worst situation of workers doing their job under constant danger. Even the most elementary of labour rights and laws are rarely enforced.

There is poverty. At the same time, there is the growing affluence among some sections of the people. Levels of health, nutrition and education of a large/very large numbers of people are distressing and appalling and one notices everywhere a tendency of denying the dignity of man and human life. The natural resources are depleted most irresponsibly and resultingly the quality of life has worsened immeasurably. The poor are neglected and the disadvantaged are uncared. In some countries, there is ultra-nationalism, perverted ideologies, ethnic differences, fundamentalism of all religions, fanaticism of many kinds. Violence erupts from both the State and sections of civil society. There is little or no security of person for large masses. There is little security of property or community. The number of refugees goes beyond human calculations/imagination.

Governments in some countries enact legislations to suppress the people's rights and freedoms. They collude with foreign firms and groups to plunder the national resources. Corruption and nepotism are seen everywhere and there is little or no accountability for those holding public or private power. There is no transparency in many things. Authoritarianism, in some States, has been raised to the level of national ideology, with the denial and deprivation of the basic rights and fundamental freedoms of their citizens. There is the wild exhortation of spurious theories of 'Asian Values' which are found to be a thin disguise for the authoritarianism. Asia is without a regional official Charter or other regional arrangements for the protection of their rights and freedoms. At the same time, the people in those countries become increasingly aware of the importance of human rights and fundamental freedoms. According to them, political and economic systems must operate within a frame work of human rights and fundamental freedoms to ensure economic justice, political participation, accountability, transparency and social peace. Respect for human rights provides the basis for a caring society. The result is the **ASEAN Human Rights Charter.**

The two International Covenants need, as repeatedly said, revision now, because the situations in which they were adopted have changed a lot. It is in 1948 that victimology has formally come into being and ever since one notices the demand for victim justice every where. Following the acceptance of the victim justice, a variety of justice came up and today, we have gender justice, sex justice, domestic justice, victimological justice, juvenile justice, justice to the old and the infirm, social justice, economic justice, cultural justice, holistic justice, equal justice, justice to the handicapped, just justice, administrative justice, political justice, bureaucratic justice and the litany goes on. 48 kinds of justice have been identified by me so far and we need the U.N. instruments which take into account all these concepts contained in very many kinds of justice. That is the reason why I insist that a total revision of the International Covenants becomes the need of the hour. This is a humble attempt to achieve that noble objective.

I am to thank my daughter Neethu, her loving husband Abhilash Varghese Koikara and her children Anna, George and Ammu for providing a very conducive atmosphere in River Vale, San Kang, Singapore to write this book in a congenial atmosphere. My wife Mary and I carried a bundle of literature collected over several decades to Singapore for writing this book and I remember all of them with a lot of love and concern. Concept Publishing Company (Pvt.) Ltd., New Delhi published all my revisions of the U.N. Declarations, Conventions, Principles etc. and I thank the Publishing Company for bringing out the unique contributions in print.

June 7, 2019 **Dr. James Vadackumchery**
Thiruvananthapuram Criminologist & Advocate

Contents

PART-1

Universal and Regional Documents on Human Rights

1. UNIVERSAL Declaration of Human Rights
2. EUROPEAN Convention on Human Rights
3. AFRICAN Charter on Human and People's Rights
4. ARAB Charter on Human Rights
5. ASEAN Human Rights Declaration
6. ASIAN Human Rights Charter
7. AMERICAN Convention on Human Rights.

Chapter 1
Universal and Regional Documents on Human Rights

UNIVERSAL DECLARATION OF HUMAN RIGHTS

"Justice is the constant desire and effort to render to every man his due"—this Justinian thought is reflected in Universal Declaration of Human Rights. Human Rights Justice is real justice with wisdom. Live and let live is the rule of human rights justice. The history of man is, no doubt, a history of human rights violations. Nevertheless, every man has great faith in human rights justice. Like the sun, it may be clouded/can be clouded by some power, yet can never be extinguished. If there was no human rights protection in this world, I am sure that many people would have committed suicide by this time.

History of the Universal Declaration of Human Rights

Four Freedoms—i.e., Freedom of speech, freedom of religion, freedom from fear and freedom from want were adopted by the Allies during World War II as their basic war aims. The Charter of the United Nations categorically stated and "reaffirmed faith in fundamental human rights, and dignity, and worth of human person" and further committed all Member States to promote "universal respect for, and observance of, human rights and fundamental freedoms for all without distinction as to race, sex, language and religion." After the World War II, the Nazi Germany continued to commit atrocities and when they became very apparent and unbearable, the consensus within the world community was the U.N. Charter which did not clearly and sufficiently define the rights to which it referred. Resultingly, a Universal Declaration that clearly specified the rights of man was necessary and inevitable to give due effect to the Charter's provisions on **Human Rights.**

Creation and Drafting

United Nations' Economic and Social Council established the Commission on Human Rights in June 1946. The said Commission consisted of 18 members from different nationalities and political backgrounds. The Commission on Human Rights was to undertake the task of preparing what was initially conceived as an **International Bill of Rights.** The Commission established a special drafting Committee for Universal Declaration of Human Rights chaired by Eleanor Roosevelt. The Committee met in two sessions over a period of two years.

John Peters Humphrey (Canada) was to work on the project and he became the Declaration's principal drafter. Other members of the drafting Committee were (i) Rene Cassin (France), Charles Malik (Lebanon), P.C. Chang (Republic of China, Taiwan). Humphrey provided the initial draft which became the working text of the Commission. The Commission found that there were divergent opinions about its contents. The Commission therefore decided to draft a Declaration of general principles. Simultaneously the Commission wanted a draft Convention containing specific rights treating legally binding obligations. Again, it was further decided to consider the question of implementation. Thus, these three documents, namely—

(1) International Declaration of Human Rights,
(2) International Covenant on Human Rights,
(3) Measures of Implementation—came into existence and they thus formed the Bill of Human Rights.

Then the draft Universal Declaration of Human Rights was considered by the Commission on Human Rights at its third session held in June 1948. The Commission finally adopted the draft Declaration of General Principles. The same was submitted to the Economic and Social Council (ECOSOC Council) which in turn adopted a resolution relating to the draft Declaration without vote and then submitted it to the General Assembly. The UDHR was finally adopted by the General Assembly (Gen. Ass. Resolution 217-A (111) of 10 December, 1948) by a vote of 48 to nil with eight abstentions. Thus, the UDHR was applauded as a **historic event of profound significance** of the United Nations. The year 2008 marked the 60th anniversary of the Declaration and it is now more than 70 years since the Declaration was adopted.

No doubt, the Declaration has influenced many national Constitutions since 1948. Ever since, the Declaration has been serving as the foundation for a growing number of national laws, international laws, treaties and for a growing number of regional, sub-national and national institutions protecting and promoting human rights. The Declaration has served as the foundation for two binding Covenants, viz.,

(1) The International Covenant on Civil and Political Rights (ICCPR), and
(2) The International Covenant on Economic, Social and Cultural Rights (ICESCR).

There was praise for the Universal Declaration since its adoption in 1948. Eleanor Roosevelt said that "it may well become the international Magna Carta of all men every where". Pope John Paul II (October 5, 1995) called the UDHR: "one of the highest expressions of human conscience of our time." While appreciating the views and opinions of a number of notable dignitaries from many parts of the world since 1948, I, for one, found it really good, but it becomes necessary to revise the 1948 Declaration to suit to the needs of the present world. Concurrently with the praise for the Declaration, there were criticisms too. Even on 10 December, 1948 when the UDHR was adopted by the General Assembly, there were 8 abstentions. They were (i) the Soviet Union, (ii) Ukrainian SSR, (iii) Byelorussiam SSR, (iv) People's Federal Republic of Yogoslavia, (v) People's Republic of Poland, (vi) Union of South Africa, (vii) Chechoslovakia and (viii) the Kingdom of Saudi Arabia.

Honduras and Yemen—both members of the UN at that time—failed to vote or abstained. Why? South Africa wanted to protect the system of apartheid. It clearly violated any number of Articles in the UDHR. Saudi Arabia has its reasoned objections. Article 18 of UDHR was about the right "to change the religion and belief." Again Article 16 UDHR was on equal marriage rights. Six communist nations' abstentions were due to the view that the UDHR did not go far enough in condemning Facism and Nazism.

Criticism from Islamic Countries

As said above, Saudi Arabia abstained from ratification vote on UDHR. They said that the Declaration violated *Sharia* Law. Iran found that the UDHR was 'a secular understanding of the Judeo-Christian tradition' and they argued that they could not implement the Declaration without conflict with *Sharia*. The members of the organization of the Islamic Conference (presently, it is called Organization of Islamic Co-operation) on June 30, 2000 officially resolved to support the Cairo Declaration on Human Rights in Islam. According to them, the people have freedom and right to a dignified life in accordance with the *Islamic Shariah* without any discrimination on grounds of race, colour, language, sex, religious belief, political affiliation, social status or other considerations.

Many scholars and human rights activists have openly criticized or expressed their concern with the UDHR's alleged western bias. I too have similar views as I find that we do not see any serious considerations given to Indian, Asian, African or Arab concepts of human rights by the UDHR. Human rights are seen in Indian mystical thoughts and the sages expressed them in very many ways. Since, I could not see many Indian Vedic thoughts in the UDHR, I brought out a book titled ***United Nations and Indian Mysticism: Parallels on Human Rights and Police*** (ISBN: 81-7022-664-2) and I said firmly and emphatically that the UN Declarations and Conventions on human rights were actually rooted in Indian mysticism. Indian mystical revelations and UN Declarations separated by thousands of years are one and the same on some aspects. The book brought out the parallels on human rights and police as they were seen in Indian mysticism and U.N. Declaration.

In Indian mysticism, the inner self is called ***Atman*** which is

Brahman immanent in man. This is in essence the basis of human rights everywhere. ***Dharma*** in Indian mysticism signifies man's obligation which includes respect for human rights and the dignity of man. The United Nations repeatedly voice against ***Adharma*** which is nothing but violation of human rights. While I appreciate the fact that UDHR contain—knowingly or unknowingly—some of the Indian mystical concepts, I do not think that the UDHR was influenced significantly by Indian mysticism. Both UDHR and Indian mystical thoughts are intended to lead people to reality, light and immortality. In my opinion, the modern human rights concept is an offshoot, though a flourishing one, of the Indian mystical parent tree. But, the UDHR did not give due consideration. Precisely therefore I wanted to revise the UDHR and a book titled—**UN Universal Declaration of Human Rights & Criminal Justice: The Total Revision**—was published. About the Book, it is written: "More than long sixty years have elapsed since the United Nations brought out the Universal Declaration of Human Rights (UDHR-1948) with high ideals and concepts for a spectacular new world order. It contained 30 Articles and certainly, it needed a revision—a total revision—in the changing and already changed situations. This is an attempt—or a good beginning towards that lofty and sublime end. Thirty Articles in the UDHR-1948 have now been revised totally and there are 56 in the new text." The question is: "Have the Articles in the UDHR-1948 become sterile and ineffective for their meaningful implementation today?" In my view, the western bias is too much in the UDHR-1948. In my view, the **Universality** of the assumptions on which the human rights concepts are based is at best suspicious—and in every way subject to questioning. Faisal Kutty, a renounced scholar in human rights says: *"A strong argument can be made that the current formulation of international human rights constitutes a cultural structure in which western society finds itself easily at home. It is important to acknowledge and appreciate that other societies may have equally valid alternative conceptions of human rights."*

A total revision of the UDHR means a total revision of the International Covenants too. I purposefully delayed the revision although they too derived their views basing on the general principles given in the UDHR-1948. As the UDHR-1948 is the fundamental constitutive document of the United Nations, it is seen that the Declaration forms part of the customary international law. No doubt, it is a very powerful and effective tool in applying diplomatic and moral pressure to Governments that violate any of the Articles in the Declaration. As said earlier, the Declaration is the foundation for the two binding Covenants. The principles are elaborated in international treaties like **(1) the International Convention on the Elimination of All Forms of Racial Discrimination, (2) the International Convention of the Elimination of Discrimination Against Women, (3) the UN Convention on the Rights of the Child, (4) The UN Convention against Torture** and many more. The Declaration continues to be elaborately quoted by Governments and cited by courts, advocates and academics. Hence, I thought that I must revise a number of UN documents before I venture to revise the two International Covenants. It took nearly 40 long years for revising the documents enumerated in the preface of this book. This revision of the International Covenants may be the last which I may do in this sphere. I think that I did a good work. Appendix I in this book gives UDHR in its original form.

EUROPEAN CONVENTION ON HUMAN RIGHTS

The **European Convention on Human Rights** (ECHR) which was earlier known as the **Convention for the Protection of Human Rights and Fundamental Freedoms** is an international treaty to protect human rights and fundamental freedoms in Europe. It was signed at Rome on November 1950 and entered into force on 3, September, 1953. All council of Europe Member States are party to the **Convention** and new members are expected to ratify the Convention at the earliest available opportunity.

The Convention established the European Court of Human Rights (ECtHR). Any individual who feels that his/her rights are violated under the Convention by a State party can/may take the matter before the Court. The verdict of the Court is binding on the States Parties concerned. The States Parties are obliged to execute the judgments of the Court.

A Committee of Ministers of the Council of Europe monitors the execution of the verdicts—especially to ensure the payment of the amounts verdicted by the Court of the litigants in compensation for the damages they have sustained.

History of European Convention

The ECHR have played an important, unique and vital role in the development and progress of Human Rights awareness in Europe. A regional system of human rights protection was developed by this and it is found to be a direct response to two concerns—namely, (i) After the World War II, Universal Declaration of Human Rights came into being on 10, December 1948. Though it was said to be universal, some countries refused to accept it to be universal. They wanted regional Conventions and it could be seen as part of a wider response to the Allied Powers in delivering a human rights agenda through which it was thought that the most serious human rights violations which had taken place during the world war II could be avoided in future, (ii) Communism in Central and Eastern Europe was growing rapidly at that time and the Convention was a response to the growth of communism then. The Convention was intended and designed to protect the Member States of the Council of Europe from communist subversion.

ECHR* was drafted by the Council of Europe after the World War II. Over 100 parliamentarians from 12 Member States of the Council of Europe gathered at Strasbourg, in 1949 (summer) to draft a Charter of Human Rights and to establish a Court to enforce it. Subsequently a Convention was drafted and a report was submitted to the Council's Consultative Assembly proposing a list of human rights to be protected. Of course, the Universal Declaration of Human Rights was of great help for the drafting of ECHR and defining how the enforcing judicial mechanism might operate. There were heated and extensive debates. Finally, the Assembly sent its final proposal to the Council's Committee of Ministers. The Committee of Ministers convened a group of experts to draft the Convention itself. The Convention was opened for signature on November 4, 1950 at Rome. It was ratified and entered into force on September 3, 1953*. The Convention was drafted in broad terms—in a similar

---

* There were 22 parties to ECHR. They were: Austria, Belgium, Cyprus, Denmark, France, Germany, Greece, Iceland, Ireland, Italy, (*Contd....*)

manner to the ***English Bill of Rights,*** the ***U.S. Bill of Rights,*** the ***French Declaration of the Rights of Man*** etc.

Articles in the Convention

The ECHR consists of three parts—say:

- **(1) Part 1** (Section I): *Main Rights and freedoms [Articles 2 to 18]*
- **(2) Part 2** (Section II): *Setting up of the Court and its rules of operation (Articles 19-51)*
- **(3) Part 3** (Section III): *Various concluding provisions.*

Article 1—Respecting Rights

Under Article I of the ECHR, the States Parties to the Convention undertake to secure to everyone within their jurisdiction the rights and freedoms defined in section I of the Convention. Thereafter, Section I enlists and defines the rights and freedoms as under:

- *(1) Article 2:* Right to life
- *(2) Article 3:* Freedom from torture etc.
- *(3) Article 4, Para 1:* Freedom from slavery or servitue
- *(4) Article 4, Para 2:* Freedom from forced or compulsory labour.
- *(5) Article 5, Para 1:* Right to liberty and security of person etc.
  Para 2: Arrested person to be brought before a judge etc.
  Para 3: Right of victims of arrest etc. for victimological compensation.
- *(6) Article 6, Para 1:* Right to a fair and public hearing etc.
  Para 2: Presumption of innocence etc.
  Para 3: Certain specified minimum rights.
- *(7) Article 7:* Non-retroductive application of criminal law etc.

Contd.... Liechtenstein, Luxembourg, Malta, the Netherlands, Norway, Portugal, San Marino, Spain, Sweden, Switzerland, Turkey and United Kingdom.

(8) *Article 8, Para 1:* Right to respect for private and family life etc.
(9) *Article 9:* Right to freedom of thought etc.
(10) *Article 10, Para 1:* Right to freedom of expression etc.
(11) *Article 11, Para 1:* Right to freedom of peaceful assembly etc.
(12) *Article 12:* Right to marry etc.
(13) *Article 13:* Right to have an effective remedy.
(14) *Article 1, Protocol 1:* Right to the peaceful enjoyment of one's possessions.
(15) *Article 2, Protocol 1:* Right to education.
(16) *Article 3, Protocol 1:* Right to have free elections etc.
(17) *Article 3, Protocol 4:* Right not to be expelled from a State.
(18) *Article 4, Protocol iv:* Freedom from collective expulsion from a State.
(19) *Article 7, Protocol 6:* Abolition of death penalty.
(20) *Article 2, Protocol 7:* Right to review a conviction by a higher court.

The full text of the ECHR is given as Appendix-2. It is made very clear in Article 14 of the Convention that the enjoyment of the rights and freedoms ensured in the Convention shall be guaranteed or secured without discrimination on any grounds—viz., sex, race, colour, language, religion, political or other opinion, national or social origin, association with a national minority, property, birth or other status.

About Life, Torture, Servitude etc.

Article 2 protects the right to one's life. However, this right is applicable only to human beings and never to non-human animals or to 'legal persons' such as corporations. There is a court decision stating that the life does not extend to human embryo—to unborn child etc. Article 2 is applicable to (i) the right for life (ii) the right to preserve life and (iii) take life to preserve life. It means that the State has three main duties under Article 2. They are:

(a) a duty to deabstain from unlawful killing.
(b) a duty to investigate suspicious deaths.

(c) a positive duty to stop or prevent foreseeable loss of life in certain circumstances.

Article 15, para 1 provides that during the time of war or public emergency threatening the life of the nation, any High Contracting party may take measures derogating from its obligations (under ECHR) to the extent strictly required by the exigencies of the situation, provided that such strategies or measures are not inconsistent with its other obligations under international law. It may be pointed out that no derogation shall be permissible under this provision from Article 2, except in case of death resulting from unlawful acts of war or from Articles 3, 4 (para 1) and 7.

Article 3 prohibits torture and inhuman or degrading treatment or punishment. The prohibition is made in absolute terms and irrespective of the victim's conduct. Article 4 prohibits slavery, servitude and forced labour. Nevertheless, it exempts labour:

(i) done as normal part of incarceration/imprisonment.
(ii) in the form of compulsory military service etc.
(iii) required to be done during a state of emergency and
(iv) considered to be a part of an individual's normal civic obligations.

About Liberty, Security and Fair Trial

Article 5 is about liberty and security of person. They are taken as a 'compound concept'. Of course lawful arrest and detention are permitted, although Article 5 provides the right to liberty. Of course, the arrested have a right to be informed, in the language they understand, of the grounds/reasons for the arrest. They have a right to be informed of any change they face along with the right of prompt access to judicial proceedings. They are aimed at to understand the legality of the arrest, detention, imprisonment etc. They have a right for a fair trial within a reasonable time or release pending trial. Of course they do have a right for victimological compensation if the arrest or detention is in violation of this Article.

What is a fair trial? Article 6 is about it. It provides a detailed right for a fair trial for a public hearing before an impartial and independent tribunal within a reasonable time. There is the presumption of innocence. Of course, those charged with a criminal offence have a right to get adequate time and facilities to prepare their defence, access to legal representation, right to examine and cross-examine witnesses and right to make use of the assistance of an interpreter free of cost etc. Whatever may be the rights under the Convention, the ground reality is that there take place excessive delays in violation of 'reasonable time' requirement, in civil and criminal proceedings before the national courts.

The right to examine witnesses and cross-examine witnesses against those charged with a criminal offence is very much affected by violations concerning the 'confrontation clause'. Here, the problem of compliance with Article 6 may come up when national laws permit the use in evidence of the testimonies of absent, anonymous and vulnerable witnesses.

About Retroactivity, Conscience and Religion

Retroactive criminalisation of acts and omissions are prohibited by Article 7 of ECHR. Retroactive means 'operative with respect to past occurrences, as a statute'. In other words, no person shall be punished for an act that was not an offence at the time he committed. The Article also prohibits a heavier (very grave) penalty being inflicted than was applicable at the time the offence was committed. In other words, the Article recognizes the principle in jurisprudence that ***nullum crimen, nulla poena sine lege*** in the Convention.

Everyone has his/her private and family life, his/her home and correspondence and Article 8 provides a right to respect them. However, this right can be enjoyed subject to certain restrictions which are 'in accordance with law' and necessary in a democratic society. It means that the Article provides a right to be free of unlawful searches. Of course, there is protection for private and family life.

About Conscience and Religion

Article 9 of the ECHR provides a right to freedom of thought, conscience and religion. This includes one's freedom to change a religion or faith or belief and to express or manifest a religion or belief in worship, teaching, practice, observance and promotion. Nevertheless, they are subject to certain restrictions that are 'in accordance with law' and 'necessary in a democratic society.'

About Expression, Association

Article 10 of ECHR is about the freedom of expression and provides the right to it subject to certain restrictions which are in 'accordance with law' and 'necessary in a democratic society'. This right includes the freedom to hold opinions and to receive and impart information and ideas, but permits restriction for—

(i) interests of national security.
(ii) territorial integrity or public safety.
(iii) protection of health or morals;
(iv) prevention of disorder or crime;
(v) protection of the reputation or the rights of others;
(vi) preventing the disclosure of information received in confidence; and
(vii) maintaining the authority and impartiality of the judiciary.

Article II provides the right to freedom of assembly and association. It also includes the right to form trade unions, subject to certain restrictions which are *in accordance with law and necessary in a democratic society.*

About Marriage

Article 12 is about the right for men and women of marriageable age to marry and establish a family. However, uni-sex marriages are not so far recognized. The Articles is applicable to 'different sex marriages' and as such the Article protects only 'different sex' couples. Can we call uni-sex marriages to be marriages at all? Marriage is intended for procreation of children and their upbringing. In uni-sex marriages, no children is born. Then what about the marriages of the transgender community or the hermaphrodites?

About Effective Remedy

Article 13 is for an effective remedy and therefore provides for the right for an effective remedy before national authorities for violations of rights under ECHR. The inability to obtain a remedy before a national court for an infringement of a right conferred under ECHR is thus a free standing and separately actionable infringement of the Convention.

About Discrimination

Discriminating people on certain grounds is a serious problem everywhere in the world and precisely therefore, Article 14 of ECHR is about prohibition of discrimination. Some critics say that the prohibition is broad while many others subscribe to the view that it is narrow. Those who attest the view that it is broad always argue that it prohibits discrimination under a potentially unlimited number of grounds. The Article 14 certainly and specifically prohibits discrimination based on 'sex, race, colour, language, religion, political or other opinion, national or social origin, association with a national minority, property, birth or similar status.' Nevertheless, the criticism is that the Article 14 does not extend its protection to many other grounds not specifically mentioned such as has been done relating to discrimination based on an individual's sexual orientation, denomination, sect in religion etc.

About Derogations

Derogate means to detract as from authority, estimation etc. Article 15 of ECHR permits contracting States to derogate from some rights guaranteed by the Convention and it is allowed in time of war or other public emergency threatening the life of the nation. The derogations allowed under Article 15 must satisfy the following three substantive conditions, namely—

(i) there should be a public emergency which threatens the life of the nation.

(ii) any measures or strategies taken in response must be 'strictly required by the exigencies of the situation'.

(iii) the measures or stratagems taken in response to it must be in compliance with the State's other obligations under the international law.

The above requirements are substantive. Nevertheless, in addition to those substantive requirements, the Article insists that the derogation must be procedurally sound. There should be some formal announcement of the derogation and the notice of the derogation. Any measures/stratagems taken under the Convention and the ending of the derogation must be communicated to the Secretary General of the Council of Europe.

It is noticed that eight Member States had ever invoked derogations (as of 2016). It may be specially mentioned that the Court is very permissive in accepting a State's derogations from the Convention. Yet, it applies a high or very high degree of scrutiny in deciding whether or not the measures/stratagems adopted by the States under a derogation are, according to Article 15—i.e., in words of the said Article strictly required by the exigencies of the situation.

In order to decide that a derogation was valid, the emergency giving rise to it must:

(i) Be actual or imminent (here the States do not have to wait for disasters to strike before taking preventive measures/stratagems).
(ii) Involve the whole nation (here, a threat confined to a specific or particular region/area may be treated/ considered as 'threatening the life of the nation' in that special or particular area).
(iii) Be such that the organized life of the community must be threatened and it should be the continuance of the organized life there.
(iv) Be exceptional such that measures and restrictions permitted/allowed by the Convention would be 'plainly inadequate' to deal with the emergency.

About Aliens

Article 16 of ECHR is about **Aliens** and it allows the States to restrict the political activity of foreigners. The Court ruled that the Member States of European Union could not consider or treat the nationals of other Member States to be **Aliens.**

About Abuse of Rights

Abuse of right is a serious matter, for, abuse means to use wrongly or improperly. Article 17 says that no person may use the rights guaranteed by the Convention to seek the abolition or limitation of rights guaranteed in the Convention. Instances are reported that the States, sometimes, seek to restrict a human right in the name of another human right. No. That is not permitted. Article 17 addresses such instances and instances where individuals rely on a human right to undermine other human rights. An individual issuing a death threat may be one example in point.

About Permitted Restrictions

Article 18 is about permitted restrictions and it provides that any limitations on the human rights provided for in the Convention may be used only for the sole purpose for which they are provided. An instance may be quoted. Article 5 of ECHR guarantees the right to personal freedom. This right may be explicitly limited in order to bring a suspect before a judge. The use of pre-trial detention as a means of intimidation of an individual under a false pretext is doubtlessly a limitation—a limitation of right to freedom. This does not serve an explicitly provided human right—i.e., to be brought before a judge-and precisely therefore is contrary to Article 18 of ECHR.

ECHR (1950) is eulogized as the first important **Regional Convention** on human rights. No doubt, this goes beyond the **Universal Declaration of Human Rights** and gives effect to civil and political rights provided therein by binding commitments. The Convention defines civil and political rights in precise terms and thus clarifies the contents well by adding exception, limitations and restrictions to which such rights are subjected. The Convention also provides a machinery for the implementation of human rights—viz., (i) The Commission, (ii) The Court, (iii) The Committee of Ministers.

International Covenant on Civil and Political Rights has

established a Human Rights Committee. The United Nations have the Human Rights Commission. It has been observed that the Commission established by ECHR is more effective and successful than the above said bodies of the ICCPR and United Nations. The Commission established under ECHR makes efforts for securing a friendly settlement of the matters. In case a settlement is not reached, the Commission transmits its report including their suggestions, recommendations and proposals as they think to the best to the Committee of Ministers. Actually this Committee of Ministers is the executive or political organ of the Council of Europe and as such, it is a strong body which has the authority to decide whether or not there has been a violation of the Convention. If it decides affirmatively, it prescribes a period within which the contracting parties concerned must make measures/stratagems required by the Committee of Ministers. It is empowered to decide what effect shall be given to its original decision. The Committee publishes its report. The decision of the Committee of Ministers is binding on States Parties as they have a binding obligation to the decision of the Committee of Ministers. In fact, the International Covenant on Civil and Political Rights does not have a similar body having any teeth.

There is the European Court of Human Rights. Of course individuals as they are—as such have no access to the Court. Only the Commission or the States Parties can bring a case to the Court. The parties to the case are bound by the decision of the Court. However, there are some drawbacks for ECHR. The Commission receives many applications and most of them are not admitted under the Convention. This is primarily because of the failure to exhaust domestic remedies, lapse of time, incompatibility with the provisions of ECHR etc. Once the application is found to be inadmissible, the procedure for its reconsideration involves great delays and a lot of money, labour and time.

AFRICAN CHARTER ON HUMAN AND PEOPLE'S RIGHTS

The African Charter on Human and People's Rights (also, known as the Banjul Charter) is an international human rights instrument (Adopted in Nairobi, June 27, 1981 and entered into force on October 21, 1986) that is aimed at/intended to promote and protect human rights and basic freedoms in the African continent. How did the Charter come into being? The African States found the European Convention on Human Rights—ECHR and the American Convention on Human Rights. They wanted a similar instrument. Hence, the African Charter on Human and People's Rights emerged under the aegis of the Organisation of African Unity (this is replaced by African Union) which at its 1979 Assembly of the Heads of the States and Governments adopted a resolution for drafting a human rights instrument. The resolution was for the creation of a committee of experts to draft a continent-wide human rights instrument in the model or similar to those which already existed in Europe (ECHR) and the Americas. They found the importance of regional Charter and the Committee thus set up produced a draft. The draft was unanimously approved at the OAU's 1981 Assembly. The African Charter on Human and People's Rights came into effect on October 21, 1986. Like December 10 is celebrated as the Human Rights Day by the United Nations, the Africans honour 21, October as the 'African Human Rights Day'.

In 1987, African Commission on Human and People's Rights was set up and the Commission was given the task of interpreting the Charter. The Commission is now headquartered in Banjul, Gambia. A **Protocol** of the Charter was adopted in 1998 whereby an African Court on Human and Peoples' Rights was to be created. The **Protocol** came into effect on 25, January 2004.

The African Union Assembly decided, on July 2004, that the African Charter on Human and Peoples' Rights would be incorporated into the African Court of Justice. It took time for the Court to come into effect. Therefore, in July 2005, the African Union took a decision that the Charter should be operationalized despite the fact that the Protocol establishing the said Court had not yet come into being or come into effect. Accordingly, the Executive Council of AU (Eight ordinary session meeting in Khartoum, Sudan) elected the first judges of the African Court on Human and Peoples' Rights on January 22, 2006. Nevertheless, the relationship between the newly created Court and the Commission is not yet decided. As of 2016, 54 States have ratified the Charter and it has been ratified by every

African Union State.

Nations throughout the world wanted and insisted upon creating regional human rights system. It was so because people in different parts of the world had their own specific and special needs. The African Charter on Human and People's Rights followed the foot-steps of (i) ECHR and (ii) Inter-American systems. The AU wanted to have a regional human rights system for Africa. As such and naturally the Charter shares many features with other regional human rights instruments. At the same time, the Charter has notably very specific and unique characteristics concerning the norms it recognizes.

The Preamble commits to the elimination of Zionism. Zionism is a world-wide Jewish movement for the establishment in Palestine of a national homeland for the Jews. The Preamble compares Zionism with colonialism and apartheid.

What are the norms contained in the Charter on Human and Peoples' Rights? The Charter accepts and recognizes most of what are accepted and recognized universally as the civil and political rights.

Civil and Political Rights

The Civil and Political rights recognized by the Charter include—

- *(i) Articles 2 and 18 (3):* Right to freedom from discrimination.
- *(ii) Article 3:* Equality.
- *(iii) Article 4:* Life and personal integrity.
- *(iv) Article 5:* Dignity, freedom from slavery, freedom from cruel, inhuman or degrading treatment or punishment.
- *(v) Article 6:* Rights to due process concerning arrest and detention.
- *(vi) Articles 7 & 25:* Right to a fair trial.
- *(vii) Article 8:* Freedom of religion.
- *(viii) Article 9:* Freedom of information and expression.
- *(ix) Article 10:* Freedom of association.
- *(x) Article 11:* Freedom to assembly.
- *(xi) Article 12:* Freedom of movement.
- *(xii) Article 13:* Freedom to political participation.

(xiii) Article 14: Right to property.

There is a view among the human rights scholars that the Charter does not cover civil and political rights elaborately and as such the coverage is inadequate. According to the critics, for example, the right to privacy or a right against forced or compulsory labour are not clearly and explicitly recognized. Again, the provision concerning fair trial and political participation are far away from being complete. They are considered incomplete by international standards. Nevertheless, there exist arguments against such views as well.

For examples—

(i) Article 5 of the African Charter is: "Every individual shall have the right to the respect of the dignity, inherent in human being and to the recognition of this legal status. All forms of exploitation and degradation of man, particularly, slavery, slave trade, torture, cruel, inhuman or degrading punishment and treatment shall be prohibited."

Again see the Article 15 which reads: "Every individual shall have the right to work under equitable and satisfactory conditions, and shall receive equal pay for equal work."

A reading to the above Articles will convince us to think that every type of forced or compulsory labour (although it is not very manifestedly or explicitly stated) is not allowed. Likewise, the African Charter does not explicitly recognize the right to vote as a means of political participation. At the same time, Article 13 of the Charter says: (1) Every citizen shall have the right to participate freely in the Government of his country either directly or through freely chosen representatives in accordance with the provisions of law.

(2) Every citizen shall have the right to equal access to the public service of his country.

(3) Every individual shall have the right to access to public property and services in strict equality of all persons before the law.

About Economic, Social and Cultural Rights

What does the African Charter tell about the economic, social and cultural rights? No doubt, the Charter recognizes some economic, social and political rights. The Charter is found to give due and considerable emphasis to these rights. For examples—

(1) *Article 15:* The right to work is recognized.
(2) *Article 16:* The right to health is recognized.
(3) *Article 17:* The right to education is recognized.

The right to housing and a right to food are understood to have been included in the Charter (see, the decision by the African Commission on Human and People's Rights, Serac v. Nigeria (2001) in an implicit way). In this context, we may assess the rights in the light of the Charter's provision on 'Right to Life (Article 4), Right to health (Article 16) and Right to development (Article 22)'.

About People's Rights and Group Rights

What are the Peoples' Rights? What are the Group Rights? The Conventions, Covenants, Charters etc. do recognize individual rights. The African Charter recognizes collective or group rights or people's rights and third generation human rights. One may not see or find such recognition of group rights, people's rights etc. either in the European (ECHR) or in the Inter-American (Americas) regional human rights instruments. Look at—

(1) *Article 18:* Awarding family protection by the State.
(2) *Article 19:* People have the right to equality.
(3) *Article 20:* Right to self-determination.
(4) *Article 21:* Right to freely dispose of their wealth and natural resources.
(5) *Article 22:* Right to development.
(6) *Article 23:* Right to peace and security.
(7) *Article 24:* Right to a generally satisfactory environment.

The special feature or characteristic of the African Charter is that it awards rights not only to individuals and peoples, but also it includes duties incumbent upon them. Article 29 contains these duties and they are as under:

(i) The duty to preserve harmonious development of the family.
(ii) To serve the national community by placing both physical and intellectual abilities at its service.
(iii) Not to compromise the security of the State.
(iv) To preserve and strengthen national independence and the territorial integrity of one's country and to contribute to its defence.
(v) To work to the best of one's abilities and competence and to pay taxes in the interest of society.
(vi) To preserve and strengthen positive African cultural values and in general to contribute to the promotion of the moral well-being of the society.
(vii) To contribute to the best of one's abilities to the promotion and achievement of African unity.

Certainly, the African Charter has many merits over the International Covenants. The concept of Group Rights, People's Right and Duties etc. are noval and are pregnant with meanings. The full text of the African Charter on Human and People's Rights may be seen in Appendix-3 of this book.

ARAB CHARTER ON HUMAN RIGHTS

The Arab Charter on Human Rights—otherwise known as ACHR—(Adopted by the Council of the League of Arab States on 22 May 2004) affirms the principles contained in UN Charter, U.N. Universal Declaration of Human Rights, U.N. International Covenants on Human Rights (ICESCR and ICEPR) and Cairo Declaration on Human Rights in Islam etc. Of course, the ACHR provides a number of traditional human rights and obviously, they include (i) the right to liberty, (ii) the right to the security of persons, (iii) the right to equality of persons before the law, (iv) the right for protection of persons from torture etc, (v) the right to own private property, (vi) the right to freedom to practise religious observance, and (vii) freedom of peaceful assembly and association.

The Arab Charter provides for the election of a Seven Person Committee of Experts on Human Rights to consider the States' reports. Interestingly enough, the first version of the Arab Charter was ready on 15th, September 1994, but no State ratified it. It took a decade more and the Charter was updated in 2004. It came into force in 2008 when seven of the members of the League of Arab States ratified it.

In the Preamble of the Charter, it is written: 'Given the Arab nations belief in human dignity since God honoured it by making the Arab world the cradle of religions and the birth place of civilizations which confirmed its right to a life of dignity based on freedom, justice and peace, pursuant to the eternal principles of brotherhood and equality among all human beings which were firmly established by the Islamic Sharia's and the other divinely-revealed religions,.' The Charter rejects racism and Zionism which according to it constitute a violation of human rights and pose a threat to world peace. The Charter has four parts and they are—

Part I: Article 1 (a) & (b),
Part II: Articles 2 to 39,
Part III: Articles 40 to 41 (1), (2) and (3),
Part IV: Articles 42 to 43.

There are 22 Member States of the League of Arab States and they are Jordan, United Arab Emirates, Bahrain, Tunisia, Algeria, Dijibouti, Saudi Arabia, Sudan, Syrian Arab Republic, Somalia, Iran, Oman, Palestine, Qatar, Comoros, Kuwait, Lebanon, Libyan Arab Jamahiriya, Egypt, Morocco, Mauritania and Yemen.

Part I

Article 1: Right of self-determination and it condemns racism, Zionism, occupation and foreign domination and make all endeavours to eliminate all such practices.

Part II

Article 2: No distinction on grounds of race, colour, sex etc.

and no discrimination between men and women.

Article 3: No restriction upon or derogation from any fundamental human rights recognized or existing in any State Party to the Charter and no derogation from the fundamental freedoms recognized and which are enjoyed by the nationals of another State that shows less respect for those freedoms.

Article 4: No restriction on the rights and freedoms deemed necessary to protect the national security etc., economy, public order, morals or the rights and freedoms of others, allowing to take measures derogating from the obligations etc. at the time of public emergency threatening the life of the nation.

Article 5: Right to life, liberty and security of person.

Article 6: No crime or punishment except as provided by law and no punishment for an act preceding the promulgation of that provision.

Article 7: Presumption of innocence in favour of the accused.

Article 8: Right to liberty and security of person.

Article 9: Equality before law.

Article 10: Imposition of death penalty only for most serious crimes.

Article 11: No death penalty for a political offence.

Article 12: No death penalty for juveniles (below 18 years of age), pregnant women, nursing mothers and so on.

Article 13: Protection from torture or cruel, inhuman or degrading treatment; also no medical or scientific experimentation on any person without his free consent.

Article 14: No imprisonment on one's proven inability to meet a debt/fulfill any civil obligation.

Article 15: Treating with humanity persons sentenced to a penalty of deprivation of liberty.

Article 16: No two trials for the same offence; right for victim compensation for those unlawfully arrested or detained.

Article 17: Right for privacy. The privacy includes private family affairs, the inviolability of home, confidentiality of correspondence etc.

Article 18: Right to recognition as a person before law.

Article 19: Right to political participation.

Article 20: Right to liberty of movement, freedom to choose a place of residence etc.

Article 21: No arbitrary or unlawful prevention to leave any

Arab country etc.

Article 22: No expelling from one's country or preventing from returning thereto.

Article 23: Right to seek political asylum in other countries to escape persecution etc.

Article 24: No arbitrarily depriving of one's nationality to acquire another nationality etc.

Article 25: Right to own private property.

Article 26: Right to freedom of belief, thought and opinion.

Article 27: Right to practice religious observances and no restrictions on the exercise of freedom of belief.

Article 28: Right to freedom of peaceful assembly and association, and no restrictions unless for national security, public safety etc.

Article 29: Right to form trade unions, right to strike.

Article 30: Right to work, comprehensive social security.

Article 31: Right to free choice of work, prohibition of forced labour etc.

Article 32: Right to enjoy equality of opportunity in regard to work, fair wages and equal remuneration for work of equal value.

Article 33: Right to access to public office.

Article 34: Right to education.

Article 35: Right to live in an intellectual and cultural environment in which Arab nationalism is a source of pride.

Article 36: Right to participate in cultural life etc.

Article 37: Minorities have a right to enjoy their culture.

Article 38: Right for care and special protection for family, mother, children and the aged.

Article 39: Right for young persons for opportunities for their physical and mental development.

Part III

Article 40: Election of the Committee of Experts and connected matters like the role of the Secretary General, term of office for Committee members, election of the chairman etc.

Article 41: Submission of the reports to the Committee of Experts on human rights etc.

Part IV

Article 42: The duties and functions of the Secretary General of the League of Arab States.

Article 43: Binding nature of the Charter and it reads: "Following its entry into forces, the present Charter shall become binding on each State."

The Charter is described as an arrangement for the promotion of human rights among Arab nations. No doubt that there is a growing realization of the fact that there are many advantages for regional Conventions and Charters over universalism. United Nations is a world body and precisely because of it, that universal organization has membership spread all over the world-comprising many and different regions which have different and various political, social and economic conditions and environments and state of development. It is accepted in fairness that respect for human rights and fundamental freedoms can be guaranteed only in countries having democratic traditions, rules and administration. The Vienna Declaration of Human Rights (1993) states that democracy, development and respect for human rights are interdependent and mutually reinforcing. Democracy is principally based on freely expressed will of the people—for the people, by the people and of the people to decide their own political, economic, social and cultural systems. It may be seen that the same is not possible in other systems of Government as monarchy, oligarchy, kingdoms, or even so-named dictatorship of the proletariat—i.e., the working class. The full text of the ARAB CHARTER is given in Appendex-4.

ASEAN HUMAN RIGHTS DECLARATION

Association of South East Asian Nations (ASEAN), in 2009, established the ASEAN Intergovernmental Commission on Human Rights to promote and propagate human rights in the ten ASEAN countries. By mid-2012, the Commission drafted the ASEAN Human Rights Declaration (AHRD) which was adopted unanimously by ASEAN Members in November, 2012 meeting held in Phnom Penh.

An overall analysis of the Declaration may show that the

first 5 Articles affirm that human rights belong to every person. They belong to all—women, children, older people, persons with disabilities, migrant workers, vulnerable and marginalized groups and so on. Article 10 affirms directly 'all the civil and political rights in the UDHR' and they are declared in Articles 11-25. Article 26 affirms all the economic, social and cultural rights in the Universal Declaration and they are seen in Articles 27 to 34.

The specialty of the ASEAN Human Rights Declaration is that it goes beyond the UDHR by making clear and explicit 'the right to safe drinking water and sanitation'. It is given in Article 28 E. Article 28 F is the 'right to safe, clean and sustainable environment'. Article 29 provides the right for protection from discrimination in treatment for 'all suffering from communicable diseases, including HIV/AIDS'. It may be noted that Article 36 provides the 'right to development aimed at poverty alleviation, the creation of conditions including the protection and sustainability of the environment'. Article 30 is all about the right to peace. All said and done, there are human rights activists and organizations which think that the ASEAN Declaration failed to include many key basic rights and fundamental freedoms. It may include even the right to freedom of association and the right to be free from enforced disappearances. A human rights organization called Human Rights Watch went to the extent of saying that the ASEAN Declaration is nothing but a 'Declaration of Government powers disguised as a Declaration of Human Rights.' Asian Civil society, Amnesty International, U.S. Department of State, U.N. High Commissioner for Human Rights etc. criticized the ASEAN Declaration in a negative way. Whatever that be, the U.S. Department of State and the U.N. High Commissioner for Human Rights welcomed the ASEAN Declaration, but with substantive reservations. In any case, it was doubtlessly an effort to develop a regional human rights declaration. Such efforts are the needs of the hour. Certainly, I am of the view that regional human rights systems must evolve and improve over time for the benefit of the people.

ASEAN (Association of South-East Asian Nations) countries are (i) Brunei Darussalam, (ii) Kingdom of Cambodia, (iii) The Republic of Indonesia, (iv) The Lao People's Democratic

Republic (v) Malaysia (vi) The Republic of the Union of Myanmar, (viii) The Republic of Philippines, (viii) The Republic of Singapore, (ix) The Kingdom of Thailand, and (x) The Socialist Republic of Vietnam. AHRD reaffirmed their adherence to the purposes and principles of ASEAN Charter, human rights, fundamental freedoms, democracy, rule of law and good governance, UDHR, Charter of the United Nations, the Vienna Declaration and programme of action and other international human rights instruments to which ASEAN Member States are parties. AHRD has further reaffirmed the importance of ASEAN's efforts in promoting human rights, including the Declaration of the Advancement of Women in ASEAN Region and the Declaration of on the Elimination of Violence against Women in the ASEAN Region. AHRD was convinced that the Declaration would help to establish a framework for human rights co-operation in the region and contribute to the ASEAN community building process.

AHRD has the following divisions, namely—

(i) General Principles.
(ii) Civil and Political Rights.
(iii) Economic, Social and Cultural Rights.
(iv) Right to Development.
(v) Right to Peace.
(vi) Co-operation in the promotion and protection of human rights.

Under General Principles come—

(i) Right to equality in dignity and rights.
(ii) Rights and freedom without distinction of any kind—say, race, gender, sex etc.
(iii) Right to recognition as a person before the law.
(iv) Rights of women, children and elderly persons and so on.
(v) Right to an effective and enforceable remedy.
(vi) Right to enjoyment of human rights and fundamental freedoms.
(vii) Realization of human rights in the regional and national context etc.

(viii) Exercise of human rights and fundamental freedoms subject to limitations determined by law.

(ix) Upholding of the principles of impartiality, objectivity etc. for the realisation of human rights.

Under civil and political rights come—

(x) Affirmation of all civil and political rights in UDHR.

(xi) Right to life.

(xii) Right to personal liberty and security.

(xiii) Right against servitude or slavery.

(xiv) Right against torture etc.

(xv) Right to freedom of movement and residence.

(xvi) Right to seek asylum in another State.

(xvii) Right to own, use, dispose property.

(xviii) Right to nationality.

(xix) Right to marry and found a family.

(xx) Right for the presumption of innocence of those accused of a crime.

(xxi) Right of ***ex post facto*** laws.

(xxii) Right against double jeopardy.

(xxiii) Right to be free from arbitrary interference with privacy, family etc.

(xxiv) Right to freedom of thought, conscience and religion.

(xxv) Right to freedom of opinion.

(xxvi) Right to freedom of peaceful assembly.

(xxvii) Right to participate in the Government.

(xxviii) Right to vote in elections.

Under ECONOMIC, SOCIAL AND CULTURAL RIGHTS come—

(xxix) Affirmation of all economic, social and cultural rights.

(xxx) Right to work.

(xxxi) Right to form trade unions etc.

(xxxii) Rights for children.

(xxxiii) Right to an adequate standing of living etc.

(xxxiv) Right to physical, mental and reproductive health etc.

(xxxv) Right to create a positive environment to overcome stigma, discrimination in the prevention, treatment etc.

of people suffering from communicable diseases.

(xxxvi) Right to social security.

(xxxvii) Right to mothers before and after child birth.

(xxxviii) Right of mothers and children.

(xxxix) Right to education.

(xl) Right to take part in cultural life.

(xli) Right for achieving progressively the full realisation of economic, social and cultural rights.

(xlii) Right to non-nationals.

Under Right to Development come—

(xliii) Right to development

(xliv) Right to meaningful people oriented and gender responsive development programmes aimed at poverty alleviation etc.

(xlv) Right to promote equitable and sustainable development, fair trade practices and effective international co-operation.

Under Right to Peace come—

(xlvi) Right to peace within ASEAN frame work of security and stability, neutrality and freedom etc.

Under Cooperation in the Promotion and Protection of Human Rights come—

(xlvii) Commitment to the promotion and protection of human rights.

(Xlviii) No undermining the purposes and principles of ASEAN, or at the destruction of any of the rights and fundamental freedoms.

The full text of AHRD is given in Appendix-5 of this book.

ASIAN HUMAN RIGHTS CHARTER

Asian Human Rights Charter is also known as **Peoples' Charter** which is declared in Kwangju, South Korea on 17, May, 1998 on the occasion of the 50th Anniversary of the Universal Declaration of Human Rights. It was part of an attempt to create in Asia a popular culture on human rights. Thousands of people from various Asian Countries and more than 200 non-governmental organizations (NGOs) participated in discussions and debates until atleast the Charter was drafted. Many NGOs and People's Organisations (POs) have endorsed the Charter.

The purpose of the Asian Charter on Human Rights was to deepen the Asian debate on human rights-and-to present the common man's views on human rights to people everywhere. There were many Asians who raised objections to the Universal Declaration of Human Rights and the two International Covenants. According to them, the human rights were not alien to Asia. They propagated the idea that the aim of their then existed international instruments of human rights was to promote their political, social and legal reforms for introducing their human rights concepts in Asian countries too. Asian Human Rights Commission said: "While drawing from the cultural wells of the region, it also points to the need for cleaning these wells that have been polluted by millenniums of prejudice, discrimination, inequality and violence."

Asian Human Rights Charter has the following contents—namely, 1. Preamble, 2. Background to the Charter, 3. General Principles, 4. Universality and Indivisibility of Rights, 5. The Responsibility and Indivisibility of Rights, 6. The Responsibility for the Protection of Human Rights, 7. Sustainable Development and the Protection of the Environment, 8. Right to Equality and Dignity 9. The Right to Life, 10. The Right to Peace, 11. The Right to Democracy, 12. The Right to Cultural Identity and the Freedom of Conscience, 13. The Right to Development and Social Justice, 14. The Rights of Vulnerable Groups, Women, Children, Differently Abled Persons, Workers, Students, Prisoners and Political Detainees, 15. The Enforcement of Rights, 16. Principles for Enforcement, 17. Strengthening the Framework for Rights, 18. The Machinery for the Enforcement of Rights, 18. Regional Institutions for the Protection of Rights etc.

The Charter says that it:

1. endorses all the rights which are contained in international instruments and it is necessary to restore

them in Asia.

2. declares the right to life as the foremost among the rights. All other rights follow from the right to life and they are (i) right to live in dignity, (ii) right to livelihood, (iii) right to a habitat or home, (iv) right to education, (v) right to a clean and healthy environment.
3. prohibits propagation of war, ethnic conflict, incitement to hatred and violence in all spheres of individual or societal or national life.

The Charter says further that—

1. The States have the responsibility to thoroughly investigate cases of torture, disappearances and custodial deaths, rapes and sexual abuses to bring culprits to justice.
2. There must be no arbitrary deprivation of life and the States must abolish the death penalty-or where it exists, it must be imposed only rarely for most serious crimes. A fair trial, independent and impartial tribunal, legal representation by a lawyer of one's choice, adequate time for preparing the defence, presumption of innocence, the opportunity to review by a higher tribunal etc. must be guaranteed rights and the execution should never be carried out in public or otherwise exhibited in public.

'Right to Peace' must be ensured. It is very much needed because, one can fully develop in his capacity only if there is peace in society. Every person and group should be entitled to protection against all forms of State violence including all forms of violence perpetuated by police and military forces.

The Charter continues to say:

1. Security of all people especially that of the vulnerable groups should be respected and protected.
2. Natural environment, the political, economic and social conditions which allow people to satisfy their needs and aspirations without recourse to oppression, exploitation, violence etc. must be protected.

3. In the background of Asian States fighting fascist invasion, colonialism and neo-colonialism, demands of national integrity or protection against the threats of foreign domination are of great importance. Hence, it is emphatically stated that the right of persons to live in peace can be guaranteed only if the States are accountable to the international community.

Right to Democracy is of paramount importance to Asians. Colonialism and other modern developments, according to the Charter, changed the nature of Asian political societies. The citizens became subjects and the Governments became very powerful. There was the hangover of the colonial laws and authoritarian habits and style of administration persisted even after the independence in Asian countries. As a result, the States became sources of corruption and oppression of people. The democratization and humanization of the States is found to be a pre-condition for the protection and respect of human rights. People were to have the right to express their views. The rights of minorities were to be respected. The States ought to become humane, accountable, open and transparent. People have a right to participate in public affairs through the electoral and other decision-making, implementing and executing processes free from all sorts of discrimination based on sex, religion, race, colour etc.

Asian traditions are important and they stress the importance of common cultural identities which help the people to cope with the pressures of economic and social change—says the Charter. No doubt, the people of Asia and Governments must respect the cultures and traditions of its diverse communities.

Asians have a traditional concept of the family based on patriarchy. They guarantee women's human rights. There exists gender inequality in Asian countries and the Charter wants to reinterpret the religious beliefs supporting gender inequality. There exists discrimination based on castes/sub-castes, ethnic origins, occupation, place of origin and many more and the Charter wants to stop practices which promote discrimination. There should be mutual tolerance and support. The national solidarity must be enforced.

Asia has many religions and precisely therefore, there should be freedom of religion and conscience. People in general may be poor and oppressed and religion is a source of comfort and solace. There is religious extremism, fundamentalism, fanaticism, terrorism, insurgency in Asian countries and they are found to be a cause of divisions and conflicts. Religious tolerance is essential for the enjoyment of the right of conscience of others, which includes the right to change one's belief—says the Charter.

All persons and groups are entitled to share the benefits of the progress of technology and of the growth of the world economy. Besides and beyond the economic development, people have a right to artistic freedom, freedom of opinion and cultivation of their cultural and spiritual capacities—the Chater emphasises so.

By virtue of historical and other reasons, there exist groups which are vulnerable. Resultingly, they require special protection for equal and effective enjoyment of their human rights. They should not be discriminated and oppressed. Refugees, for example, come under this category. Minorities and indigenous too come under this category as their basic rights are frequently violated. There is discrimination against gays, transgender hermaphrodites and lesbians denying them their identity and causing them great anguish and misery—observes the Charter.

Women in most of the Asian countries suffer from discrimination and oppression. The history, social and economic systems may be responsible for the same. To quote from the Charter: *The roots of patriarchy are systematic and its structures dominate all institutions, attitudes, social norms and customary laws, religions and values in Asian societies, crossing the boundaries of class, culture, caste and ethnicity. Oppression takes many forms, but is most evident in sexual slavery, domestic violence, trafficking in women and rape. They suffer discrimination in both public and private spheres.* Doubtlessly, there is violence against women in Asia. They are denied of justice, rehabilitation, compensation and reparation of the war crimes against them. There exists discrimination in the field of employment, right to work, free choice of profession, job security, equal remuneration, right to compensation, protection of health and safe working conditions and the litany is very long.

They have a right against all these maladies. There is the need for legislations in this field. They have a right to participate in the political and public life. Women empowerment is essential for the defence of their legal rights—finds the Charter.

What about the children in Asia? Child labour, sexual slavery, child pornography, sale and trafficking of children, child prostitution, sale of organs, psychological abuse of children, conscription into drug trafficking, forced religious conversion etc. are seen in Asia. Widespread poverty, lack of access to education and social dislocation in rural areas are seen. They are exploited and abused. Bonded labour, use of children for begging or sexual gratification are rampant. There is female infanticide owing to patriarchal gender preference and female genital mutilation are widely practised in some Asian countries—observes the Charter.

How are the differently abled persons in Asian countries? Physically or mentally handicapped people suffer enormous discrimination in very many ways. They are unable to enjoy many of their human rights—especially to have access to education, employment and housing. They are not allowed to live in dignity with security and respect. Resultingly, they do not get opportunities to realize their full potential. They do have a right to live and die with dignity.

As far as the workers in Asia are concerned, the situation is really pathetic. Traditional forms of works have no place now amidst the rapid urbanization and industrialization. The workers go after wage employment, often, in industries working under abhorring and appalling conditions. No labour laws for their protection. The right to form trade unions may be denied and the wages are grossly inadequate and the working environment is loathsome and often grim and dangerous. Globalization affects the job market and adds to the pressures on workers. There is tight competition and the collusion is with foreign corporations and international financial institutions. The migrant workers are plenty. Some of them have broken family setup and they are exploited by foreign States. Usually the migrant workers do not know the laws of the foreign States or if at all they know them, they are very much afraid to invoke them. Therefore they are denied of their basic rights and conditions which the local workers enjoy. No accommodation, no health care, no sanitary environment, no drinking water, no food of nutritional value and no legal protection. The migrant workers are found to suffer from xenophobia. Domestic workers are subjected to humiliation and sometimes, sexual abuses. These are the issues which were not taken notice of by the framers of the Universal Declaration of Human Rights and the two International Covenants.

There are internationally accepted norms for prisoners and I have revised the **U.N. Standard Minimum Rules for the Treatment of Prisoners** to suit to the needs of the hour. In Asian countries, one observes massive violations of internationally recognized norms for prisoners and detainees. The prisoners, in my opinion, do not exist. They are people who need personality development in an upright way in the right direction.

Arbitrary arrest, illegal detention, forced imprisonment, ill-treatment, torture, cruel and inhuman treatment are seen everywhere in Asian countries. The prisoners and detainees live in horrible conditions and in unhygienic environments, without any food of nutritional value, without health care, with no facility for communication etc. All types of prisoners are mixed together in one cell—which may be overcrowded. Deaths in custody are frequent and the prisoners are denied to have access to lawyers. Thus, their right for fair and speedy trial is often denied. There is detention without arrest/trial. Political opponents are arrested misusing the provisions of national security legislations. The UDHR and the Covenants have no much value in some of the Asian countries.

The Constitutions of many of the Asian countries provide fundamental rights and have guarantees of human rights. Many of the Asian countries have ratified the UDHR and the two International Covenants. According to the Asian Charter, there continues to be a wide gap between rights enshrined in these documents and the reality that denies people their rights. No doubt, a total revision of the UDHR and the two International Covenants incorporating the needs of the countries in Africa, Asia, Europe, Australia and Arab States becomes the most important need of the present times. Asian Human Rights Charter is given in Appendix-6.

AMERICAN CONVENTION ON HUMAN RIGHTS

The American Convention on Human Rights—also called the **'Pact of San Jose'** is an instrument of international importance. (Adopted by many countries in the Western Hemisphere in San Jose, Costa Rica on 22, November, 1969) This international instrument came into force after the eleventh instrument of ratification (that of Grenada) was deposited on 18, July, 1978 (cf. *Wikipedia*).

Inter-American Commission on Human rights and the Inter-American Court of Human Rights—these two bodies have the responsibility for overseeing compliance with the American Convention on Human Rights. Both are organs of the Organization of American States (OAS).

What is seen in the Preamble? The Preamble says: The purpose of the Convention is *to consolidate in this hemisphere within the framework of democratic institutions, a system of personal liberty and social justice based on respect for the essential rights of man.*

American Convention on Human Rights was adopted seven months before the adoption of the Universal Declaration of Human Rights (UDHR) of the United Nations. The Bogota Charter of the Organization of American States (OAS), the American Counterpart of the Council of Europe, was adopted by the ninth Inter-American Conference in 1948. Besides establishing new bodies or institutions of the OAS, 1948, Bogota Conference also adopted the American Declaration on the Rights and Duties of Man. Doubtlessly, there existed some differences between the two instruments—namely the Universal Declaration of Human Rights and the American Declaration. It is seen that the UDHR contains only **Rights** and the American Declaration has **duties of man** as well. It is very interesting to note that there are as many as eight Articles dealing with the **duties of man** in the American Declaration. Twenty eight Articles provide the Rights of Man. Strangely enough, out of 30 Articles in UDHR, only one Article—say Article 29, deals with the duties of man.

The Bogota Conference requested the Inter-American Judicial Committee to prepare a Statute for the American Courts to guarantee the rights of man. The Committee recommended to the Judicial Council of the OAS to prepare a draft Statute for a

Convention on Human Rights. It was thought that such a Convention would involve a radical transformation of the constitutional system of American countries.

Five years after the 10th Conference of the American States, the meeting of the consultation of the foreign ministers established an Inter-American Commission on Human Rights. They requested the Juridical Council to prepare a draft Convention on Human Rights and a Statute of the Court of Human Rights. The Juridical Council thus prepared the draft Convention on Human Rights. This draft was considered at the second special Inter-American conference in Rio de Janiero in 1965. Two other drafts (one by Chile and another by Uruguay) were also considered.

The Conference referred those drafts to the Council of OAS. The Commission on Human Rights was formally recognized as a statutory organ of the OAS at Bones Airs (in the third special Inter-American Conference) in 1967. By 1968, the Commission prepared a draft Convention on Human Rights. In order to adopt this Convention, a special conference on Human Rights was called at San Jose, Costa Rica on 22, November 1969. The Conference thus adopted the **American Convention on Human Rights**. The Convention came into force in 1978. Like the ECHR (European Convention on Human Rights), the American Convention incorporates only civil and political rights.

Rights recognized under the Convention

The American Convention on Human Rights—1969 guarantees the following civil and political rights—

- *(i)* *Article 3*: The right to juridical personality.
- *(ii)* *Article 4*: The right to life.
- *(iii)* *Article 5*: The right to human treatment.
- *(iv)* *Article 6*: The right to freedom from slavery and involuntary servitude.
- *(v)* *Article 7*: The right to personal liberty.
- *(vi)* *Article 8*: The right to fair trial.
- *(vii)* *Article 9*: The right to freedom from *expost facto laws.*
- *(viii)* *Article 10*: The right to compensation for miscarriage of justice.

(*ix*) *Article 11*: The right to privacy.
(*x*) *Article 12*: The right to freedom of conscience and religion.
(*xi*) *Article 13*: The right to freedom of thought and expression.
(*xii*) *Article 14*: The right to reply.
(*xiii*) *Article 15*: The right to assembly.
(*xiv*) *Article 16*: The right to freedom of association.
(*xv*) *Article 17*: The right to family.
(*xvi*) *Article 18*: The right to a name.
(*xvii*) *Article 19*: The rights of a child.
(*xviii*) *Article 20*: The right to a nationality.
(*xix*) *Article 21*: The right to property.
(*xx*) *Article 22*: The right to freedom of movement and residence.
(*xxi*) *Article 23*: The right to participate in Government.
(*xxii*) *Article 24*: The right to equal protection before law.
(*xxiii*) *Article 25*: The right of judicial protection.

Both ECHR and the American Convention contain a non-discrimination provision. They guarantee the free and full exercise of the rights and freedoms without any discrimination on the grounds of race, colour, sex, religion, political or other opinion, national or social origin, economic status, births or any other social conditions. Both allow the States Parties to achieve progressively the full realization of the rights implicit in the economic, social, educational, scientific and cultural standards set forth. Both instruments allow the States Parties to suspend rights and freedoms in time of war, public or the emergency that threaten the security and independence of a State Party. They have a right to derogate from the obligations in such situations. Of course, there may be some conditions for derogation—i.e., the derogation must not be inconsistent with other obligations under the international law and that no discrimination is made on the ground of race, colour, sex etc. There are other conditions too for exercising the right of derogation. In other words, the States availing the right of derogation from obligations are not allowed to suspend certain specified rights and freedoms. They may be—

(i) The right to juridical personality (Article 3).

(ii) The right to life (Article 4).
(iii) The right to freedom from torture etc. (Article 5).
(iv) The right to freedom from slavery (Article 6).
(v) The right to freedom from *ex post facto* laws (Article 9).
(vi) The right of the family (Article 17).
(vii) The right to a name (Article 18).
(viii) The right of the child (Article 19).
(ix) The right to a nationality (Article 20).
(x) The right to participate in Government (Article 23).

Why is it so? The reasons are simple. Those **rights** are regarded and treated as so fundamental that no derogation will be permissible. Moreover a State Party which avails the right of derogation is required to inform immediately the other State Party/ies through the Secretary General of the OAS of the provisions it has suspended and application thereof. The date fixed for termination of such suspension must also be intimated.

In a nutshell, as a summary, it can be said:

1. Chapter 1 establishes the general obligations of the States Parties. They are to uphold the rights set forth in the Convention.
2. 23 Articles of Chapter II give a list of civil and political rights due to every person. They include—
   (i) The right to life.
   (ii) The right to human treatment.
   (iii) The right to a fair trial.
   (iv) The right to privacy.
   (v) The right to freedom of conscience.
   (vi) The right to freedom of assembly.
   (vii) The right to freedom of movement etc.

Article 15 of the Convention prohibits *any propaganda for war and any advocacy of national, racial or religious hatred that constitute incitement to lawless violence or to any other similar action against any person on any ground including those of race, colour, religion, language or national origin* to be considered as an offence punishable under law. Article 20 of the International Covenant of Civil and Political Rights has its influence for making such a provision.

Chapter IV is an important one as it provides the situations in which certain rights can be temporarily suspended. During a state of emergency, as said above, certain rights can be suspended following formalities which are valid for suspending the rights. Nevertheless, it does not allow or authorize any suspension of—

(1) *Article 3:* Right to juridical personality.
(2) *Article 4:* Right to life.
(3) *Article 5:* Right to human treatment.
(4) *Article 6:* Right to freedom from slavery.
(5) *Article 9:* Right to freedom from *ex post facto* laws.
(6) *Article 12:* Right to freedom of conscience and religion.
(7) *Article 17:* Right to family.
(8) *Article 18:* Right to the name.
(9) *Article 19:* Right of the child.
(10) *Article 20:* Right to nationality.
(11) *Article 23:* Right to participate in Government.

Chapter V emphasizes the fact that the individuals have rights as well as duties or responsibilities. There should be a balance between the rights and duties. They were enshrined in the earlier American Declaration of the Rights and Duties of man.

The Inter-American Commission based in Washington, D.C. (U.S.A.) and the Inter-American Court with its headquarters in San Jose, Costa Rica are two important bodies under the Convention. Hence, Chapters VI, VII, VIII and IX contain the provisions for the creation and operation of the two bodies for overseeing compliance with the American Convention. Finally, Chapter X deals with the mechanisms for ratifying the Convention. Various transitory provisions are set forth in Chapter XI.

Implementation of the Convention

As shown above, there are two specialized enforcement mechanisms, namely,

(1) Inter-American Commission of Human Rights.
(2) Inter-American Court of Human Rights.

The Inter-American Commission of Human Rights consists of 7 members. They are to be people of high moral character and integrity. They should possess recognized competence in the field of human rights (see, Article 34). The Inter-American Court of Human Rights, like the European Court of Human Rights, is not accessible to individuals. It is accessible only to the Inter-American Commission and to those States Parties which have expressly recognized its jurisdiction. The Court consists of seven judges who are jurists of the highest morality and integrity. They must possess recognized competence in the field of human rights. The ACHR is given in Appendix-7.

Looking into the regional Conventions, Charters, Declarations etc. we come to the conclusion that the Universal Declaration of Human Rights as well as the two International Covenants did not take into account the regional variations, changes and differences. India is not America and America is not Australia, Australia is not Africa. Africa is not Afghanistan and Afghanistan is not Canada. Arab nations are not European countries. Even in a single country, differences and variations are seen. What is seen in South America may not be seen in all countries alike in South America. What is noted in the northern part of Canada may not be seen in the South, West or East of Canada. Nevertheless, human beings live everywhere. As far as the **essence** of man is concerned, everyone living anywhere in the world has the same **essence** and in that way, everyone is alike every other one. As far as the **existence** of man is concerned, there are many differences among the people. One may be having the existence of a Hindu while another may have the existence of a Jew. There may be Christians belonging to many denominations just like the Muslims are seen in different sects or divisions. Different kinds of existence will be noticed in colour, creed, race, caste, sex, economy and in many other ways. Any universal instrument which does not take into account the various kinds of **existence** of man will not be universal. It can not be called international. Similarly, the **environment** will be different for each one. The social, cultural, economic, physical, political, educational environments are different. The environments seen in Arab nations may not be the environments noticed in American countries. The developed countries will have an environment different from the same found in developing countries. Any international instrument of human rights should take into account the **Essence, Existence and Environments (3 Es)** of the people and I doubt seriously that the two International Covenants on human rights that we have today are international at all! The framers of the International Instruments were not representing the various nations in the world. As a result, many nations—viz., Algeria, Bangladesh, Belgium, China, Egypt, France, India, Indonesia, Ireland, Japan, Kuwait, Mexico, Monaco, New Zealand, Norway, Pakistan, Thailand, Trinidad and Tobago, Turkey, United Kingdom etc. have made reservations and interpretative declarations to their application of the Covenant—**International Covenant on Economic, Social and Cultural Rights.** What were their reservations and interpretative declarations are given in the Chapter **ICESCR. The Complete Revision.** Again, Argentina, Australia, Austria, Bahamas, Bahrain, Bangladesh, Barbados, Belgium, Belize, Congo, Denmark, Gambia and United States had made reservations and interpretative declaration to their application of the Covenant namely, **International Covenant on Civil and Political Rights.** What are their reservations and interpretative declarations are given in the chapter **ICCPR: The Complete Revision.**

It may be specially noted that even in 1951 session (The Commission commenced the work of drafting articles on economic, social and cultural rights), there were differences of opinion. The draft of the Human Rights Commission was then submitted to ECOSOC Council for its consideration. During the consideration of the draft by ECOSOC Council, many countries, as pointed out earlier, did not like the idea of including of articles on economic, social and cultural rights, in the Covenant dealing with civil and political rights. Thus came into existence two Covenants—one dealing with civil and political rights and the other dealing with economic, social and cultural rights. Thus, in 1952, the Commission decided to prepare two draft Covenants (see, General Assembly Resolution 543 (vi) and 545 (vi), February 5, 1952). Thus came into existence two Covenants.

A study of the two Covenants will show that there exists some relationship between the two. Both Covenants contribute to **the ergo omens** principle. Both Covenants codified in treaty form the rights in UDHR. The States Parties cannot terminate both

Covenants once they are ratified. It is an obligation that cannot be denounced. Both Covenants believe in 'Collective right to self-determination.' The right permits all people to freely determine their political status and freely pursue their economic, social and cultural development. Both instruments are legally binding. They are treaties that must be respected at any cost. Both instruments copied largely from UDHR. The compactness and interdependency show in their Articles—(e.g., the right to trade unions; education and liberty of parents). The Preamble of both the Covenants are the same and so is the case with Articles 1, 3 and 5. It is seen that both Covenants are supplementary to each other. The 1993 (June 14 to 25) Conference finally recognized and affirmed the interdependence and interrelationship of both Covenants. The Conference found: 'While the significance of the national and regional particularities and various historical, cultural and religious backgrounds must be borne in mind, it was the duty of the States, regardless of their political, economic and cultural systems to promote and protect all human rights'. (See, *U.N. Chronicle,* Vol. XXX, No. 3, September 1993). This happened in 1993 and it is now 2019, i.e., 25 years elapsed since the view was expressed—and still, we do not give due importance to the revision of the international Covenants keeping in view the differences existing in various countries. This is a humble attempt to do the same by me. In my view, some of the human rights—as given in the two Covenants—cannot become universal, for, they differ from region to region and from State to State in view of the economic, social and political conditions prevailing there. Of course, this view is challenged by vested interests saying that there is nothing which prevents the States of different regions to adopt regional Conventions, Charters and Declarations on Human Rights. In my view, **International is International** and **Regional is Regional.** An instrument of human rights adopted by the United Nations cannot be compared with regional instruments of human rights. The chapters that follow are my wholistic revision of the two International Covenants taking into account the current concepts of human rights and various differences seen in many parts of the world.

PART 2

International Covenant on Civil and Political Rights

Chapter 2
ICCPR: Introduction

The International Covenant on Civil and Political Rights (ICCPR) is a multilateral treaty. The General Assembly of the United Nations adopted it on 16, December, 1966 and came into force from 23, March 1976—i.e., after 28 years since the U.N. Universal Declaration of Human Rights came into existence. It is part of the International Bill of Human Rights, along with the International Covenant on Economic, Social and Cultural Rights (ICESCR) and Universal Declaration of Human Rights (UDHR). The Covenant is monitored by the UN Human Rights Committee (a separate Body of the UN Human Rights Council), which makes reviews regularly the reports of the States Parties on how the rights are being enforced or implemented. States must report initially one year after ascending to the Covenant and then whenever, the Committee wants (as a rule, every four years). The Committee usually meets in Geneva and normally holds three sessions every year.

At the very outset, it may be stated that the ICCPR has its roots in the same process that paved the way to the Universal Declaration of Human Rights (UDHR). It may be noted that the 1945 San Francisco Conference which led to the founding of the United Nations proposed a 'Declaration of the Essential Rights of Man.' Subsequently, the Economic and Social Council was given the responsibility of preparing a draft. Early in the process, the document was split into a Declaration setting forth general principles of human rights, and a Convention or Covenant containing binding commitments. As everyone knows, the former evolved into the Universal Declaration of Human Rights (UDHR) and was adopted by the United Nations on 10, December 1948.

The International Covenant on Civil and Political Rights has the structure of the Universal Declaration of Human Rights (UDHR) and the International Covenant on Economic, Social and Cultural Rights (ICESCR) with (1) a **preamble** and (2) **fifty three articles** divided into six parts in the following way.

1. **Preamble.**
2. **General (Articles 1 to 3 and 5).**
3. **Rights in Emergency (Article 4).**
4. **Substantive Rights (Articles 6 to 27).**
5. **Implementation or Enforcement Machinery (Articles 28 to 45).**
6. **Interpretation or saving provision (Articles 46 and 47).**
7. **Final or concluding provisions, regarding ratification, of accession of the Covenant, amendments etc.**

Part 1—i.e., Article 1 of the ICCPR says that all peoples have the right of self-determination including the right to 'freely determine their political status.' By virtue of that right they freely pursue their economic, social and cultural development or goals (Article 1, Para 1) and manage and depose of their own resources and natural wealth without prejudice to any obligations arising out of international economic co-operation, based upon the principle of natural benefit and international law. It accepts and recognizes a negative right of all the people not to be deprived of its means of subsistence (Article 1, Para 2) and imposes an obligation on States Parties, including those having the responsibility for administration of Non-Self Governing and Trust Territories to promote the realization of the right of self-determination and to respect that right in conformity with the provisions of the U.N. Charter (Article 1, Para 3).

Part 2—i.e., Articles 2-5 of the ICCPR obliges Parties to legislate where necessary to give effect to the rights recognised in the present Covenant. It also provides an effective or meaningful legal remedy for any violation of those rights. The Covenant requires the rights to be recognized 'without distinction of any kind such as race, colour, sex, language, religion, political or other opinion, national or social origin, property, birth or other status' (Article 2, Para 1). Where legislative or other measures do not exist to give effect to the rights recognized in the present Covenant, each State Party undertakes to take the necessary steps, in accordance with its Constitutional processes and with provisions of the Covenant, to adopt such legislative or other measures, to give an effect to the rights (Article 2, Para 2). The rights are to be enjoyed equally by women. The rights can only be limited 'in time of public emergency which threatens the life of the nation' and even then no derogation is permitted from the rights to life, freedom from torture and slavery, the freedom from retrospective law, the right to personhood, and freedom of thought, conscience and religion.

"Each State Party to the Covenant undertakes:

(a) to ensure that any person whose rights or freedoms recognised in the Covenant are violated shall have an effective remedy, notwithstanding that the violation has been committed by persons acting in official capacity.
(b) to ensure that any person claiming such a remedy shall have his right thereto determined by competent judicial, administrative, or legislative authorities, or by any other competent authority provided for by the legal system of the State and to develop the possibilities of judicial remedy;
(c) to ensure that the competent authorities shall enforce such remedies when granted (Article 2, Para 3).

As said above, by virtue of Article 3, the States Parties to the present Covenant undertake to ensure the principle of equal right of men and women to the enjoyment of all civil and political rights enumerated in the Covenant.

Article 5 makes it very clear and specific that nothing in the Covenant may be interpreted as implying for any State, group or person any right to engage in any activity or perform any act aimed at the destruction of any of the rights and freedoms recognized herein or at their limitation to a greater extent than is provided for in the present Covenant (Article 5, Para 1). Moreover, there shall be no restriction upon or derogation from any of the fundamental human rights recognized or existing in any State party to the present Covenant pursuant to law,

Conventions, regulations or custom on the pretext that the present Covenant does not recognize such rights or that it recognizes them to a lesser extent (Article 5, Para 2).

Civil and Political Rights in Emergency

It may be noted that many of the above rights include specific actions which must be initiated or undertaken for realizing them. Public emergency which usually threatens the life of the people required very emergent, drastic or exceptional measures which are not normally allowed or permissible. It may be noted that Article 4 of the present Covenant permits the States Parties to take all measures during such emergency provided that the existence of which is officially proclaimed, derogating from their obligation under the Covenant to the extent strictly required by the exigencies of the situation, provided that such measures are not inconsistent with their other obligations under international law. Of course, they do not involve discrimination on the ground of race, colour, sex, language, religion or social origin. It has been well clarified that this provision will not allow the States Parties to make any derogation from Article 6 *(dealing with inherent right to life),* Article 7 *(dealing with prohibition of torture, or cruel, inhuman or degrading treatment or punishment etc.),* Article 8 *(dealing with prohibition of slavery, slave trade or servitude),* Article 11 *(prohibition of punishment on any criminal offence not constituting a criminal offence under national or international law and ex post facto laws),* Article 16 *(recognition everywhere as a person before law) and* Article 18 *(dealing with freedom of thought, conscience, and religion).* In Article 4, Para 2, it is, moreover, provided that any State Party which avails the right of derogation shall inform other Parties of the Covenant of such derogation and reasons thereof and shall also inform the date on which such derogation is allowed (Article 4, Para 3).

Part 3—i.e., Articles 6-27—lists the rights which include the rights to—

* Physical integrity, in the form of right to life and freedom from torture and slavery (Articles 6, 7 and 8).
* Liberty and security of the person in the form of freedom from arbitrary arrest and detention and the

right to *habeas corpus* (Article 9-11).

* Procedural fairness in law in the form of rights to due processes, a fair and impartial trial, the presumption of innocence, and recognition as a person before the law (Articles 14, 15 and 16).
* Individual liberty in the form of freedom of movement, thought, conscience and religion, speech, association and assembly, family rights, the right to a nationality and the right to privacy (Articles 12, 13, 17-24).
* Prohibition of any propaganda for war as well as any advocacy of national or religious hatred that constituted incitement to discrimination, hostility or violence by law (Article 20).
* Political participation, including the right to the right to vote (Article 25).*
* Non-discrimination, minority rights and equality before

---

* More specifically, it may be shown as under:

Article 6: Right to life.
Article 7: Prohibition of torture or cruel, inhuman treatment etc.
Article 8: Prohibition of slavery etc.
Article 9: Right to liberty etc.
Article 10: Right to all persons deprived of their liberty to be treated with humanity etc.
Article 11: Prohibition of imprisonment.
Article 12: Right to liberty of movement etc.
Article 13: Freedom of aliens lawfully.
Article 14: Right to equality.
Article 15: Non-retroactive application of criminal law.
Article 16: Right to be recognized everywhere as a person.
Article 17: Right of everyone not to be subjected to arbitrary or unlawful interference with privacy etc.
Article 18: Freedom of thought.
Article 19: Right to freedom of opinion.
Article 20: Prohibition of propaganda of war etc.
Article 21: Right to peaceful assembly.
Article 22: Right to freedom of association etc.
Article 23: Right to marry.
Article 24: Right of every child to be protected.
Article 25: Right of every citizen to take part in the conduct of public affairs.

the law (Articles 26, 27).*

It may be remembered that the rights in the ICCPR are not absolute. Of Course, they are subject to limitations.

Right to Physical Integrity

Individual's inhererent right to life is a supreme right from which no derogation can be permitted. Hence, the rights must be interpreted widely. It therefore required States Parties to take positive measures to reduce infant mortality and increase life expectancy as well as prohibiting arbitrary killings by security forces.

It may be specially noticed that the Article 6 does not prohibit capital punishment/death penalty. Nevertheless, it restricts its application to the rarest of rare cases—i.e., to the most serious cases only. It forbids it to be used on children and pregnant women or in a manner contrary to the Convention on the Prevention and Punishment of the Crime of Genocide. The Human Rights Committee of the United Nations interprets the Article 6 as 'strongly suggesting that abolition is most desirable' and regards any progress towards abolition of capital punishment/death penalty as advancing towards this right. The Second Optional Protocol commits its signatories to the abolition of capital punishment/death penalty within their borders. I firmly support this view.

Article 7 prohibits torture and cruel, inhuman or degrading treatment or punishment. As with Article 6 in the Covenant, it cannot be derogated from under any circumstances. The Article is now interpreted to impose similar obligations to those required by the U.N. Convention Against Torture or Cruel, Inhuman or Degrading Treatment or Punishment, including not just prohibition of torture, but active measures to prevent its use and a prohibition on refoulement. In response to Nazi human experimentation during World War II, this Article explicitly included a prohibition on medical and scientific experimentation

---

* *Article 26:* Equality before law
Article 27: Right of ethnic, religious etc. to enjoy their own culture etc.

without consent. This Convention against Torture was revised by me and published in my book titled HUMAN RIGHTS—A Fair Trail of United Nations (ISBN: 13: 978-93-86682-13-0 Part-1).

Article 8 prohibits slavery and enforced/compulsory servitude to all situations. It also prohibits forced labour with exceptions for criminal punishment, military service and civil obligations.

Liberty and Security of Person

Article 9 of the Covenant recognizes the rights of everyone to liberty and security of the person. It forbids arbitrary arrest and detention; requires any deprivation of liberty to be in accordance to law; obliges States Parties to allow those deprived of their liberty to challenge their imprisonment through the courts of law. These provisions are applicable not only just to those imprisoned as part of the criminal justice process, but also to those detained owing to mental illness, psychic disorders, drug addition or for educational or immigration purposes.

What do Articles 9.3 and 9.4 say? They impose procedural safeguards around arrest, requiring anyone arrested to be promptly informed of the charges against him/her, and to be brought promptly before a Judge. It further restricts the use of pre-trial detention requiring it to be imposed only in exceptional circumstances and for as short period of time as possible.

Article 10 of the Covenant requires everyone deprived of liberty to be treated with dignity and humanity. It is applied not just to prisoners in an institution for correction, but also to all those detained for immigration purposes or psychiatric care. This right compliments the rights conferred under Article 7 about prohibition on torture and cruel, inhuman or degrading treatments or punishments. The Articles also impose specific obligations around criminal justice, requiring prisoners in pre-trial detention to be separated from convicted prisoners, and children to be separated from adults. It requires prisoners to be focused on reform and rehabilitation rather than punishment.

Article 11 is about prohibition of imprisonment merely on the ground of inability to fulfil a contractual obligation. In other words, it prohibits the use of imprisonment as a punishment for breach of contract.

Procedural Fairness and Rights of the Accused

Article 14 is about the Right to equality before the courts and tribunals; right to a fair and public hearing; and a right of everyone charged with a criminal offence to be presumed innocent (Accusatorial or Adversary system) until proved guilty according to law. In other words, Article 14.1 establishes the ground rules: i.e., everyone must be equal before the courts, and any hearing must take place in open court—before a competent, independent and impartial tribunal, with any judgement or ruling made in public in a transparent way. Of course, closed hearing is permitted. But, they are limited or permitted for reasons of privacy justice, sex justice for women or national security. Judgements may only be suppressed in divorce cases or to protect the interest of children. These obligations apply to both criminal and civil hearings, and to all courts and tribunals.

The rest of the Article imposes very special, specific and detailed obligations around the process of criminal trials in order to protect the rights of the accused. The accused has a right to for a fair and just trial. The presumption of innocence is ensured and the article forbids double jeopardy. Those who are convicted for a crime has a right for an appeal to a higher court/tribunal. The victims of miscarriage of justice has a right for victimological compensation/restitution. Speedy trial is guaranteed. The Article establishes the right to counsel against self-incrimination, and for the accused to be present and call and examine witnesses.

Prosecutions under *ex post facto* law is prohibited. The imposition of retrospective criminal penalties is prohibited. The Article requires the imposition of the lesser penalty where criminal sentences have changed between the offence and conviction. The right to be recognized everywhere as a person before the law is accepted by Article 16 of the Covenant.

Individual Liberties

As said earlier, Article 12 of the Covenant ensures freedom of movement, including the right of individuals to choose their residence and to leave a country. Both the legal aliens and the citizens of a State enjoy this right. It can be restricted only where and only when necessary to protect the national security, public order or health, and the rights and the freedoms of others. The Article also recognizes the right of the individuals to enter their own country. The U.N. Human Rights Committee interprets this right broadly as applying not just to citizens, but also to those stripped of or denied their nationality. They also regard it as near-absolute. However, there are few, if any, circumstances in which deprivation of the right to enter one's own country could be reasonable.

Article 13 is about the freedom of aliens lawfully in the territory of a State Party to Covenant from arbitrary expulsion. It also requires such decisions to be able to be appealed or reviewed. What about Article 17? It deals with the right of everyone not to be subjected to arbitrary or unlawful interference with his privacy, family, home or correspondence and freedom from unlawful attacks on his honour and reputation. In other words, Article 17 mandates the right of privacy. Article 17(1) protects private adult consensual sexual activity thereby nullifying prohibitions on homosexual behaviour. Nevertheless, the wordings of this Covenant's marriage right (see, Article 23) excludes the extrapolation of a uni-sex marriage right from this provision. What about the marriages of the transgenders? Article 17 also protects the individuals against unlawful attacks to their honour and reputation and grants the protection of the law against such attacks.

Freedom of thought, conscience and religion is mandated by Article 18 of the Covenant. Article 19 mandates the right to freedom of opinion and expression. Article 20 mandates sanctions against inciting hatred—i.e., prohibition of propaganda of war and advocacy of national, racial or religious hatred constituting incitement to discrimination, hostility or violence.

Articles 21 and 22 mandate right of peaceful assembly and freedom of association respectively. Freedom of association includes the right to form and join trade unions for the protection of interests. These provisions define the International Labour Organization.

The Article 23 is about the right to marry and found a family. The wording of this provision does not prohibit uni-sex marriages. What about the marriage of transgenders? Article 24 is about the right of every child to be protected according to his status as minor on the part of his family, society and the State. Every child has a right to acquire a nationality. The Article mandates special protection for the right to a name and the right to a nationality for every child.

Article 25 speaks about the right of every citizen to take part in the conduct of public affairs. It mandates the right to vote and to be selected, and to have access, on general terms of equality to public service in his country.

The Article 27 mandates the right of ethnic, religious or linguistic minorities to enjoy their own culture to profess and practise their own religion or to use their own language.

Political Rights

Article 3 of the Covenant provides an accessory non-discrimination principle—necessary in the sense and in the way that it cannot be used independently. It can only be relied upon in relation to another right protected by the Covenant. This Article ensures the principle of equal rights for men and women for the enjoyment of all civil and political rights conferred by the Covenant.

In contrast, Article 26 contains a revolutionary norm. It provides an autonomous principle of equality which is not dependent upon another right under Convention being infringed. Surely it has the effect of widening the scope of the non-discrimination principle beyond and besides the scope of ICCPR.

As said above, the rights conferred under ICCPR are not absolute. They are subject to limitations. The formulation of limitations differs from Article to Article. Nevertheless, the ICCPR provides that it shall not be subjected to restrictions except those specified by law and those which are needed to safeguard or protect national security, public order, public health or morals or the rights and freedoms of others.

It may be specially noted that some of the rights are not subject to any special or specific restrictions. Example is the right to freedom of thought, conscience etc. In time of public emergency (threatening the very life of the nation), the States Parties can make all measures (derogating from the obligations under ICCPR to the extent strictly required by the exigencies of the situation) to protect their interests. In such situations, the measures taken should not be inconsistent with other obligations under international law. They must not involve any discrimination purely or solely on the ground of race, colour, sex, language, religion or social origin.

Implementation or Enforcement Machinery

U.N. Human Rights Committee is the machinery for implementation. The Committee consists of 18 members. They are nationals of States Parties to the Covenant. They are experts having high moral integrity or caliber and specially recognized competence in the area of human rights. Certainly, they will have good legal expertise and wide experience. They are elected by secret ballot from a list of people having the required qualifications and quality (see, Article 28) and nominated for the purpose by the States Parties to ICCPR.

Each State Party to the Covenant may nominate not more than 2 persons who are its national. The Committee may not include more than one national of the same State Party. Consideration shall be given to the equitable geographical distribution of membership in the election of the Committee. Consideration will also be given to the representation of the different forms of civilization and of the principal legal systems.

The term of service for the members of the Committee is four years and the members are eligible for re-election in case they are nominated again. The terms of nine of the members elected at the first election shall expire at the end of 2 years. Immediately after the first election, the names of these nine members shall be chosen by lot by the Chairman of the meeting referred in Article 30, Para 4. According to Article 30, the initial election shall be held not later than six months after the date of entry into force of the Covenant.

At least four months before the date of each election to the Committee (other than an election to fill a vacancy declared in accordance to Article 34), the Secretary General of the United Nations shall address a written invitation to the States Parties to the Covenant to file their nomination for membership of the Committee within 3 months. The Secretary General of the United

Nations shall thereafter prepare a list in alphabetical order of all the persons thus nominated and submit it to the States Parties to the present Covenant not later than one month before the date of each election. Thereafter, election of the members of the Committee shall be held at a meeting of the States Parties to the Covenant convened by the Secretary General of the United Nations at his Headquarters. At that meeting, 2/3rd of the States Parties will constitute the quorum. The person elected to the Committee shall be those nominees who get the largest number of votes and an absolute majority of votes of the representatives of States Parties present and voting (Article 30, Para 4).

Methods or Ways of Implementation

The Committee implements the human rights in the following ways.

(1) The system of reporting.
(2) Inter-State Communication system.
(3) Conciliation procedure.

The States Parties are required to file the reports—reports on the measures they adopted to give effect to the rights recognized and the progress made—within one year of the entry into force of the Covenant whenever the Committee so requests. The Secretary General receives the reports and transmits them to the Committee for consideration. He may, after consultation with the Committee, transmit them to the specialized agencies. The Committee transmits its reports with their comments to the States Parties. The Committee may also transmit it to ECOSOC Council their comments along with the copies of the reports. The States Parties may submit to the Committee observations on any Covenants that the Committee made. Thus one may understand that the 18 member Human Rights Committee is a watch-dog body to ensure that the States Parties do apply the ICCPR.

ICCPR also provides for a system of State to State or inter-state communication. If one of the States Parties finds that the rights recognized by the Covenant are not implemented by another State Party, then it may send a communication to the Human Rights Committee. The provision relating to inter-state communication is provided in Article 41 of the Covenant. What about the conciliation procedure? If the inter-state communication provided under Article 41 is not resolved to the satisfaction of the States Parties concerned, then the Committee may appoint an *ad-hoc* Conciliation Commission. The Commission may make an amicable solution to the matter. As (1) the system, of reporting, (2) Inter-state communications system, and (3) conciliation procedure etc. do not come within the scope of this book, I am not inclined to elaborate the same further. There are two optional protocols to this Covenant. The first Optional Protocol establishes an individual complaints mechanism, permitting individuals to complain to the Human Rights Committee about any violations of the Covenant. The second Optional Protocol abolishes capital punishment/death penalty. However, countries are allowed to make a reservation permitting the use of capital punishment/death penalty for the most serious/heinous crimes of a military nature committed during war time. The optional protocols too do not come within the purview/scope of this book. It may be pointed out for academic interest that as of July 2013 the second Optional Protocol has 77 Parties.

Chapter 3
ICCPR: The Complete Revision

This Covenant, as said before, has its foundation in the Universal Declaration of Human Rights-1948 and U.N. Charter. The States Parties to the Covenant recognized the civil and political rights in UDHR and duties of individual to other fellow beings and community at large. The **Preamble** of the Covenant was adopted in 1966. The Covenant came into force in 1976. The Covenant has a **Preamble** and six parts. Articles 1 to 28 are in Parts I, II & III and they constitute the civil and political rights. They are comparable almost to European and American Conventions on Human Rights. Later came African Charter on Human and People's Rights, Arab Charter on Human Rights, ASEAN Human Rights Declaration, Asian Human Rights Charter etc. The rights are—

1. Right to self determination.
2. Right to life.
3. Right to freedom from torture etc.
4. Right to freedom from slavery etc.
5. Right to liberty etc.
6. Right of detained persons.
7. Right to freedom from imprisonment from debt.
8. Right to freedom of movement etc.
9. Right to freedom of aliens from arbitrary expulsion.
10. Right to fair trial.
11. Right to prohibition against retroactivity of criminal law.
12. Right to recognition everywhere as a person before law.
13. Right to privacy etc.
14. Right to freedom of thought etc.
15. Right of opinion etc.

16. Right to prohibition of propaganda for war etc.
17. Right to peaceful assembly.
18. Right to freedom of association.
19. Right to marry etc.
20. Right of the child.
21. Political rights.
22. Right to equality before law.
23. Right of person belonging to the minorities.

Articles 28 to 53 in Part IV to VI are about monitoring provisions, interpretation and final clauses. The first optional protocol has 14 articles with nexus to procedures on individual complaints. Second Optional Protocol basically amended the right to life in article 6 of the International Covenant on Civil and Political Rights.

Look at the rights given in the Covenant. Many of them are seen in the UDHR. The UDHR is a Declaration and precisely therefore, it is soft. Conventions or Covenants are international laws and therefore, they are not soft—rather are 'hard laws' in every sense. The Principle of *Pacta Sunt Servanda* applies to both Covenants. ICCPR and ICESR are legally binding instruments. Accordingly, they give or confer legal obligation on the States Parties. There is a treaty behind the obligation. It is well established that the ICCPR is the most comprehensive and well established treaty of the United Nations on civil and political rights. I do admit it, nevertheless, I am of the firm opinion that the rights are not that comprehensive as they are claimed to be. They need a through revision and this is an attempt for it. Already, there is a criticism that some rights are given in a very detailed manner—e.g., Articles 6, 9, 10 and 14 (restriction) whereas others are generally mentioned. They need rethinking and revision.

As said elsewhere, the Preamble to ICESCR and ICCPR is one and the same. I have suggested that we must put 'good governance' to the existing ICESCR to make it more meaningful. I do recommend the same in the Preamble of my revised ICCPR. Again I have added *'maintained'* in the Preamble of ICESCR as under—

"...can only be achieved if conditions are created and maintained whereby everyone may enjoy." I want to retain it in the revised Preamble of ICCPR. *Conducive environment for development* suggested by me in ICESCR is retained here too.

In the Preamble of ICCPR, I want to put *'favourable'* before conditions to read: 'Recognizing that, in accordance with the Universal Declaration of Human Rights. want can only be achieved if 'favourable conditions are created.' Why do I want 'favourable?' I think that many a time, civil and political rights are denied by creating unfavourable conditions by vested interests. Favourable means providing aid, advantage or convenience. It is very essential to have such a situation for the enjoyment of civil and political rights. Hence the amended Preamble will be.

Preamble

The States Parties to the present Covenant,

Considering that, in accordance with the principles proclaimed in the Charter of the United Nations, recognition of the inherent dignity and of equal and inalienable rights of all members of the human family is the foundation of freedom, justice, peace and good governance.

Recognizing that these rights derive from the inherent dignity of human person.

Recognizing that, in accordance with the Universal Declaration of Human Rights, the ideal of free human beings enjoying civil and political freedom and freedom from fear and want can only be achieved if favourable conditions are created and maintained whereby everyone may enjoy his civil and political rights, as well as his economic, social and cultural rights in a conducive environment for development.

The Universal Declaration of Human Rights contains only normative declarations and statements of guidance in observance of human rights universally. Of course, the ICCPR, as said earlier, relied very much on UDHR and in fact copied copiously from it. (See, Articles 3,4,5,6,9 & 10 of the UDHR and read them along with ICCPR)

Part I of ICCPR contains only Article I which reads:

PART I

Article 1

1. All peoples have the right of self-determination. By virtue of that right they freely determine their political status and freely pursue their economic, social and cultural development.

2. All peoples may, for their own ends, freely dispose of their natural wealth and resources without prejudice to any obligations arising out of international economic co-operation, based upon the principle of mutual benefit, and international law. In no case may a people be deprived of its own means of subsistence.

3. The States Parties to the present Covenant, including those having responsibility for the administration of Non-Self-Governing and Trust Territories, shall promote the realization of the right of self-determination, and shall respect that right, in conformity with the provisions of the Charter of the United Nations.

No amendment is suggested. A number of parties to the Covenant have made reservations and interpretative declarations to their application of this Covenant. For example, Argentina, Australia, Austria, Behamas, Baharian, Bangladesh, Barbados, Belgium, Belize, Congo, Denmark, Gambia, the United States have made reservations. But none of them has any reservation to Article 1 of ICCPR.

Articles 2 to 5 are in Part II of the Covenant. Article 2 may be reproduced:

PART II

Article 2

1. "Each State Party to the present Covenant undertakes to respect and to ensure to all individuals within its territory and subject to its jurisdiction the rights recognized in the present Covenant, without distinction of any kind, such as race, colour, sex, language, region, political or other opinion, national or social origin, property, birth or other status.

2. Where not already provided by existing legislative or other measures, each State Party to the present Covenant undertakes to take the necessary steps, in accordance with its Constitutional processes and with the provisions of the present Covenant, to adopt such laws or other measures as may be necessary to give effect to the rights recognized in the present Covenant.

3. Each State Party to the present Covenant undertakes:

(a) to ensure that any person whose rights or freedoms as herein recognized are violated shall have an effective remedy, not withstanding that the violation has been committed by persons acting in an official capacity;

(b) To ensure that any person claiming such a remedy shall have his right thereto determined by competent judicial, administrative or legislative authorities, or by any other competent authority provided for by the legal system of the State and to develop the possibilities of judicial remedy;

(c) To ensure that the competent authorities shall enforce such remedies when granted."

As far as Article 2.1 is concerned, I notice that distinctions are made on grounds other than what are given there. 'Other Status' does not mean much when it is not specified. Now, the complaint is that the 'Transgenders' and 'hermaphrodites' are neglected everywhere. Their human rights are not respected. They are treated as subhuman and therefore, my suggestion is to specially include them in the Article 2.1 'Religion' is fine, but within the same religion, one sees castes, sub-castes, denominations, converts, sects, creed etc. Hence stating religion in a sweeping way may not be enough. Within the same caste, one may see many sub-castes and I find distinction being made among the sub-castes. It means that some sub-castes are found to be superior to others within the same castes.

'Taking necessary steps' is fine, nevertheless, they may not be effective. Some countries slow down the steps and therefore, I suggest to put *'effective and time bound'* steps in the Article 2.2 *'Give effect' to the rights recognized in the present Covenant* is not enough. I add 'and to get them legally enforced in case violations take place.'

Article 2.3 (a). Here too, the effective remedy should be given *within a time frame.* I have noticed that the remedy is given after several years and it itself is injustice. When the violations take place and they are done by a person in his official capacity, then the matter becomes serious. On one side, there is a mammoth power and on the other side, there is a fragile and weak person. Therefore I am of the firm opinion that the victim must get everything done 'free of cost'. No amendment is suggested to Article 2.3 (b), whereas there must be a provision for victim compensation/restitution in Article 2.3 (c). Hence, the amended Article 2 will be—

Article 2

1. Each State party to the present Covenant undertakes to respect and to ensure to all individuals within its territory and subject to its jurisdiction the rights recognized in the present Covenant, without distinction of any kind, such as race, colour, sex including transgender or hermaphrodites, language, religion, sect, caste, subcaste, denomination, creed, political or other opinion, national or social origin, aborigines and tribals, property, birth, '*...ologies, ...isms, ...sophies*' or other status.

2. Where not already provided by existing legislative or other measures, each State Party to the present Covenant undertakes to take the necessary, effective and time bound steps, in accordance with its Constitutional processes and with the provisions of the present Covenant, to adopt such laws or other measures as may be necessary to give effect to the rights recognized in the present Covenant and to get them legally enforced in case violations take place.

3. Each State Party to the present Covenant undertakes:

(a) to ensure that any person whose rights or freedoms as hereinafter recognized are violated shall have an effective remedy within a time-frame not withstanding that the violation has been committed by person/s acting in an official capacity in which case, it shall be free of cost to the victim/s.

(b) To ensure that any person claiming such a remedy shall have his right thereto determined by competent judicial, administrative or legislative authorities or by any other competent authority provided for by the legal system of the State, and to develop the possibilities of judicial remedy;

(c) To ensure that the competent authorities shall enforce such remedies when granted along with victim compensation/restitution or both.

Article 3 is about equal rights and it reads: "The States Parties to the present Covenant undertakes to ensure equal right to men and women to the enjoyment of all civil and political rights set forth in the present Covenant."

The complaint often heard is that there is no sex justice ensured to the transgender. Transgenders do not have any specific sex and therefore, they are neglected or ignored everywhere. Likewise, the hermaphrodites as well are treated. The amended article is:

Article 3

The States Parties to the present Covenant undertake to ensure the equal right of men and women including transgenders and hermaphrodites to the enjoyment of all civil and political rights set forth in the present Covenant.

Article 4 reads:

Article 4

1. "In time of public emergency which threatens the life of the nation and the existence of which is officially proclaimed, the States Parties to the present Covenant may take measures derogating from their obligations under the present Covenant to the extent strictly required by the exigencies of the situation provided that such measures are not inconsistent with their other obligations under international law and do not involve discrimination solely on the ground of race, colour, sex, language, religion or social origin.

2. No derogation from articles 6,7,8 (paragraph 1 and 2), 11, 15,16 and 18 may be made under the provision.

3. Any State Party to the present Covenant availing itself of

the right of derogation shall immediately inform the other States Parties to the present Covenant, through intermediary of the Secretary General of the United Nations, of the provisions from which it has derogated and of the reasons by which it was actuated. A further communication shall be made, through the same intermediary, on the date of which it terminates such derogation."

Emergency may be internal or external or both. If the emergency is internal, then the State Party needs not necessarily derogate from their obligations. Again, taking 'measures' alone may not be enough. There should be 'taking stratagems' as well. I am unable to understand why does the Covenant limit or restrict discrimination solely on the ground of race, colour, sex, language, religion or social origin? There can be or there are many more and I am of the firm opinion that they too must be included in article 4.1.

Why is the phrase 'may be' in article 4.2? In my view, it must be 'shall be' because, it is a period of proclaimed emergency which threatens the very life of the nation. That is the precise reason why I insist that 'the reasons along with the measures and stratagems taken' should be informed to the Secretary General of the United Nations. Certainly the Secretary General can act upon it and give suitable advice if needed. The amended article will be—

Article 4

1. In time of public emergency—internal, external or both—which threatens the life of the nation and the existence of which is officially proclaimed, the States Parties to the present Covenant may take measures and stratagems derogating from their obligations under the present Covenant to the extent strictly required by the exigencies of the situation, provided that such measures are not inconsistent with their other obligations under international law and do not involve discrimination solely on the ground of race, colour, creed, sex including transgender or hermaphrodites, languages, religion, caste or subcaste, sect, denomination, political or other opinions, national or social origin, aborigines and tribals, property, birth, '*...ologies, ...isms, ...sophies*', or other status.

2. No derogation from articles 6,7,8 (paragraphs 1 and 2), 11,15,16 and 18 shall be made under this provision.

3. Any State Party to the present Covenant availing itself of the right of derogation shall immediately inform the other States Parties to the present Covenant, through the intermediary of the Secretary General of the United Nations, of the provisions from which it has derogated and of the reasons, measures and stratagems by which it was actuated. A further communication shall be made through the same intermediary on the date of which it terminates such derogation.

What rights are given by Article 5? Article 5 reads:

1. "Nothing in the present Covenant may be interpreted implying for any State, group or person any right to engage in any activity or perform any act aimed at the destruction of any of the rights and freedoms recognized herein or at their limitation to a greater extent than is provided for in the present Covenant.
2. There shall be no restriction upon or derogation from any of the fundamental human rights recognized or existing in any State Party to the present Covenant pursuant to law, Conventions, regulations, customs on the pretext that the present Covenant does not recognize such rights or that it recognizes them to a lesser extent."

Article 5.1 speaks about 'rights' first and later it says rights and freedoms. It needs to be amended to read 'rights and freedoms' throughout. Again, doing an act or omitting to do an act—both are to be considered. For, commissions and omissions are taken together and there must be such an amendment. There may be dilution as well as destruction. Both expression should be there. Again, the same expressions are lacking in article 5.2 as well. The amended article will be:

Article 5

1. Nothing in the present Covenant may be interpreted as implying for any State, group or persons any rights or freedoms to engage in any activity or omit to engage in an activity or perform any act or omit to perform an act aimed at the dilution

or at the destruction of the rights and freedoms recognized herein or at their limitation or to a greater extent than is provided for in the present Covenant.

2. There shall be no restriction upon or derogation from or dilution of any of the fundamental human rights and freedoms recognized or existing in any State Party to the present Covenant pursuant to law, Conventions, regulations, rules, precedents, customs or traditions on the pretext that the present Covenant does not recognize such rights and freedoms or that it recognizes them to a lesser extent.

Here, precedents, traditions and rules are as important as the laws and customs etc.

PART III

Part III consists of articles 6-27. Article 6.1, 2, 3, 4, 5, 6 is as under-

Article 6

1. "Every human being has the inherent right to life. This right shall be protected by law. No one shall be arbitrarily deprived of his life.

2. In countries which have not abolished the death penalty, sentence of death may be imposed only for the most serious crimes in accordance with the law in force at the time of the commission of the crime and not contrary to the provisions of the present Covenant and to the Convention on the Prevention and Punishment of the Crime of Genocide. The penalty can be carried out pursuant to a final judgement rendered by a competent Court.

3. When deprivation of life constitutes the crime of genocide, it is understood that nothing in this article shall authorize any State Party to the present Covenant to derogate in any way from any obligation assumed under the provisions of the Convention on the Prevention and Punishment of the Crime of Genocide.

4. Anyone sentenced to death shall have the right to seek pardon or commutation of the sentence. Amnesty, pardon or commutation of the sentence of death may be granted in all cases.

5. Sentence of death shall not be imposed for crimes committed by persons below eighteen years of age and shall not be carried out on pregnant women.

6. Nothing in this article shall be invoked to delay or to prevent the abolition of capital punishment by any State Party to the present Covenant."

Inherent means existing in something as a permanent and inseparable element, quality, or attribute. When the law says so categorically that *every human being has the inherent right to life,* there is no relevance or meaning to what is said after that. Hence, there is no need or necessity to state "No one shall be arbitrarily deprived of his life." Here the amended article 6.1 will be—

Article 6

1. Every human being has the inherent right to life. This right shall be protected by law.

Right is inseparable from life and then it is protected. No question of arbitrarily depriving of one's life arises in such a situation. Hence, it is deleted. Once, the right is inherent, inseparable and permanent to life, and it is protected by law, then there is no meaning in saying that the countries where death penalty exists should limit the imposition of the punishment to the most serious crimes. Under this Covenant, the question of death penalty does not arise.

Death penalty is no penalty for a crime. It is a judicial murder of a criminal or crime-doer. Penalty for a crime has noble aims and objectives. It is, as accepted now, is nothing but the development of personality in an upright way in the right direction. If that is so, what is the meaning of annihilating a man? He can not benefit by the penalty. Again, a murder committed by an individual or by the judicial system is a murder. Precisely therefore, one cannot call murder to be a penalty. In my view, the death sentence shall be converted to 'life imprisonment upto or until the natural death of the imprisoned in a Centre for Personality Development (Prison). Hence, the amended version of article 6.2 will be-

2. Countries which still consider judicial murder to be a penalty to crimes, shall immediately abolish such judicial

murder in accordance to the provisions of the present Covenant.

No amendment is suggested to article 6.3 and hence it reads:

3. When deprivation of life constitute the crime of genocide, it is understood that nothing in this article shall authorize any State Party to the present Covenant to derogate in any way from any obligation assumed under the provisions of the Convention of the prevention and punishment of the crime of Genocide.

Genocide means the deliberate and systematic extermination of a national or racial group. As the judicial verdict for the commission of a *'Judicial murder'* is not recognized, the article 6.4 is to be amended in the following way—i.e.,

4. Anyone sentenced to life imprisonment up to or until his natural death in a Centre for Personality Development shall have the right to seek remission and get a pre-mature release under the parole system or otherwise.

Article 6.5 is deleted. Article 6.6 is retained to read:

5. Deleted

6. Nothing in this article shall be invoked to delay or to prevent the abolition of capital punishment (Judicial Murder as it is called) by any State Party to the present Covenant.

My recommendation is to abolish Judicial Murder (capital punishment) for all sorts of crimes. In some countries, the so-named capital punishment is given in rarest of rare cases. In such countries, the decision whether or not, it is a 'rarest of rare' case is decided by the Judge simply by applying his subjective scales. When it is challenged in the Appeal Court, the earlier judgement is sometimes cancelled and the Appeal Court judge applies his subjective scales. In any case, there is very strong criticisms against the verdicts of so-called capital punishment which is now discouraged in several countries—nearly 150 countries or more have already abolished judicial murder as a penalty for any type of crimes.

What is stated under Article 7? It reads:

Article 7

"No one shall be subjected to torture or to cruel, inhuman or degrading treatment or punishment. In particular, no one shall be subjected without his free consent to medical or scientific experimentation."

This article was written at a time when torture in various forms were not fully known. Today, physical, psychological, moral, spiritual and pharmacological torture in different forms are identified. Hence, they need to be specified. Moreover, a number of interrogation methods—sometimes, harmful to physical, psychological or both—have come into existence. They may be scientific or psychological or pharmacological aids to investigation. Allegations are sometimes heard that some of such methods are torturous in nature. Finally, we may add psychiatric too along with medical or scientific experimentation. The amended article is as under:

Article 7

1. No one shall be subjected to torture—physical, psychological, moral, spiritual, pharmacological or any other kind either alone or in combination of more than one—or cruel, inhuman, or degrading treatment or punishment.

2. No one shall be subjected to interrogation by using drugs or hypnosis, or a polygraph test or other such procedure designed to determine the truthfulness of statements by body reactions, unless, after such procedure has been proposed, such person has had an opportunity to consult with counsel for a period adequate to obtain advice concerning such procedure and consented thereto.

3. No one shall be subjected without his free and willing consent to medical, psychiatric or scientific experimentation.

Article 8 is as follows:

Article 8

1. "No one shall be held in slavery; slavery and the slave trade in all their forms shall be prohibited.
2. No one shall be held in servitude.
3. (a) No one shall be required to perform forced or compulsory labour;
   (b) Paragraph 3 (a) shall not be held to preclude in countries where imprisonment with hard labour

may be imposed as a punishment for a crime, the performance of hard labour in pursuance of a sentence to such punishment by a competent court;

(c) For the purpose of this paragraph, the term "forced or compulsory labour" shall not include:
   (i) Any work or service, not referred to in subparagraph (b), normally required of a person who is under detention in consequence of a lawful order of a court, or of a person during conditional release from such detention;
   (ii) Any service of a military character and in countries where conscientious objection is recognized, any national service required by law of conscientious objection;
   (iii) Any service exacted in cases of emergency or calamity threatening the life or well-being of the community;
   (iv) Any work or service which forms part of normal civil obligations."

Here, *slavery* means ownership of a person or persons by another or others; the condition of a slave.

'Slave-trade' means the act or process of buying, selling or exchanging slaves (like commodities) at either wholesale or retail prices, within a country or between countries. There were slave traders.

Servitude means slavery or bondage of any kind; compulsory service or labour as a punishment for criminals.

Slavery, slave trade, servitude, as they are, may not be nakedly seen today. Nevertheless, the children of those who were slaves once upon a time live in deplorable conditions financially and socially. They need an upliftment which is not possible unless they are given special aid and support. There are countries where special scholarship, financial assistance, housing etc. are provided to them for their upliftment. Hence, the amended article will be:

Article 8

1. No one shall be held in slavery; Slavery and the slave in

all their forms shall be declared as offences under the domestic law and shall be prohibited.

2. No one shall be held in servitude.

3. Special aids and support shall be provided to the children of those who were slaves once upon a time for their upliftment socially, culturally, financially and educationally.

4. (a) No one shall be required to perform forced or compulsory labour. Exploiting the financial weakness of the labourers shall be prohibited.

(b) Paragraph 4 (a) shall not be held to preclude, in countries where imprisonment with hard labour may be imposed as a punishment for a crime, the performance of hard labour in pursuance of a sentence to such punishment by a competent court. In such situations, the provisions contained in the U.N. Standard Minimum Rules for the Treatment of Prisoners shall be meticulously followed.

(c) For the purpose of this paragraph, the terms 'forced or compulsory labour' shall not include:

(i) Any work or service, not referred to in subpragraph (b), normally required of a person who is under detention in consequence of a lawful order of a court, or of a person during conditional release from such detention.

(ii) Any service of a military character and, in countries where conscientious objection is recognized, any national service required by law of conscientious objectors.

(iii) Any service exacted in cases of emergency or calamity threatening the life, welfare or well-being of the community;

(iv) Any work or service which forms part of normal civil obligations.

Article 9 is about the rights to liberty etc. and it reads:

1. "Everyone has the right to liberty and security of person. No one shall be subjected to arbitrary arrest or detention. No one shall be deprived of his liberty except on such grounds and in accordance with such procedure as are established by law.

2. Anyone who is arrested shall be informed, at the time of arrest, of the reasons for his arrest and shall be promptly informed of any charges against him.

3. Anyone arrested or detained on a criminal charge shall be brought promptly before a judge or other officer authorized by law to exercise judicial power and shall be entitled to trial within a reasonable time or to release. It shall not be the general rule that persons awaiting trial shall be detained in custody, but release may be subject to guarantees to appear for trial, at any other stage of judicial proceedings, and, should occasion arises, for execution of the judgement.

4. Anyone who is deprived of his liberty by arrest or detention shall be entitled to take proceedings before a court, in order that that court may decide without delay on the lawfulness of his detention and order his release if the detention is not lawful.

5. Anyone who has been the victim of unlawful arrest or detention shall have an enforceable right to compensation."

There is no difficulty to accept in theory that everyone has the right to liberty and security of person. But, in practice, the right is often violated. The number of people who die in police custody/jail custody many be many. Often allegations are raised that people are murdered and in many cases there may not be any arrest at all. The article 9 says that arbitrary arrest and detention are prohibited. Nevertheless, there exist informal arrests, unnecessary arrests, illegal arrests, unauthorized arrests etc. Infact, they are not 'arrests' in law. They are just taking people in custody by misusing or abusing the muscle power of the law enforcement officials. Some times, they exercise pseudo-authority too. In some countries, there exist clandestine lock-ups to detain those who are thus taken into custody in an illegal or informal way. Muscle power is a powerful energy and therefore law enforcement officials take people with or without any cause/s. There may not be any grounds for arrest and the courts are found to be, many a time, very lenient to those officials who abuse their power or misuse their authority or exercise pseudo-authority. They do not adopt any procedure established by law. The arrest or taking into custody are arbitrary and it seems that there is no one to question those who misuse the power/abuse the authority or exercise pseudo-authority. Hence, the amendment:

Article 9

1. (i) Everyone has the right to liberty and security of person. No one shall be subjected to arbitrary arrest or detention. Informal taking into custody and unauthorised detention are offences under law.
   (ii) No one shall be deprived of his liberty except on such grounds and in accordance with such procedure as are established by law.
   (iii) Victims of arbitrary arrest, informal taking into custody, unauthorized detention are entitled to get victimological compensation decided *suo motu* or otherwise by an impartial Tribunal.

What is happening today in some countries? People are taken into custody just like that and are detained in an unauthorised manner in clandestine lock-ups! They are subjected to torture to gather information or to obtain a confession. If the attempts fail, they are just released just like that and no victim justice is ensured. No one considers the illegal (informal) taking into custody as 'abduction' and unauthorized detention as 'wrongful confinement'. This is bad in law and in every sense a violation of the human rights justice.

When a person is informally taken into custody or arbitrarily arrested, no body is told anything about the grounds of taking into custody or arrest. Even when the taking into custody or arrest is legal and justified, no reasons for the arrest is given. No charges against them are told. The fact that some one is taken into custody or arrested, the fact is not communicated to the near and dear ones or atleast to some one interested in the arrestees and so on. Nothing is said about the place of detention, time of arrest etc. There may not be any witnesses to the arrest. No medical examination is conducted to note down the injuries seen on the arrestees or those taken into custody at the time of arrest or taken into custody. In my considered view, there must be an **arrest/custody memo** issued by the authorities at the time of arrest or taken into custody and such a memo should contain all details containing the reasons for the arrest, taking into custody, time of arrest/taking into custody, names of the arresting officials/official taking into custody, place of detention, persons informed about the arrest, taking into custody and detention etc. Hence, the amended article will be—

2. (i) Anyone who is taken into custody or arrested shall be informed, at the time of taking into custody/arrest of the reasons for his taking into custody/arrest.

(ii) An arrest/custody memo shall be prepared and given to the arrested/person taken into custody. The arrest/custody memo shall contain all information such as the name of the officer, time of arrest/taking into custody, reason for the arrest/taking into custody, medical examination, place of detention, name of witnesses, persons informed about the arrest/taking into custody etc. and such other information needed for the purpose. Every State Party to the present Covenant shall enact special legislations to this end.

(iii) Anyone arrested shall be promptly informed of any charges against him.

(iv) Any violation to the above provisions in the present Covenant is an offence under law and the victim is entitled to receive victim compensation/restitution decided, *suo motu* or otherwise, by an impartial Tribunal.

What is seen today in some countries? People are taken into custody/informally arrested and they are detained in an unauthorized manner. They are not even fed properly and not produced before a judge. They are subjected sometimes to interrogation—continuous interrogation—indepth interrogation by underqualified, unqualified or ill-qualified officials for days together and then released after threatening them that they would be subjected to painful consequences if they leak out their informal arrest, illegally taking into custody or unauthorized detention etc. Usually, they do not say anything to anybody. This is a serious violation of human rights justice. Hence the following amendment:

3. (i) Anyone taken into custody on legal reasons shall be promptly arrested if needed, and anyone arrested or detained on a criminal charge shall be brought promptly before a judge or other officer authorized by law to exercise judicial power. There shall be a judge or other judicial officer authorized by law to

exercise judicial power for 24 hours and seven days during a week.

In some countries, there exist a funny law. The law is that anyone arrested can be kept under detention for 24 hours before he is produced before a judge or other officer authorized by law. The provision of law is abused/misused by the officials. They use the 24 hours for interrogating the arrested in many ways to gather information or to get a confession. In some cases death takes place owing to the severity of interrogation and some officials detain those taken into custody for days/weeks/months together without making any record of taking into custody. As a result, it is very necessary to enact a law stating that the arrested shall be promptly produced before a judge or other officer authorized by law. The old legislations enacted at a time when roads, vehicles or transport system were deplorably poor and hopeless can not serve any useful or just purpose now. They are misused or abused. Hence, the amendment—

(ii) Anyone produced promptly after arrest before a judge or other officer authorized by law is entitled to get a bail in bailable offences or shall be remanded to custody as per law. Those released to judicial custody shall be housed in an institution manned and managed by the Judiciary.

(iii) Anyone released on bail or remanded to custody is entitled to trial within a reasonable time or to release.

Why so? The reason is that there are under trial prisoners (in some countries) who stay in custody for 6-10 years without any trial and in some cases, they spend more time under remand than the period of imprisonment if they were punished otherwise by a court after a fair trial for the offence/s committed by them. Instances have been reported that some in custody become insane or exhibit signs of mental disorder. Hence, the amendment as under—

(iv) Anyone remanded to custody is detained for an unreasonable period is entitled to get victimological compensation on his release without trial. States Parties to this Covenant shall enact special legislations showing the period of remand for each and every offence alleged to have been committed by the detained.

(v) It shall not be the general rule that persons awaiting trial shall be detained in custody, but release may be subject to guarantees to appear for trial, at any other stage of the judicial proceedings, and should occasion arise, for execution of judgement.

My researches show that an arrest/taking into custody is the beginning of a series of hardships and financial loss to the victim. People suffer a lot and some of them become financially zero after the criminal proceedings against them. Article 9.4 is amended as under-

4. Anyone who is deprived of his liberty by taking him in custody or by arrest or detention shall be entitled to take proceedings before a court, in order that court may decide without delay on the lawfulness of his detention and order his release if the detention is found to be not lawful. In such cases, the victim is entitled to get victim compensation decided by an impartial Tribunal.

5. Anyone who has been the victim of unlawful taking into custody, illegal arrest or detention shall have an enforceable right to compensation and the compensation shall be decided by an impartial Tribunal after taking an action *suo motu* or otherwise to decide the amount of compensation.

6. Officials responsible for illegally taking into custody, unlawful arrest or detention are liable to be prosecuted and punished in addition to departmental action for imposing punishment on them.

7. The amount of compensation decided by the Tribunal may be realized from the officials responsible, if that is needed and possible.

Criminal prosecution and departmental action against officials violating the above provisions will work as a deterrent on them. Article 10 is about treating those persons deprived of their liberty and connected matters and it reads:

Article 10

1. "All persons deprived of their liberty shall be treated with humanity and with respect for the inherent dignity of the human person.

2. (a) Accused persons shall, save in exceptional circumstances, be segregated from convicted persons and shall be subject to separate treatment appropriate to their status as unconvicted persons;

(b) Accused juvenile persons shall be separated from adults and brought as speedily as possible for adjudication.

3. The penitentiary system shall comprise treatment of prisoners, the essential aim of which shall be their reformation and social rehabilitation. Juvenile offenders shall be segregated from adults and be accorded treatment appropriate to their age and legal status."

All persons deprived of their liberty means mostly those taken in custody, arrested or legally detained. Necessarily they need to be treated with humanity and with respect to the inherent dignity of the human person. If that is not found, then those who ill treat them deserve to be punished and the victims of their ill treatment become entitled to victim compensation. The amended article 10.1 will be—

Article 10

1. All persons deprived of their liberty in a lawful manner shall be treated with humanity and with respect for the inherent dignity of the human person. Those who violate this shall be punished both criminally and by taking departmental action for misconduct. The victims of ill treatment are entitled to get victim compensation as per law decided by a competent Tribunal.

Detention may be of two types—namely detention under police custody or detention under judicial custody—prior to conviction to a jail. There are countries where detention under judicial custody is either in an institution manned and managed by the judiciary or in an institution manned and managed by the prisons department (i.e., Department of Correction/Department of Personality Development). A person is treated as an accused person only when the case is under trial before a court of law. Such persons are called under trial prisoners. The amendment will be:

2. (a) Persons who are suspected to have committed an offence/s are remanded to (i) police custody (ii) to judicial custody manned and managed by judicial officials or (iii) in rare and exceptional cases under the custody of prison officials. Those remanded to any custody shall be housed separately from people who are housed otherwise;

(b) Accused persons or under trial inmates in an institution for remanding them shall be segregated from people who are housed otherwise—including civil prisoners, security prisoners, political prisoners, convicted prisoners and so on.

(c) Accused persons or under-trial inmates shall be subject to separate treatment appropriate to their status as unconvicted persons. Special Rules shall be framed and enacted for the purpose of interaction between different categories of inmates and the staff, their accommodation, stay, food and living there.

The suspects, the under trial inmates, and the accused persons in a crime are not convicted people for any offence and precisely therefore, they should not suffer any punishment in an institution for personality development (prison).

Again, there may be juvenile persons who are suspects in a crime or are accused in a crime or are under-trial inmates. Juveniles may be below 12 years of age or between 12-18 years of age. It is found to be a good suggestion to separate children (below 12 years of age) from the juveniles who are senior in age (between 12-18 years of age). The amendment is:

(d) The suspected, the accused or the under-trial children (below 12 years of age) shall be separated from the juvenile (senior) persons (between 12 and 18 years of age) when they are housed. Both categories of the juvenile persons shall be separated from adults (between 18 and 35 years of age). Under no circumstances, the juvenile and adult persons—suspected, accused or under—trial—shall stay with the middle aged (between 35 and 60 years of age) and still senior persons (60 + years of age). The juvenile persons shall be brought as speedily as possible for adjudication.

My studies show that mixing them together will be dangerous from many angles. Their association is likely to transfer some of their evil characters and instances have been reported that there took place, sometimes, sexual abuses including homosexuality and lesbian contacts.

I can not and do not want to call 'penitentiary system, treatment of prisoners etc. and I find that they are time worn—very old terms now considered as meaningless. The objective of punishment, in my studied opinion, is *development of personality in an upright way in the right direction* and I have repeatedly used that objective in my revised old Standard Minimum Rules for the Treatment of Prisoners. Reformation is alright but prior to it, there is something called 'correction' and after it we may see 'rehabilitation, resocialization and reintegration to the society back'. Putting everything together—say, correction, reformation, rehabilitation, resocialization and reintegration to the society back—we may call such a process to be development of personality in an upright way in the right direction. This is the true objective of incarceration. The amendment is:

(4) The system for 'development of personality in an upright way in the right direction' shall comprise nothing but the personality development of an inmate in a Centre For Personality Development via correction, reformation, rehabilitation, resocialization and reintegration back to society. Juveniles who are in conflict with law shall be segregated from adults, middle aged and 60 + persons and be accorded special and specialized training and treatment appropriate to their age and legal status with an aim to develop their personality in an upright way in the right direction.

Prisons are called by me the 'Centre For Personality Development.' 'Juvenile Offenders'—this is considered to be an expression used not for the 'best interest' of the children. The new expression is 'children or juvenile in conflict with law'. What is required is not just 'correction', but the development of their personality in an upright way in the right direction.

Article 11 speaks about imprisonment for the inability to fulfil a contractual obligation. No amendment is recommended as the article 11 is:

Article 11

No one shall be imprisoned on the ground of inability to fulfill a contractual obligation.

Article 12 needs no amendment as it reads:

Article 12

1. Everyone lawfully within the territory of a State shall within that territory, have the right to liberty of movement and freedom to choose his residence.

2. Everyone shall be free to leave any country, including his own.

3. The above—mentioned rights shall not be subject to any restrictions except those which are provided by law, are necessary to protect national security, public order *(ordre public)*, public health or morals or the rights and freedoms of others and are consistent with the other rights recognized in the present Covenant.

4. No one shall be arbitrarily deprived of the right to enter his own country.

Article 13 too does not require any amendment.

Article 13

An alien lawfully in the territory of a State Party to the present Covenant may be expelled therefrom only in pursuance of a decision reached in accordance with law and shall, except where compelling reasons of national security otherwise require, be allowed to submit the reasons against his expulsion and to have his case reviewed by, and be represented for the purpose before the competent authority or a person or persons especially designated by the competent authority.

Article 14 says that all persons shall be equal before law. One doubts very much whether or not such a pious and wishful thinking will be a truth ever? Experience and researches in the area show that some are 'more equal' and some are 'less equal'. Equality before the courts and tribunals is a pious wish—nice to hear—but never to happen in this terrestrial world. Nevertheless, the article 14 reads:

Article 14

1. "All persons shall be equal before the courts and tribunals. In the determination of any criminal charge against him, or of his rights and obligations in suit at law, everyone shall be entitled to a fair and public hearing by a competent, independent and impartial tribunal established by law. The press and the public may be excluded from all or part of a trial for reasons of morals, public order *(ordre public)* or national security in a democratic society or when the interest of the private lives of the parties so requires, or to the extent strictly necessary in the opinion of the court in special circumstances where publicity would prejudice

the interests of justice, but any judgement rendered in a criminal case or in a suit at law shall be made public except where the interest of juvenile persons otherwise requires or the proceedings concern matrimonial disputes or the guardianship of children;

2. Everyone charged with a criminal offence shall have the right to be presumed innocent until proved guilty according to law;

3. In the determination of any criminal charge against him, everyone shall be entitled to the following minimum guarantees in full equality;

(a) To be informed promptly and in detail in a language which he understands of the nature and cause of the charge against him;
(b) To have adequate time and facilities for the preparation of his defence and to communicate with counsel of his own choosing;
(c) To be tried without undue delay;
(d) To be tried in his presence, and to defend himself in person or through legal assistance of his own choosing; to be informed, if he does not have legal assistance, of his rights; and to have legal assistance assigned to him, in any case where the interests of justice so require, and without payment by him in any such case if he does not have sufficient means to pay for it;
(e) To examine or have examined the witnesses against him and to obtain the attendance and examination of witnesses on his behalf under the same conditions as witnesses against him;
(f) To have the free assistance of an interpreter if he cannot understand or speak the language used in court;
(g) Not to be compelled to testify against himself or to confess guilt;

4. In the case of juvenile persons, the procedure shall be such as will take account of their age and the desirability of promoting their rehabilitation.

5. Everyone convicted of a crime shall have the right to his conviction and sentence being reviewed by a higher tribunal or court according to law.

6. When a person has by a final decision been convicted of a

criminal offence and when subsequently his conviction has been reversed or he has been pardoned on the ground that a new or newly discovered fact shows conclusively that there has been a miscarriage of justice, the person who has suffered punishment as a result of such conviction shall be compensated according to law unless it is proved that the non-disclosure of the unknown fact in time is wholly or partly attributable to him.

7. No one shall be liable to be tried or punished again for an offence for which he has already been finally convicted or acquitted in accordance with the law and penal procedure of each country."

Can the human society and the people treat all persons equal before the court and tribunals? How many political leaders are ever punished? Go to a prison and look at the inmates. How many of them are affluent? Many are poor and in one country, it was seen that most of the people convicted for death penalty were socially and financially poor ones. Do we see human sharks?—Meat eater criminals?—*Mafia* Chiefs?—religious leaders in the prisons? If not, how can we say that all are equal before the courts and tribunals? Many of the politicians, businessmen, lawyers, high ranking officials, judges and 'religious' men have got unholy nexus and they are equal in many respects. Still, the amended article 14.1 will be—

Article 14

1. All persons shall be equal before the courts and tribunals. In the determination of any criminal charge against him, or of his rights, obligations and privileges in a suit at law, everyone shall be entitled to a fair and public hearing by a competent, highly specialized, trained, independent and impartial Court or Tribunal established by law. The press, the media including the visual and social media and the public may be excluded from all or part of a trial for reasons of moral, public order *(ordre public),* national security or integrity of a nation in a democratic society, or when the interest of the private lives of the parties especially of women's sex justice so requires or to the extent strictly necessary in the opinion of the Court or Tribunal as the case may be in special circumstances where publicity would prejudice or destroy the interests of justice, but any judgement rendered in a

criminal case or in a suit at law shall be made public except where the interest of juvenile persons otherwise requires or the proceedings concern matrimonial disputes or the guardianship of children.

Many of the judges are found to be not specialists—who are trained in the special subjects or special areas of law and to that extent their judgements may lack the contents of just justice. Therefore, I emphatically recommend to highly specialized, trained and experienced Court or Tribunal in the amended article. Social media in these days are very powerful or more powerful than the print and visual media. Therefore, it is necessary to put it along with the press in the new article.

The presumption of innocence now applauded in administration of justice does not have much meaning. Why? In accusatorial system of justice, the accused is presumed to be innocent. How is it possible to presume that a guilty person is innocent? Man cannot conceive of such an innocence. In the inquisitorial system of justice, the accused is presumed to be guilty. How is it possible to presume so? Precisely therefore, I have suggested **'Noquisitorial System'** of justice in my other books. In **'Noquisitorial System'**, no presumption either in favour or in disfavour to the accused is made. The presumption is 'the accused may or may not be guilty'-or-'the accused may or may not be innocent'. Hence, the amended article 14.2 will be—

2. Everyone charged with a criminal offence shall have the right to be presumed or conceived *'may or may not be guilty/innocent'* until proved otherwise under a *noquisitorial* system of justice administration according to law.

In article 14.3, I am unable to understand the meaning and relevance of informing the accused about the *cause of the charge against him. Nature* of the charge is fine, but the *cause* of the charge may be unnecessary. The suggested amendment of article 14.3 (a) is:

3. In the determination of any criminal charge against him, everyone shall be entitled to the following minimum guarantees, in full equality:

(a) To be informed promptly and in detail in a language which he understands of the nature of the charge against him quoting the provision of law which he has violated.

Why I suggest that the provisions of law should be quoted.

It is necessary that the one who is charged should know clearly the charge/s against him and the charge/s must be couched in clarity. Charges made in a sweeping manner or in a general way cannot be accepted.

Instances are reported that even very poor people who do not have a lawyer's services are charged with criminal offences. If that is the case, then he should be entitled to have the lawyer's services free of cost. The amendment is:

(b) To have adequate time and facilities for the preparation of his defence and to communicate or consult with a counsel of his choice. If he does not have a counsel, he is entitled to get the services of a lawyer free of cost.

Allegations are plenty against the police and the judiciary for undue delay in investigation and trial. Instances are reported that some cases in some countries are investigated for 10 or more years and the trial takes place for more than 3 years in many cases. I have taken note of criminal cases whose delay was found to be more than 16 years. Hence, the amendment for article 14.3 (c) as under.

(c) To be investigated, prosecuted and tried without undue delay.

In my view, everything must be over within 1-2 years. There may be appeal from the trial court to the higher court. There may be a second appeal from the first appellate court to the next higher court. Everything taken together, the investigation, prosecution, trial and adjudication and appeals must be done and over within 4-5 years. 4-5 years period is a lengthy period for an ordinary man whose life-span is about 60-70-80 years.

Lawyer's services to be given free of cost has been put in the amended article 14.3 (b). Nevertheless, it needs more clarification. Earlier, I spoke about the financial status of many convicted for imprisonment. In other words, my researches show that many who are imprisoned are those who had no good lawyer to defend them or who had received a lawyer free of cost or a lawyer who is poorly paid. Many of them, as a rule, are not very much interested to defend the person charged with a criminal offence. Some have become pauper after a court trial. The amended article 14.3 (d) is:

(d) To be tried in his presence, and to defend himself in person or through legal assistance of his own choosing; to be informed, if he does not have legal assistance of this right; and to have legal assistance from a panel of lawyers already available chosen by him and assigned to him, in case where the interests of justice so requires and without payment by him in any such case if he does not have sufficient means to pay for it. He has this right not only before the trial court but also before the court/s of appeal, if that is necessary.

A panel of lawyers becomes necessary. Usually good and efficient lawyers may not come forward to offer legal assistance as it is not lucrative for them. Therefore, it is necessary to give an option to the one charged with criminal offence/s to choose a lawyer from a panel already prepared for the purpose.

Article 14.3 (d) is about examination of witnesses. That is not enough. There should be the right for cross-examination, re-examination and re-cross examination and the right to declare a witness to be 'hostile' as well. The amended version is:

(e) To examine, cross-examine, re-examine and re-cross examine or have examined, cross-examined, re-examined and re-cross examined the witnesses against him and to obtain the attendance and examination and re-examination of witnesses on his behalf under the same conditions as witnesses against him. He has a right to declare his witnesses as hostile if that is needed.

Why should the right to declare a witness as hostile be given? It so happens that the witnesses who appear for him (i.e., in the pretext of giving testimony to his favour) are purchased, influenced, threatened or abused by interested parties in prosecution. In such a desperate situation, he has no option but to declare him as a hostile witness.

No amendment is suggested to article 14.3 (f and g). They read:

(f) To have the free assistance of an interpreter if he cannot understand or speak the language used in court.

(g) Not to be compelled to testify against himself or to confess guilt.

About 14.4, it may be remembered that anything done in the case of juvenile persons shall be to the best interest of the child. Rehabilitation of the juvenile is just only one aspect of his total personality development. The aim and objective should be the development of his personality in an upright way in the right direction. Therefore, a thorough amendment is required in the following way.

(4) In the case of juvenile persons—either in the case of a child in conflict with law or in the case of a child in need of care and protection—the procedure shall be such as will take account of their age and the desirability of promoting the development of their total personality in an upright way in the right direction via correction, reformation, resocialization, rehabilitation and reintegration to society back. The principle of *'parens patriae'* is recognized in all the procedures taken in favour of juvenile persons.

A minor change is needed in the following way in the case of article 14.5:

(5) Every one convicted of a crime shall have the right to his conviction and sentence being reviewed by a higher Court or Tribunal, as the case may be, according to laws. In case, he is acquitted in the appeal and the acquittal is with honour and not under benefit of doubt, he is entitled to get victim compensation/restitution as decided by an impartial Victim Compensation Tribunal instituted for the purpose.

Above, the need to provide victim compensation/restitution to all those who are acquitted with honour has been discussed. Under article 14.6, the victim compensation is extended to other cases as well in the following way—i.e.,

When a person has by a final decision been convicted of a criminal offence and when subsequently his conviction has been reversed or he has been pardoned on the ground that a new or newly discovered fact shows conclusively that there has been a miscarriage of justice, the person who has suffered punishment as a result of such conviction shall be compensated according to law, unless it is proved that the non-disclosure of the unknown fact in time is wholly or partly attributable to him.

The above provision contained in article 14 (6) needs a through revision. The amended version is:

(6) When a person has by a final decision been convicted of a criminal offence and when subsequently his conviction has been reversed or he has been pardoned on the ground that a new or newly discovered fact shows conclusively that there has been a miscarriage of justice by way of administration of wounded justice, less justice, injustice, partial justice, ill-justice etc. during the course of investigation, prosecution, trial or adjudication, the

person who has suffered losses—physical, psychological, financial—and punishment as a result of such a conviction shall be compensated according to law, unless it is proved that the non-disclosure of the unknown fact in time is wholly or partly attributable to him. Necessary laws shall be enacted for this purpose in countries where no laws for victim compensation/restitution is now in force.

No amendment is recommended to article 14.7 as it reads:

7. No one shall be liable to be tried or punished again for an offence for which he has already been finally convicted or acquitted in accordance with the law and penal procedure of each country.

Ex post facto theory is accepted in jurisprudence. Article 15 is about it and it reads:

Article 15

1. No one shall be held guilty of any offence on account of any act or omission which did not constitute a criminal offence, under national or international law, at the time when it was committed. Nor shall a heavier penalty be imposed than the one that was applicable at the time when the criminal offence was committed. If subsequent to the commission of the offence, provision is made by law for the imposition of the lighter penalty, the offender shall benefit thereby.

No amendment is suggested to the above Article 15.1. Again Article 15.2 reads:

2. Nothing in this article shall prejudice the trial and punishment of any person for any act or omission which, at the time when it was committed, was criminal according to the general principles of law recognized by the community of nations.

No amendment is proposed for article 15.2, above. Likewise, no amendment is suggested to article 16 which reads:

Article 16

Everyone shall have the right to recognition everywhere as a person before the law.

Article 17 is as follows.

Article 17

1. "No one shall be subjected to arbitrary or unlawful interference with his privacy, family, home or correspondence, nor to unlawful attacks on his honour and reputation.

2. Everyone has the right to the protection of the law against such interference or attacks."

There is shadowing of people by police and surveillance of certain individuals. This is a time of electronic surveillance and CCTV camera may be found everywhere. Police surveillance/ shadowing, media surveillance/shadowing, surveillance by private detective agencies, political parties, those who want to black mail people etc. are seen. Hence, the amended article 17.1 will be:

Article 17

1. No one shall be subjected to arbitrary or unlawful or unnecessary or unwarranted interference with his privacy, morality, family, home or correspondence by any means or methods—electronic or otherwise—nor to unlawful, immoral or unjustified attacks on his honour, good name and reputation.

2. Everyone has the right to the protection of the law against such interference or attacks.

3. Persons who are incarcerated or are under the lawful custody of an authority shall enjoy the above stated freedom and the authorities who have their care and custody have only limited powers to interfere in the correspondence of those who are under their custody and their power shall be restricted by duly enacted laws. Correspondence here means correspondence by letters, internet, telephone, social media or through personal communications etc. and it shall be restricted or controlled by laws to that effect.

Article 18 is as follows.

Article 18

1. "Everyone shall have the right to freedom of thought, conscience and religion. This right shall include freedom to have or to adopt a religion or belief of his choice, and freedom, either

individually or in community with others and in public or private to manifest his religion or belief in worship, observance, practice and teaching.

2. No one shall be subject to coercion which would impair his freedom to have or to adopt a religion or belief of his choice.

3. Freedom to manifest one's religion or belief may be subject only to such limitations as are prescribed by law and are necessary to protect public safety, order, health, or morals or the fundamental rights and freedoms of others.

4. The States Parties to the present Covenant undertake to have respect for the liberty of parents and, when applicable, legal guardians to ensure the religious and moral education of their children in conformity with their own convictions."

'We eat the same food, but what a variety of thoughts'—this is a village saying and it means that man has the freedom of thought over which no one has any control. When one's thought is put into action, it should not affect the freedom of others to behave in a way they think provided the action is lawful. Necessarily, it means that man has the right to freedom of thought and article 18.1 recognizes this freedom. What is called the *'freedom of conscience?'* Conscience means, as said elsewhere, the sense of what is right or wrong in one's conduct or motives; impelling one toward right action, ethical and moral principles that control or inhibit the actions or thoughts of an individual. In other words, conscience is very much related to morality/ethics. This Article says that man has the right to freedom of conscience and it means that man may behave in any way he likes provided he is prepared to enjoy or suffer the consequence of his action. Finally, man has the right to freedom of religion which is otherwise called the 'spirituality' which is based on faith or belief or both. In my **push—pull—ego factor theory of crime causation,** I have explained that man has (i) intelligence, (ii) morality/ethics and, (iii) spirituality with faith or belief or both. This Article recognizes the freedom of man in (i) intelligence (thought), (ii) morality/ethics (conscience) and spirituality (religion/eternity) based on faith or spirituality based on belief (not religious) or both. The amended article 18.1, will be:

Article 18

1. Everyone shall have the right to freedom of thought, conscience, and religion. This right shall include (a) freedom to think in the way he wants and act/omit accordingly provided that he is willing to enjoy or suffer the consequence of his act/omission; (b) freedom to act/omit to act morally/ethically provided that he is prepared to live in guilty or no guilty conscience; (c) to have or to adopt a religion or creed of his choice, and freedom, either individually or in community with others and in public or in private, to manifest his religion or creed in worship, observance, practice, propagation and teaching.

I have changed 'belief' to 'creed' as I find creed having more affinity and relation with religion. *Creed* means *an accepted system of religious belief.* Belief does not necessarily mean a belief in a religion, sect, denomination, division of a religious faith. Accordingly, article 18.2 is amended as:

2. No one shall be subject to coercion which would impair his freedom to have or to adopt a religion or creed of his choice.

Allegations are always heard that there is pressured conversion into a religion by force or into a creed/sect/ denomination of a particular religion. This is bad and is against the declared principles of the present Covenant. The amended version of article 18.3 is as under:

3. Freedom to manifest one's religion or belief may be subject only to such limitations as are prescribed by law and are necessary to protect public safety, good order, health, religious harmony, communal co-existence, or morals/ethics or the fundamental rights and freedoms of others.

No amendment is proposed in article 18.4 which is reproduced down as:

4. The States Parties to the present Covenant undertake to have respect for the liberty of parents and when applicable, legal guardians to ensure the religious and moral education of their children in conformity with their own convictions.

What does article 19 say?

Article 19

1. "Everyone shall have the right to hold opinion without interference.

2. Everyone shall have the right to freedom of expression. This right shall include freedom to seek, receive and impart information and ideas of all kinds regardless of frontiers, either orally, in writing or in print, in the form of art or through any media of his choice.

3. The exercise of the rights provided for in paragraph 2 of this article carries with it special duties and responsibilities. It may, therefore be subject to certain restrictions, but these shall only be such as are produced by law and are necessary.

(a) For respect of the rights or reputation of others.

(b) For the protection of national security or of public order *(ordre public)*, or of public health or morals."

This is a time of extremism, fundamentalism, fanaticism, terrorism, insurgency, Nazism, Naxalism or such *'...isms, ...ologies and ...sophies'* which are dangerous for human coexistence and national security. Hence, I may suggest to qualify 'opinion' by prefixing *'independent and legally* sustainable' to it to read:

Article 19

1. Everyone shall have the right to hold independent and legally sustainable opinions without interference.

2. Everyone shall have the right to freedom of expression; this right shall include freedom to speak, to seek, receive, hold and impart information and ideas of all kinds, regardless of frontiers, either orally, in writing, or in print. It may as well be imparted electronically or in the form of art or through any other means including cultural or performing arts or making use of the social media of his choice.

This is a period of social media and internet transmissions. Revolution in information technology has crossed all frontiers and therefore they must be invariably included. Article 19.3 is amended as:

3. The exercise of the rights provided for in paragraph 2 of this article carries with it special duties, responsibilities and legal

liabilities. It may therefore be subject to certain controls and restrictions, but these shall only be such as are provided by law and are necessary:

(a) For respect of the rights and freedoms or honour and reputation of others;

(b) For the protection of national security, integrity of the nation or of public order *(ordre public)* or of social harmony and human co-existence or public health or morals.

4. The legal liability in paragraph 2 of this article means victimological compensation if that becomes necessary.

Article 20 is about propaganda for war or advocacy of national, racial or religious hatred etc. It says:

Article 20

1. "Any propaganda for war shall be prohibited by law.

2. Any advocacy of national, racial or religious hatred that constitutes incitement to discrimination, hostility or violence shall be prohibited by law."

I am inclined to think that any propaganda preceeds planning and preparation and therefore they too must be included in article 20.1. The amended article will be:

Article 20

1. Any planning, preparation, incitement or propaganda for war shall be prohibited by law.

2. Any advocacy of national, racial, ethnic, religious, denominational, communal, caste, sub-caste, sect hatred that constitutes incitement to discrimination, hostility, bigotry or violence shall be prohibited by law. Victims of such atrocities are entitled to receive victim compensation/restitution. Necessary laws shall be enacted to this end.

As a result of an advocacy, there may result in massive damages to the people and the victims of such atrocious acts must be compensated for their loss in many and various ways. Article 21 is about the right of peaceful assembly.

Article 21

"The right of peaceful assembly shall be recognized. No restrictions may be placed on the exercise of this right other than those imposed in conformity with the law and which are necessary in a democratic society in the interests of national security or public safety, public order *(ordre public),* the protection of public health or morals or the protection of the rights and freedoms of others."

The amended article 21 will be:

Article 21

The right to peaceful assembly and association shall be recognized. No restrictions may be placed on the exercise of this right other than those imposed in conformity with the law and which are necessary in a democratic society in the interests of national security, integrity of the nation on public safety, public order *(ordre public),* human co-existence, social welfare, the protection of public health or faith, creed or morals/ethics or the protection of the rights and freedoms of others.

The strength of the associations is, sometimes, misused or abused for creating chaos in society. It affects adversely the human co-existence, social welfare, integrity of the nation and therefore they are included in the amended article.

Article 22 of the Covenant is about freedom of association and allied matters. Above, in the previous article, it is about the right of peaceful assembly and association. Here, it is mainly to form and join trade unions for the protection of collective interests and bargaining.

Article 22

1. "Everyone shall have the right to freedom of association with others, including the right to form and join trade unions for the protection of his interests.

2. No restrictions may be placed on the exercise of this right other than those which are prescribed by law and which are necessary in a democratic society in the interests of national security or public safety, public order *(ordre public),* the

protection of public health or morals or the protection of the rights and freedoms of others. This article shall not prevent the imposition of lawful restrictions on the members of the armed forces and of the police in their exercise of this right.

3. Nothing in this article shall authorize States Parties to the International Labour Organization Convention of 1948 concerning Freedom of Association and Protection of the Right to organize, to take legislative measures which would prejudice, or to apply the law in such a manner as to prejudice the guarantees provided for in that Convention."

Trade unions have a purpose—a noble purpose of collective bargaining. They have a right to strike if that is found necessary and inevitable. Nevertheless, I notice that many of the trade unions are politicized and political leaders become the leaders of trade unions as well. It so happens that, many a time, they politicize the powers of the unions for political purposes and they are found to involve in all sorts of activities which sometimes work for the disadvantages of labour-interests. In other words, they misuse or abuse the labour strength to achieve political gains. The amended article 22.1 will be:

Article 22

1. Everyone shall have the freedom of lawful association with others, including the right to form, join and work in trade unions for the protection of his interest and social welfare.

Today associations are formed for unlawful purposes, terrorists' activities, fundamentalist and fanatic actions etc. Goverments in some countries prohibit the formation and working of such unlawful associations. The trade unions work for protecting their interests alone causing serious damages to the social welfare. They misuse their right to strike and often paralize the life of the ordinary, helpless people in society. Sometimes, they cause serious damages to public property and deny the essential services to the people in society. Hence—

2. No restrictions may be placed on the exercise of this right other than those which are prescribed by law and which are necessary in a democratic society in the interest of national security, integrity of the nation or public safety, public order *(ordre public),* protection of public property, public health or

morals or maintenance of essential services, care and protection of children and the elderly, the infirm and the handicapped or the protection of the rights and freedoms of others. This article shall not prevent the imposition of lawful restrictions and reasonable controls on the members of armed forces and of the police services in their exercise of this right.

No amendment is suggested to article 22.3 of this Covenant.

3. Nothing in this article shall authorize States Parties to the International Labour Organization Convention of 1948 concerning Freedom of Association and Protection of the Right to Organize to take legislative measures which would prejudice, or to apply the law in such a manner as to prejudice, the guarantees provided for in that Convention.

Article 23 is about family, marriage etc. and it says:

Article 23

1. "The family is the natural and fundamental group unit of society and is entitled to protection by society and the State.

2. The right of men and women of marriageable age to marry and to found a family shall be recognized.

3. No marriage shall be entered into without the free and full consent of the intending spouses.

4. States Parties to the present Covenant shall take appropriate steps to ensure equality of rights and responsibilities of spouses as to marriage, during marriage and its dissolution. In the case of dissolution, provision shall be made for the necessary protection of any children."

Family does not mean a nuclear family alone. A nuclear family means a family consisting of parents and their children only. Nuclear family can be many types. There may be family where the father is a step-father or mother is a step-mother. Accordingly a family may have children of the same father and same mother living together or of the step-father/step-mother living together with the children of the earlier marriages. Whatever that be, nuclear family means a social unit composed of father (step-father), mother (step mother) and children and they may be living together or not. Family also means a joint family and it means a group of persons closely related by blood, as parents, children, uncles, aunts and cousins living together under the same roof or all those persons considered as descendants of a common progenitor.

Again a nuclear family may be a problem family, disorganized family, separated family or broken family, unemployed, under-employed family, poor family etc. Taking everything together, the amended article 23.1 will be.

Article 23

1. The normal nuclear family is the natural, necessary, inevitable and fundamental unit of the society and is entitled to protection by society and the State.

Family and home are interrelated. A home is built by emotions of 'give and take', sharing the pain and pleasure, living together in love, concern and care etc. Such a home is the best family and therefore—

2. The right of men and women of marriageable age to marry and to found a home and thereby a family shall be recognized. Families which are not *homes* need special care and protection from the society and the State.

Will and Consent are two faculties of human mind. St. Thomas Aquinas (1225?-74), the Scholastic philosopher, a major theologian of the Roman Catholic Church is said to have brought these concepts of will and consent. Will means voluntarily—i.e., without any external force and therefore it was thought that there should be the *free will* and *full consent* of the intending spouses for the marriage. In other words there should not be any external force to give consent. Therefore—

3. No marriage shall be entered into without the free will and full consent of the intending spouses. The same principle is accepted in the living together of the gays, lesbians, hermaphrodites and transgenders who need protection by the society and State.

The question of protecting the old parents arises now. The allegation is that the old are neglected and are treated as 'waste' by many. Hence—

4. States Parties to the present Covenant shall take appropriate steps to ensure equality of rights and responsibilities of spouses as to marriage, during marriage and at its dissolution. In the case of dissolution, provision shall be made for the

necessary protection of any children and their old parents, if that is necessary.

Article 24 of the Covenant is about children and it is:

Article 24

1. "Every child shall have, without any discrimination as to race, colour, sex, language, religion, national or social origin, property or birth, the right to such measures of protection as are required by his status as a minor, on the part of his family, society and the State.

2. Every child shall be registered immediately after birth and shall have a name.

3. Every child has the right to acquire a nationality."

This Covenant has come into existence at a time the transgenders and hermaphrodites were not officially recognized. As a result, they were ignored. It is necessary to give them an identity and recognize them as human person with dignity. Therefore article 24 is amended.

Article 24

1. Every child shall have, without any discrimination as to race, colour, sex including transgender or hermaphrodites, language, religion, caste, sub-caste, creed and belief, denomination, sects, national or social origin, property or birth, the right to such measures of care and protection as are required by his status as a minor on the part of his family, society and the State.

Protection alone is not enough. There should be care as well. Religion may have different sects, divisions, denominations on the basis of the creed. There are tribals who have no religion as such (They may have their tribal gods) and there are castes and subcastes within a religion and even outside.

2. Every child shall be registered immediately after birth specifying the sex including transgenders or hermaphrodites and shall have a name.

It becomes very difficult for the transgenders and hermaphrodites to specify their sex in later life. As a result, they are denied the status of human person with dignity. Hence, I recommend that their sexual status should be specified when they are registered officially. The certificate can specify that fact as well.

3. Every child has the right to acquire a nationality.

No amendment is proposed to article 24.3 above. Article 25 is about citizen's right to take part in the conduct of public affairs and connected matters.

Article 25

1. Every citizen shall have the right and the opportunity, without any distinction mentioned in article 24 and without unreasonable restrictions:

(a) To take part in the conduct of public affairs, directly or through freely chosen representatives;

(b) To vote and be elected at genuine periodic elections which shall be by universal and equal suffrage and shall be held by secret ballot, guaranteeing the free expression of the will of the electors;

(c) To have access on general terms of equality to public service in his country.

I have no suggestion for any amendment to article 25 above. Nevertheless, I disfavour the use of electronically operating voting machines—I have an addition to it in the following way as (d):

(d) To make special reservations for transgenders, hermaphrodites, differently abled persons, members of socially and economically handicapped people and so on for appointment in public services in his country.

Article 26 is about equality before law and reads:

Article 26

"All persons are equal before the law and are entitled without any discrimination and guarantee to all persons equal and effective protection against discrimination on any ground such as race, colour, sex, language, religion, political or other opinion, national or social origin, property, birth or other status:"

Again, no concern is given to transgenders, hermaphrodites,

people in low castes/sub-castes and so on. Hence, the amendment:

Article 26

All persons are equal before the law and are entitled without any discrimination to the equal protection of the law. In this respect, the law shall prohibit any discrimination and guarantee to all persons equal and effective protection against discrimination on any ground, such as race, colour, sex including transgender and hermaphrodites, language, religion, sect, castes, sub-castes, creed and belief, political or other opinion, national or social origin, property, birth or other status.

Minorities are important in any country. Protection of the interests of the minorities is a measure of honour and dignity for the nation. Minorities may be on the basis of religion, culture, language etc. and all must be honoured. Article 27 is about it and it reads:

Article 27

In those countries in which ethnic, religious or linguistic minorities exist, persons belonging to such minorities shall not be denied the right, in community with the other members of their group, to enjoy their own culture, to profess and practise their own religion or to use their own language.

No change is suggested. Some nations made reservations and have made interpretative declarations to their application of the Covenant. For examples:

1. Belgium interpreted the freedom of speech, assembly and association in a manner consistent with the European Convention on Human Rights. It did not consider itself obliged to ban war propaganda as required by article 20 and interpreted that article in the light of expression in the Universal Declaration of Human Rights.

2. Bahrain interpreted article 3 (i.e., no sexual discrimination), article 18 (i.e., freedom of religion) and article 23 (i.e., family rights) within the context of Islamic Sharia law.

3. Australia reserved the right to progressively implement the present standards of article 10, to compensate for miscarriage

of justice by administrative means rather than through the courts, and interpreted the prohibition on racial incitement as being subject to the freedoms of expression, association and assembly. It also declared that its implementation would be effected at each level of its federal system.

4. Denmark reserved to exclude the press and the public from trials as per its own laws. Reservation was also made to article 20, paragraph 1. It was in accordance with the vote cast by Denmark in the XVI General Assembly of the United Nations in 1961 when Danish Delegation, referring to the preceding article concerning freedom of expression, voted against the prohibition against propaganda for war.

Thus, we may see Gambia, Congo, Belize, Barbados, Bahamas, Austria, Argentina making reservations and interpretative declarations to their application of the Covenant. The Covenant is not directly enforceable in Australia, but its provisions support a number of domestic laws which confer enforceable rights on individuals. United States of America ratified the Covenant in 1992 with five reservations, five understandings and four declarations.

I am of the firm opinion that we must add more Articles to the present ICCPR to make it more meaningful and relevant to the needs of the present day society. They are about the right to information, the right to services within a specified time, special rights to transgenders and hermaphrodites, to the old and infirm, to the girls and women etc. Hence, article 28—

Article 28

(i) Everyone has the right to information and thereby to secure access to information under the control of public authorities.

(ii) In order to promote transparency and accountability in the working of every public authority, each State Party shall enact legislations to provide the right to information to every citizen within a specified time prescribed by the domestic Act and any violation to provide information within the specified time will necessarily entitle him to get victim compensation/restitution.

Why should the people enjoy the right to information? Any democracy requires informed citizenry. The transparency of information which are vital to the functioning of the democracy should be provided to the people and the public service is accountable to the people in a democracy. The people are the masters in a democracy. Usually the Government officials refuse to provide information to the people without recommendations, introductions and corruption or malpractices. This right will protect the citizenry with information which they need.

Right to information alone is not enough. The people should have the right to services. Hence, the Article 29.

Article 29

(1) Everyone has the right to services and the Governments are to provide for the delivery of services to the people within the specified time limit. Any violation to provide services within the specified time will necessarily entitle him for victim-compensation/restitution.

(2) Every State Party shall enact legislations to provide the delivery of services to the general public within the time limit specified in the Act.

My studies show that the services are denied to people for several years for no justifiable reasons. There is an allegation that hoarding of files is a normal phenomenon not only in the executive sphere but also in judiciary. In many countries, the hoarding of files without taking decisions is linked with bribery/corruption and malpractices. The vested interests are after hoarding of files and there is a strong argument that hoarding of files should be treated as an offence punishable under law.

Sexual offences are plenty and they are seen in many and various forms. Sexual harassment of women at work places takes place making women to suffer. Hence, Article 30:

Article 30

Every woman has the right to get protection against sexual harassments at work places as they result in her right to life and live with dignity is adversely affected. Her right to practise any profession or to carry on any occupation, trade or business which includes a right to a safe environment free from sexual harassments shall be recognised and protected. Victims of sexual harassment are entitled to get victim compensation decided by an impartial Tribunal and necessary domestic laws shall be enacted by every State Party to the present Covenant.

While men and women are recognised and respected, the transgenders and hermaphrodites are often viewed with contempt and disrespect. They are sometimes looked down upon as sex workers and thus, they are not able to live in dignity in society. Hence, Article 31:

Article 31

1. States Parties to the present Covenant recognize the transgenders and hermaphrodites as human persons with dignity. They are entitled to get every respect and regard which any other human person has in society. They are entitled to get reservations in employment in public services and to get admission to various academic courses offered by the Government or otherwise.

2. Transgenders and hermaphrodites of marriageable age have a right to live together either with a person of their sexual status or with a person of male/female status. No living together thus shall be entered into without the free will and full consent of the indending parties.

3. States Parties to the present Covenant shall take appropriate legislative and other steps to ensure equality of rights and responsibilities of the intending parties as to living together, during their living together and at their dissolution. In the case of dissolution, provision shall be made for the necessary protection of the victimized by such a dissolution.

4. Unisex marriages are no marriages at all but are living together. States Parties to the present Covenant recognize paragraphs 2 and 3 in this Article, *mutatis mutandis* to those parties who live together.

Elder population is increasing day by day. Concurrently, elder mistreatment, abuse and neglect, harassment also go up in geometric proportion. Violence and related forms of abuses against the elders is a global public health and human rights problem resulting in death, disability and exploitation of the elderly. Hence, the Article 32:

Article 32

The States Parties to the present Covenant recognize the rights of older persons (60 +):

(i) to be free from financial, spiritual and emotional abuses and exploitations;

(ii) to qualitatively good food to maintain their health, good drinking water, shelter and adequate health care, community and family support and financial independence;

(iii) to autonomy in decision-making relating to legal and medical services;

(iv) to comprehensive medical care, health care facilities, continuing medical attention for those with terminal diseases or permanent disabilities and it includes adequate pain relief provided by the State;

(v) to social security schemes including social insurance and pension schemes in accordance with the domestic laws;

(vi) to form movements and associations for the elderly.

(vii) to not to be subjected to euthanasia (mercy killing) as they have a right to have a natural death.

(viii) to live in an environment including old-age homes that are safe and adaptable to personal preferences and changing capacities.

Prisoners suffer a lot and are subjected to a variety of human rights violations. They are invisible to all in society and precisely therefore, the sufferings they undergo are not known to many. My opinion is that they deserve to be treated in accordance with the provisions contained in the Standard Minimum Rules for the Treatment of Prisoners (now under revision by the United Nations) which I have revised in my personal capacity and the revised Rules have been published. I am not giving a separate article for it here. Nevertheless, there must be special institutions to house those under judicial custody and those who are under-trials. Such institutions must be under the judiciary (not under-the Prisons Department/Department of Correction). They must have special rules enacted and enforced keeping in mind their life in dignity under judicial custody or as under-trials. The revised (draft) of ICCPR is given in the chapter that follows.

Chapter 4
International Covenant on Civil and Political Rights (ICCPR): The Draft

Every one has civil and political rights. People living in different continents in the two hemispheres have their special and, sometimes, unique rights. Certainly, there exist differences. Exploding population, growing industrialisation, expanding urbanization, skyrocketing unemployment, alarming agitations, demonstrations, disputes, conflicts, frustrations, terrorism, communal clashes, racial fights, organized crimes etc., etc. add constantly newer and newer dimensions in civil and political rights. The United Nations may be fully aware of them, but they do not come forward to make periodical amendments to the articles in existence in the Covenant. This is an honest attempt to make a holistic revision of the Covenant—ICCPR—to update the articles contained in the international instrument to suit to the expectations and aspirations of the changing world. This draft is for international discussion and debate.

INTERNATIONAL COVENANT ON CIVIL AND POLITICAL RIGHTS

Preamble

The States Parties to the present Covenant,

Considering that, in accordance with the principles proclaimed in the Charter of the United Nations, recognition of the inherent dignity and of equal and inalienable rights of all members of the human family is the foundation of freedom, justice, peace and good governance.

Recognizing that these rights derive from the inherent dignity of human person.

Recognizing that, in accordance with the Universal Declaration of Human Rights, the ideal of free human beings enjoying civil and political freedom and freedom from fear and want can only be achieved if favourable conditions are created and maintained whereby everyone may enjoy his civil and political rights, as well as his economic, social and cultural rights in a conducive environment for development.

PART I

Article 1

1. All peoples have the right of self-determination. By virtue of that right they freely determine their political status and freely pursue their economic, social and cultural development.

2. All peoples may, for their own ends, freely dispose of their natural wealth and resources without prejudice to any obligations arising out of international economic co-operation, based upon the principle of mutual benefit, and international law. In no case may a people be deprived of its own means of subsistence.

3. The States Parties to the present Covenant, including those having responsibility for the administration of Non-Self-Governing and Trust Territories, shall promote the realization of the right of self-determination, and shall respect that right, in conformity with the provisions of the Charter of the United Nations.

PART II

Article 2

1. Each State Party to the present Covenant undertakes to respect and to ensure to all individuals within its territory and subject to its jurisdiction the rights recognized in the present Covenant, without distinction of any kind, such as race, colour, sex including transgender or hermaphrodites, language, religion, sect, caste, subcaste, denomination, creed, political or other opinion, national or social origin, aborigines and tribals, property, birth, '*...ologies, ...isms, ...sophies*' or other status.

2. Where not already provided by existing legislative or other measures, each State Party to the present Covenant undertakes to take the necessary, effective and time bound steps, in accordance with its Constitutional processes and with the provisions of the present Covenant, to adopt such laws or other measures as may be necessary to give effect to the rights recognized in the present Covenant and to get them legally enforced in case violations take place.

3. Each State Party to the present Covenant undertakes:

(a) to ensure that any person whose rights or freedoms as hereinafter recognized are violated shall have an effective remedy within a time-frame not withstanding that the violation has been committed by person/s acting in an official capacity in which case, it shall be free of cost to the victim/s.

(b) To ensure that any person claiming such a remedy shall have his right thereto determined by competent judicial, administrative or legislative authorities or by any other competent authority provided for by the legal system of the State, and to develop the possibilities of judicial remedy;

(c) To ensure that the competent authorities shall enforce such remedies when granted along with victim compensation/restitution or both.

Article 3

The States Parties to the present Covenant undertake to ensure the equal right of men and women including transgenders and hermaphrodites to the enjoyment of all civil and political rights set forth in the present Covenant.

Article 4

1. In time of public emergency—internal, external or both—which threatens the life of the nation and the existence of which is officially proclaimed, the States Parties to the present Covenant may take measures and stratagems derogating from their obligations under the present Covenant to the extent strictly required by the exigencies of the situation, provided that

such measures are not inconsistent with their other obligations under international law and do not involve discrimination solely on the ground of race, colour, creed, sex including transgender or hermaphrodites, languages, religion, caste or subcaste, sect, denomination, political or other opinions, national or social origin, aborigines and tribals, property, birth, *'...ologies, ...isms, '...sophies'*, or other status.

2. No derogation from articles 6, 7, 8 (paragraphs 1 and 2), 11, 15, 16 and 18 shall be made under this provision.

3. Any State Party to the present Covenant availing itself of the right of derogation shall immediately inform the other States Parties to the present Covenant, through the intermediary of the Secretary General of the United Nations, of the provisions from which it has derogated and of the reasons, measures and stratagems by which it was actuated. A further communication shall be made through the same intermediary on the date of which it terminates such derogation.

Article 5

1. Nothing in the present Covenant may be interpreted as implying for any State, group or persons any rights or freedoms to engage in any activity or omit to engage in an activity or perform any act or omit to perform an act aimed at the dilution or at the destruction of the rights and freedoms recognized herein or at their limitation or to a greater extent than is provided for in the present Covenant.

2. There shall be no restriction upon or derogation from or dilution of any of the fundamental human rights and freedoms recognized or existing in any State Party to the present Covenant pursuant to law, Conventions, regulations, rules, precedents, customs or traditions on the pretext that the present Covenant does not recognize such rights and freedoms or that it recognizes them to a lesser extent.

PART III

Article 6

1. Every human being has the inherent right to life. This right shall be protected by law.

2. Countries which still consider judicial murder to be a penalty to crimes, shall immediately abolish such judicial murder in accordance to the provisions of the present Covenant.

3. When deprivation of life constitute the crime of genocide, it is understood that nothing in this article shall authorize any State Party to the present Covenant to derogate in any way from any obligation assumed under the provisions of the Convention of the prevention and punishment of the crime of Genocide.

4. Anyone sentenced to life imprisonment up to or until his natural death in a Centre for Personality Development shall have the right to seek remission and get a pre-mature release under the parole system or otherwise.

5. Deleted

6. Nothing in this article shall be invoked to delay or to prevent the abolition of capital punishment (Judicial Murder as it is called) by any State Party to the present Covenant.

Article 7

1. No one shall be subjected to torture—physical, psychological, moral, spiritual, pharmacological or any other kind either alone or in combination of more than one-or cruel, inhuman, or degrading treatment or punishment.

2. No one shall be subjected to interrogation by using drugs or hypnosis, or a polygraph test or other such procedure designed to determine the truthfulness of statements by body reactions, unless, after such procedure has been proposed, such person has had an opportunity to consult with counsel for a period adequate to obtain advice concerning such procedure and consented thereto.

3. No one shall be subjected without his free and willing consent to medical, psychiatric or scientific experimentation.

Article 8

1. No one shall be held in slavery; Slavery and the slave-trade in all their forms shall be declared as offences under the domestic law and shall be prohibited.

2. No one shall be held in servitude.

3. Special aids and support shall be provided to the children

of those who were slaves once upon a time for their upliftment-socially, financially, culturally and educationally.

4. (a) No one shall be required to perform forced or compulsory labour. Exploiting the financial weakness of the labourers shall be prohibited.

(b) Paragraph 4 (a) shall not be held to preclude, in countries where imprisonment with hard labour may be imposed as a punishment for a crime, the performance of hard labour in pursuance of a sentence to such punishment by a competent court. In such situations, the provisions contained in the U.N. Standard Minimum Rules for the Treatment of Prisoners shall be meticulously followed.

(c) For the purpose of this paragraph, the terms 'forced or compulsory labour' shall not include:

(i) Any work or service, not referred to in subpragraph (b), normally required of a person who is under detention in consequence of a lawful order of a court, or of a person during conditional release from such detention.

(ii) Any service of a military character and, in countries where conscientious objection is recognized, any national service required by law of conscientious objectors.

(iii) Any service exacted in cases of emergency or calamity threatening the life, welfare or well-being of the community;

(iv) Any work or service which forms part of normal civil obligations.

Article 9

1. (i) Everyone has the right to liberty and security of person. No one shall be subjected to arbitrary arrest or detention. Informal taking into custody and unauthorised detention are offences under law.

(ii) No one shall be deprived of his liberty except on such grounds and in accordance with such procedure as are established by law.

(iii) Victims of arbitrary arrest, informal taking into custody, unauthorized detention are entitled to get victimological compensation decided *suo motu* or otherwise by an impartial Tribunal.

2. (i) Anyone who is taken into custody or arrested shall be informed, at the time of taking into custody/arrest of the reasons for his taking into custody/arrest.

(ii) An arrest/custody memo shall be prepared and given to the arrested/person taken into custody. The arrest/custody memo shall contain all information such as the name of the officer, time of arrest/taking into custody, reason for the arrest/taking into custody, medical examination, place of detention, name of witnesses, persons informed about the arrest/taking into custody etc. and such other information needed for the purpose. Every State Party to the present Covenant shall enact special legislations to this end.

(iii) Anyone arrested shall be promptly informed of any charges against him.

(iv) Any violation to the above provisions in the present Covenant is an offence under law and the victim is entitled to receive victim compensation/restitution decided, *suo motu* or otherwise, by an impartial Tribunal.

3. (i) Anyone taken into custody on legal reasons shall be promptly arrested if needed, and anyone arrested or detained on a criminal charge shall be brought promptly before a judge or other officer authorized by law to exercise judicial power. There shall be a judge or other judicial officer authorized by law to exercise judicial power for 24 hours and seven days during a week.

(ii) Anyone produced promptly after arrest before a judge or other officer authorized by law is entitled to get a bail in bailable offences or shall be remanded to custody as per law. Those released to judicial custody shall be housed in an institution manned and managed by the Judiciary.

(iii) Anyone released on bail or remanded to custody is entitled to trial within a reasonable time or to release.

(iv) Anyone remanded to custody is detained for an unreasonable period is entitled to get victimological compensation on his release without trial. States Parties to this Covenant shall enact special legislations showing the period of remand for each and every offence alleged to have been committed by the detained.

(v) It shall not be the general rule that persons awaiting trial shall be detained in custody, but release may be subject to guarantees to appear for trial, at any other stage of the judicial proceedings, and should occasion arise, for execution of judgement.

4. Anyone who is deprived of his liberty by taking him in custody or by arrest or detention shall be entitled to take proceedings before a court, in order that court may decide without delay on the lawfulness of his detention and order his release if the detention is found to be not lawful. In such cases, the victim is entitled to get victim compensation decided by an impartial Tribunal.

5. Anyone who has been the victim of unlawful taking into custody, illegal arrest or detention shall have an enforceable right to compensation and the compensation shall be decided by an impartial Tribunal after taking an action *suo motu* or otherwises to decide the amount of compensation.

6. Officials responsible for illegally taking into custody, unlawful arrest or detention are liable to be prosecuted and punished in addition to departmental action for imposing punishment on them.

7. The amount of compensation decided by the Tribunal may be realized from the officials responsible, if that is needed and possible.

Article 10

1. All persons deprived of their liberty in a lawful manner shall be treated with humanity and with respect for the inherent dignity of the human person. Those who violate this shall be punished both criminally and by taking departmental action for misconduct. The victims of ill treatment are entitled to get victim compensation as per law decided by a competent Tribunal.

2.(a) Persons who are suspected to have committed an offence/s are remanded to (i) police custody (ii) to judicial custody manned and managed by judicial officials or (iii) in rare and exceptional cases under the custody of prison officials.

Those remanded to any custody shall be housed separately from people who are housed otherwise;

(b) Accused persons or under-trial inmates in an institution for remanding them shall be segregated from people who are housed otherwise—including civil prisoners, security prisoners, political prisoners, convicted prisoners and so on.

(c) Accused persons or under-trial inmates shall be subject to separate treatment appropriate to their status as unconvicted persons. Special Rules shall be framed and enacted for the purpose of interaction between different categories of inmates and the staff; their accommodation, stay, food and living there.

(d) The suspected, the accused or the under-trial children (below 12 years of age) shall be separated from the juvenile (senior) persons (between 12 and 18 years of age) when they are housed. Both categories of the juvenile persons shall be separated from adults (between 18 and 35 years of age). Under no circumstances, the juvenile and adult persons—suspected, accused or under—trial—shall stay with the middle aged (between 35 and 60 years of age) and still senior persons (60 + years of age). The juvenile persons shall be brought as speedily as possible for adjudication.

(4) The system for 'development of personality in an upright way in the right direction' shall comprise nothing but the personality development of an inmate in a Centre For Personality Development via correction, reformation, rehabilitation, resocialization and reintegration back to society. Juveniles who are in conflict with law shall be segregated from adults, middle aged and 60 + persons and be accorded special and specialized training and treatment appropriate to their age and legal status with an aim to develop their personality in an upright way in the right direction.

Article 11

No one shall be imprisoned on the ground of inability to fulfil a contractual obligation.

Article 12

1. Everyone lawfully within the territory of a State shall within that territory, have the right to liberty of movement and freedom to choose his residence.
2. Everyone shall be free to leave any country, including his own.
3. The above-mentioned rights shall not be subject to any restrictions except those which are provided by law, are necessary to protect national security, public order *(ordre public),* public health or morals or the rights and freedoms of others and are consistent with the other rights recognized in the present Covenant.
4. No one shall be arbitrarily deprived of the right to enter his own country.

Article 13

An alien lawfully in the territory of a State Party to the present Covenant may be expelled therefrom only in pursuance of a decision reached in accordance with law and shall, except where compelling reasons of national security otherwise require, be allowed to submit the reasons against his expulsion and to have his case reviewed by, and be represented for the purpose before the competent authority or a person or persons especially designated by the competent authority.

Article 14

1. All persons shall be equal before the courts and tribunals. In the determination of any criminal charge against him, or of his rights, obligations and privileges in a suit at law, everyone shall be entitled to a fair and public hearing by a competent, highly specialized, trained, independent and impartial Court or Tribunal established by law. The press, the media including the visual and social media and the public may be excluded from all or part of a trial for reasons of moral, public order *(ordre public),* national security or integrity of a nation in a democratic society, or when the interest of the private lives of the parties especially of women's sex justice so requires or to the extent strictly

necessary in the opinion of the Court or Tribunal as the case may be in special circumstances where publicity would prejudice or destroy the interests of justice, but any judgement rendered in a criminal case or in a suit at law shall be made public except where the interest of juvenile persons otherwise requires or the proceedings concern matrimonial disputes or the guardianship of children.

2. Everyone charged with a criminal offence shall have the right to be presumed or conceived *'may or may not be guilty/innocent'* until proved otherwise under a *noquisitorial* system of justice administration according to law.

3. In the determination of any criminal charge against him, everyone shall be entitled to the following minimum guarantees, in full equality:

(a) To be informed promptly and in detail in a language which he understands of the nature of the change against him quoting the provision of law which he has violated.

(b) To have adequate time and facilities for the preparation of his defence and to communicate or consult with a counsel of his choice. If he does not have a counsel, he is entitled to get the services of a lawyer free of cost.

(c) To be investigated, prosecuted and tried without undue delay.

(d) To be tried in his presence, and to defend himself in person or through legal assistance of his own choosing; to be informed, if he does not have legal assistance of this right; and to have legal assistance from a panel of lawyers already available chosen by him and assigned to him, in case where the interests of justice so requires and without payment by him in any such case if he does not have sufficient means to pay for it. He has this right not only before the trial court but also before the court/s of appeal, if that is necessary.

(e) To examine, cross-examine, re-examine and re-cross examine or have examined, cross-examined, re-examined and re-cross examined the witnesses against him and to obtain the attendance and examination and re-examination of witnesses on his behalf under the same conditions as witnesses against him. He has a right to declare his witnesses as hostile if that is needed.

(f) To have the free assistance of an interpreter if he cannot understand or speak the language used in court.

(g) Not to be compelled to testify against himself or to confess guilt.

(4) In the case of juvenile persons—either in the case of a child in conflict with law or in the case of a child in need of care and protection—the procedure shall be such as will take account of their age and the desirability of promoting the development of their total personality in an upright way in the right direction via correction, reformation, resocialization, rehabilitation and reintegration to society back. The principle of *'parens patriae'* is recognized in all the procedures taken in favour of juvenile persons.

(5) Every one convicted of a crime shall have the right to his conviction and sentence being reviewed by a higher Court or Tribunal, as the case may be, according to laws. In case, he is acquitted in the appeal and the acquittal is with honour and not under benefit of doubt, he is entitled to get victim compensation/restitution as decided by an impartial Victim Compensation Tribunal instituted for the purpose.

(6) When a person has by a final decision been convicted of a criminal offence and when subsequently his conviction has been reversed or he has been pardoned on the ground that a new or newly discovered fact shows conclusively that there has been a miscarriage of justice by way of administration of wounded justice, less justice, injustice, partial justice, ill-justice etc. during the course of investigation, prosecution, trial or adjudication, the person who has suffered losses—physical, psychological, financial—and punishment as a result of such a conviction shall be compensated according to law, unless it is proved that the non-disclosure of the unknown fact in time is wholly or partly attributable to him. Necessary laws shall be enacted for this purpose in countries where no laws for victim compensation/restitution is now in force.

7. No one shall be liable to be tried or punished again for an offence for which he has already been finally convicted or acquitted in accordance with the law and penal procedure of each country.

Article 15

1. No one shall be held guilty of any offence on account of any act or omission which did not constitute a criminal offence, under national or international law, at the time when it was committed. Nor shall a heavier penalty be imposed than the one that was applicable at the time when the criminal offence was committed. If subsequent to the commission of the offence, provision is made by law for the imposition of the lighter penalty, the offender shall benefit thereby.

2. Nothing in this article shall prejudice the trial and punishment of any person for any act or omission which, at the time when it was committed, was criminal according to the general principles of law recognized by the community of nations.

Article 16

Everyone shall have the right to recognition everywhere as a person before the law.

Article 17

1. No one shall be subjected to arbitrary or unlawful or unnecessary or unwarranted interference with his privacy, morality, family, home or correspondence by any means or methods—electronic or otherwise—nor to unlawful, immoral or unjustified attacks on his honour, good name and reputation.

2. Everyone has the right to the protection of the law against such interference or attacks.

3. Persons who are incarcerated or are under the lawful custody of an authority shall enjoy the above stated freedom and the authorities who have their care and custody have only limited powers to interfere in the correspondence of those who are under their custody and their power shall be restricted by duly enacted laws. Correspondence here means correspondence by letters, internet, telephone, social media or through personal communications etc. and it shall be restricted or controlled by laws to that effect.

Article 18

1. Everyone shall have the right to freedom of thought, conscience, and religion. This right shall include (a) freedom to think in the way he wants and act/omit accordingly provided that he is willing to enjoy or suffer the consequence of his act/omission; (b) freedom to act/omit to act morally/ethically provided that he is prepared to live in guilty or no guilty conscience; (c) to have or to adopt a religion or creed of his choice, and freedom, either individually or in community with others and in public or private, to manifest his religion or creed in worship, observance, practice, propagation and teaching.

2. No one shall be subject to coercion which would impair his freedom to have or to adopt a religion or creed of his choice.

3. Freedom to manifest one's religion or belief may be subject only to such limitations as are prescribed by law and are necessary to protect public safety, good order, health, religious harmony, communal co-existence, or morals/ethics or the fundamental rights and freedoms of others.

4. The States Parties to the present Covenant undertake to have respect for the liberty of parents and when applicable, legal guardians to ensure the religious and moral education of their children in conformity with their own convictions.

Article 19

1. Everyone shall have the right to hold independent and legally sustainable opinions without interference.

2. Everyone shall have the right to freedom of expression; this right shall include freedom to speak, to seek, receive, hold and impart information and ideas of all kinds, regardless of frontiers, either orally, in writing, or in print. It may as well be imparted electronically or in the form of art or through any other means including cultural or performing arts or making use of the social media of his choice.

3. The exercise of the rights provided for in paragraph 2 of this article carries with it special duties, responsibilities and legal liabilities. It may therefore be subject to certain controls and restrictions, but these shall only be such as are provided by law and are necessary:

(a) For respect of the rights and freedoms or honour and reputation of others;

(b) For the protection of national security, integrity of the nation or of public order *(ordre public)* or of social harmony and human co-existence or public health or morals.

4. The legal liability in paragraph 2 of this article means victimological compensation if that becomes necessary.

Article 20

1. Any planning, preparation, incitement or propaganda for war shall be prohibited by law.

2. Any advocacy of national, racial, ethnic, religious, denominational, communal, caste, sub-caste, sect hatred that constitutes incitement to discrimination, hostility, bigotry or violence shall be prohibited by law. Victims of such atrocities are entitled to receive victim compensation/restitution. Necessary laws shall be enacted to this end.

Article 21

The right to peaceful assembly and association shall be recognized. No restrictions may be placed on the exercise of this right other than those imposed in conformity with the law and which are necessary in a democratic society in the interests of national security, integrity of the nation on public safety, public order *(ordre public),* human co-existence, social welfare, the protection of public health or faith, creed or morals/ethics or the protection of the rights and freedoms of others.

Article 22

1. Everyone shall have the freedom of lawful association with others, including the right to form, join and work in trade unions for the protection of his interest and social welfare.

2. No restrictions may be placed on the exercise of this right other than those which are prescribed by law and which are necessary in a democratic society in the interest of national security, integrity of the nation or public safety, public order

(ordre public), protection of public property, public health or morals or maintenance of essential services, care and protection of children and the elderly, the infirm and the handicapped or the protection of the rights and freedoms of others. This article shall not prevent the imposition of lawful restrictions and reasonable controls on the members of armed forces and of the police services in their exercise of this right.

3. Nothing in this article shall authorize States Parties to the International Labour Organization Convention of 1948 concerning freedom of Association and Protection of the Right to Organize to take legislative measures which would prejudice, or to apply the law in such a manner as to prejudice, the guarantees provided for in that Convention.

Article 23

1. The normal nuclear family is the natural, necessary, inevitable and fundamental unit of the society and is entitled to protection by society and the State.

2. The right of men and women of marriageable age to marry and to found a home and thereby a family shall be recognized. Families which are not *homes* need special care and protection from the society and the State.

3. No marriage shall be entered into without the free will and full consent of the intending spouses. The same principle is accepted in the living together of the gays, lesbians, hermaphrodites and transgenders who need protection by the society and State.

4. States Parties to the present Covenant shall take appropriate steps to ensure equality of rights and responsibilities of spouses as to marriage, during marriage and at its dissolution. In the case of dissolution, provision shall be made for the necessary protection of any children and their old parents, if that is necessary.

Article 24

1. Every child shall have, without any discrimination as to race, colour, sex including transgender or hermaphrodites, language, religion, caste, sub-caste, creed and belief,

denomination, sects, national or social origin, property or birth, the right to such measures of care and protection as are required by his status as a minor on the part of his family, society and the State.

2. Every child shall be registered immediately after birth specifying the sex including transgenders or hermaphrodites and shall have a name.

3. Every child has the right to acquire a nationality.

Article 25

1. Every citizen shall have the right and the opportunity, without any distinction mentioned in article 24 and without unreasonable restrictions:

(a) To take part in the conduct of public affairs, directly or through freely chosen representatives;

(b) To vote and be elected at genuine periodic elections which shall be by universal and equal suffrage and shall be held by secret ballot, guaranteeing the free expression of the will of the electors;

(c) To have access on general terms of equality to public service in his country.

(d) To make special reservations for transgenders, hermaphrodites, differently abled persons, members of socially and economically handicapped people and so on for appointment in public services in his country.

Article 26

All persons are equal before the law and are entitled without any discrimination to the equal protection of the law. In this respect, the law shall prohibit any discrimination and guarantee to all persons equal and effective protection against discrimination on any ground, such as race, colour, sex including transgender and hermaphrodites, language, religion, sect, castes, sub-castes, creed and belief, political or other opinion, national or social origin, property, birth or other status.

Article 27

In those countries in which ethnic, religious or linguistic minorities exist, persons belonging to such minorities shall not be denied the right, in community with the other members of their group, to enjoy their own culture, to profess and practise their own religion or to use their own language.

Article 28

(i) Everyone has the right to information and thereby to secure access to information under the control of public authorities.

(ii) In order to promote transparency and accountability in the working of every public authority: each State Party shall enact legislations to provide the right to information to every citizen within a stipulated time prescribed by the domestic Act and any violation to provide information within the specified time will necessarily entitle him to get victim compensation/restitution.

Article 29

(1) Everyone has the right to services and the Governments are to provide for the delivery of services to the people within the specified time limit. Any violation to provide services within the specified time will necessarily entitle him for victim—compensation/restitution.

(2) Every State Party shall enact legislations to provide the delivery of services to the general public within the time limit specified in the Act.

Article 30

Every woman has the right to get protection against sexual harassments at work places as they result in her right to life and live with dignity is adversely affected. Her right to practise any profession or to carry on any occupation, trade or business which includes a right to a safe environment free from sexual harassments shall be recognised and protected. Victims of sexual harassment are entitled to get victim compensation decided by an impartial Tribunal and necessary domestic laws shall be enacted by every State Party to the present Covenant.

Article 31

1. States Parties to the present Covenant recognize the transgenders and hermaphrodites as human persons with dignity. They are entitled to get every respect and regard which any other human person has in society. They are entitled to get reservations in employment in public services and to get admission to various academic courses offered by the Government or otherwise.

2. Transgenders and hermaphrodites of marriageable age have a right to live together either with a person of their sexual status or with a person of male/female status. No living together thus shall be entered into without the free will and full consent of the intending parties.

3. States Parties to the present Covenant shall take appropriate legislative and other steps to ensure equality of rights and responsibilities of the intending parties as to living together, during their living together and at their dissolution. In the case of dissolution, provision shall be made for the necessary protection of the victimized by such a dissolution.

4. Unisex marriages are no marriages at all but are living together. States Parties to the present Covenant recognize paragraphs 2 and 3 in this Article, *mutatis mutandis* to those parties who live together.

Article 32

The States Parties to the present Covenant recognize the rights of older persons (60 +):

(i) to be free from financial, spiritual and emotional abuses and exploitations;

(ii) to qualitatively good food to maintain their health, good drinking water, shelter and adequate health care, community and family support and financial independence;

(iii) to autonomy in decision-making relating to legal and medical services;

(iv) to comprehensive medical care, health care facilities, continuing medical attention for those with terminal diseases or permanent disabilities and it includes adequate pain relief provided by the State;

(v) to social security schemes including social insurance and pension schemes in accordance with the domestic laws;

(vi) to form movements and associations for the elderly.

(vii) to not to be subjected to euthanasia (mercy killing) as they have a right to have a natural death.

(viii) to live in an environment including old-age homes that are safe and adaptable to personal preferences and changing capacities.

PART-3

International Covenant on Economic, Social and Cultural Rights

Chapter 5
ICESCR: Introduction

The International Covenant on Economic, Social and Cultural Rights (ICESCR) is a multilateral treaty. It was adopted by the United Nations' General Assembly on 16, December 1966. The treaty came into force from 3, January 1976. Thus the Covenant is part of the International Bill of Human Rights, along with the Universal Declaration of Human Rights (UDHR) and the International Covenant on Civil and Political Rights (ICCPR), including the latter's first and second optional protocols. This Covenant is monitored by the United Nations Committee on Economic, Social and Cultural Rights.

As in the case of ICCPR, this Covenant—i.e., ICESCR—had its roots in the same process that resulted in the Universal Declaration of Human Rights. To start with, a **Declaration of the essential rights of man** had been proposed at the 1945 San Francisco Conference. It paved the way for the founding of the United Nations. The Economic and Social Council was given the task of preparing it. Early on in the process, the document was split into a Declaration giving birth to the General Principles of Human Rights, and a Convention or Covenant containing binding commitments. The first one above became the UDHR and was adopted by the United Nations, as stated earlier, on December 10, 1948.

Besides the **Preamble**, the ICESCR comprises of 31 Articles. They are divided into 5 parts. They are—

Part 1
Part 2—**General** (Article 1 to 5)
Part 3—**Substantive Rights** (Article 6-15)
Part 4—**Measures for Implementation** (Articles 16-25)

Part 5—**Final or concluding provisions** (Article 26-31).

The **Preamble** of this Covenant is almost the same as the **Preamble** of the Covenant on Civil and Political Rights. The **why** of this similarity is that the common source for both the Covenants are the U.N. Charter provisions and UDHR-1948.

Part 2, i.e., Article 1: Article 1 "recognizes the right of all peoples to self-determination, including the right to freely determine their political status, pursue their economic, social and cultural goals, and manage and dispose of their own resources. It recognizes the negative right of a people not to be deprived of its means of subsistence and imposes an obligation on those parties still responsible for non-self governing and trust territories (colonies) to encourage and respect their self-determination" (Wikipedia).

Articles 1, 3 and 5 of the ICESCR-1966 are similar to the Articles 1, 3 and 5 of the Covenant on Civil and Political Rights. However, there is a difference and that is, Article 3 speaks about the enjoyment of all economic, social and cultural rights in place of civil and political rights given in Article 2 of the Covenant on Economic, Social and Cultural Rights-1966. It is as under—

(1) Each State Party to the present Covenant undertakes to take steps, individually and through internal assistance and co-operation especially economic and technical to the maximum of its available resources, with a view to achieving progressively the full realization of the rights recognized in the present Covenant by all appropriate adoption of legislative measures.

(2) The States Parties to the present Covenant undertake to guarantee that the rights enunciated in the present Covenant will be exercised without discrimination of any kind as to race, colour, sex, language, religion, political or other opinion, national or social origin, property, birth or other status.

(3) Developing countries with due regard to human rights and their national economy, may determine to what extent they would guarantee the economic rights recognized in the present Covenant to non-nationals.

Though Article 4 of ICESCR states that the States Parties to the Covenant recognize that, in the enjoyment of those rights provided by the State in conformity with the present Covenant, they may subject such rights only to such limitations as are determined by law only in so far as this may be compatible with the nature of these rights and society for the purpose of promoting the general welfare in a democratic society.

Why do we notice the difference in the contents of the above articles? The reason for the difference is the difference in the nature of both the Covenants. Moreover, the economic, social and cultural rights are by their very nature more vague as compared to civil and political rights.

Part 2 (i.e., Articles 2-5) establishes the principle of **Progressive Realization.** It also requires the rights to be recognized "without discrimination of any kind as to race, colour, sex, language, religion, political or other opinion, national or social origin, property, birth or other status". Obviously the rights can only be limited by law, in a manner compatible with the nature of the rights, and only for the purpose of 'promoting the general welfare in a democratic society.'

What is meant by the **Principle of Progressive Realization**? Article 2 of ICESCR imposes a duty on all parties and it reads as stated above—*'Each State Party to the present Covenant undertakes to take steps, individually and through internal assistance and co-operation especially economic and technical to the maximum of its available resources with a view to achieving progressively the full realization of the rights recognized in the present Covenant by all appropriate means including particularly the adoption of legislative measures'*. This is known as the principle of **Progressive Realization.** It accepts and appreciates the truth that some of the rights may be difficult to achieve in a short span of time. The States may have its own problems and resource constraints. Nevertheless, it requires the States to act as best as they can within their limitations and means.

The principle of **Progressive Realization** certainly differs from the same of ICCPR which obliges the parties to "respect and to ensure to all individuals within its territories and subject to jurisdiction" the rights in that Convention. It does not mean that such an obligation renders the Covenant meaningless. What is the requirement? The requirement is to 'take steps' and it imposes a continuing obligation to work towards the realisation of the rights. Certainly it means that there is no scope for any deliberate regressive measures to be taken for impeding the goal.

This is the prime reason why the Committee on Economic, Social and Cultural Rights interpreted the principle as imposing minimum core obligations to provide at the least, minimum essential levels of each of the rights. If resources are highly constrained, then it must include, no doubt, the use of targeted programmes aimed at the vulnerable.

The Committee on Economic, Social and Cultural Rights considers legislation as a *conditio sine qua non* or indispensable and inevitable means for realizing the rights which are unlikely to be limited by resource constraints. The enactment of anti-discrimination laws and the establishment of enforceable rights with judicial remedies/relief's within the national legal systems are considered to be appropriate means. Certainly provisions such as anti-discrimination provisions are already required under other human rights instruments, such as the ICCPR.

Part-3 is about the **Substantive Rights** and it contains Articles 6 to 15 and it deals with Economic, Social and Cultural Rights. They are—

(i) Right to work freely chosen (Article 6), (ii) Right to the enjoyment of just and favourable conditions of work (Article 7), (iii) Right to form trade union and join the trade union of choice (Article 8), (iv) Right to social security including social insurance (Article 9), (v) Rights relating to family, motherhood, childhood and of young persons to protection and assistance and the right of free consent to marriage (Article 10), (vi) right to adequate standard of living for himself and his family including adequate food, clothing and housing and to the continuous improvement of living conditions (Article 11), (vii) Right to the enjoyment of the highest attainable standard of physical and mental health (Article 12), (viii) Right to education—including compulsory and free primary education (Article 13), (ix) Undertaking to implement the principle of compulsory education free of charge of all within a reasonable number of years (Article 14) and (x) Rights to (a) take part in cultural life, (b) enjoy the benefits of scientific progress and its applications and (c) benefit from the protections of the moral and material interests resulting from any scientific, literary or artistic production of which he is the author (Article 15)

Labour Rights

As seen in Article 6 of the Covenant, the ICESCR recognises the right to work, defined as the opportunity of every individual to make his living by freely chosen or accepted work. The Covenant makes it clear and specific that the parties are required to initiate and implement 'appropriate steps' to safeguard this right. It includes technical and vocational training as well. Further, it consists of economic policies aimed at the steady economic growth and development and ultimately full employment. The right means and implies parties to guarantee equal access to employment and protect workers from being unfairly/unjustly deprived of employment. Of course, they ought to prevent discrimination in the workplace and ensure access for the disadvantaged. No forced labour or child labour is ever thought of and they must be stopped forthwith with iron hands. The work must be freely chosen and accepted.

What type of work is contemplated under Article 6? The work referred to in Article 6 must be *decent* work. Article 7 of ECESCR describes the nature of the *decent* work. It says that the right of every person must be in 'just and favourable' working conditions. These are in otherwords and in turn explained as *'fair wages'* with *'equal pay'* for *'equal work'* and the wages must be sufficient to provide a decent living for the workers, their family and dependents. Safe working conditions must be ensured and equal opportunity in the work places ought to be guaranteed. There should be sufficient rest and leisure including limited or fixed working hours and regular paid holidays.

There are trade unions and Article 8 recognizes the workers' right to form and join trade unions. The objective here is to protect their rights—especially, their right to strike. However, this right to strike is very much restricted in the case of the members of armed forces, police and government administration. Nevertheless, several parties have their reasoned reservations on the above clause—allowing it to be interpreted in a manner consistent with their Constitutions or extending the restriction of human rights to groups such as fire fighters and so on.

Right to Social Security

What does Article 9 of ICESCR say? It recognizes the right of everyone to social security, including social insurance. It requires the parties to provide some form of social insurance scheme to ensure protection to people against the risks of sickness, disability, maternity, employment injury, unemployment or old age; to provide for survivors, orphans and those who cannot afford health care and to ensure that families are suitably or adequately, supported. No doubt, the benefit from such a scheme must be adequate and accessible to everyone. It must be provided to all without any discrimination. The Covenant does not restrict the form of the scheme. It permits both contributory and non-contributory schemes. All said and done, the Committee on Economic, Social and Cultural Rights has frustratingly noted persistent problems with the implementation of this right, with very low level of access.

Right to Family Life

According to Article 10 of ICESCR, family is 'the natural and fundamental group unit of society' and therefore it requires parties to accord it 'the widest possible protection and assistance.' Doubtlessly, every citizen is freely free to establish families and this right must be ensured by the parties. Marriage is a contract and it must be freely contracted and not forced. The Article insists that the parties should provide paid leave or adequate social security to mothers before, during and after child birth. It is an obligation which, it appears, overlaps with that of Article 9. The children are the nation's wealth and precisely, therefore, parties must take *'special measures'* to safeguard or protect children from social and economic exploitation. It requires the parties to set a minimum age of employment and to bar children from dangerous and harmful works and occupations.

Right to Adequate Standard of Living

Every one has a right to an adequate standard of living and Article 11 of the ICESCR recognises this right. It includes, but not limited to, the right to adequate food, clothing, housing and the continuous improvement of living conditions. It says further that the parties have an obligation to work in unison or to work together to establish a good world order.

Right to food means the **Right to adequate and nutritious food.** It is interpreted as requiring the availability of food in a quantity and quality sufficient to satisfy the dietary needs of individuals, free from adverse substances, and acceptable within a given culture. Every one must have an access to adequate food- and it implies an obligation to provide special programmes for the vulnerable. Certainly, it must ensure an equitable distribution of world food supplies in relation to need, taking into account the issues and problems connected with food—importing and food—exporting countries. Right to food also means a right to clean and pure **water.**

What is meant by the **right to adequate housing?** It is nothing but the **right to live somewhere in security, peace and dignity.** It necessitates adequate privacy, adequate space, adequate security, adequate lighting and ventilation, adequate basic infrastructure and adequate location with regard to work and basic amenities and facilities—all at a reasonable cost. Parties must make sure that there is security of tenure and that the access is free of discrimination and progressively work to eliminate homelessness. Forced evictions are prohibited and the **Forced Eviction** is described as 'the permanent or temporary removal against the will of the individuals, families and/or communities from the homes and/or land which they occupy, without the provision of and access to, appropriate forms of legal or other protection.' Forced evictions are gross violation of this Covenant.

The Right to adequate clothing is nothing but the right to clothing. This is not authoritatively defined and precisely therefore, it has attracted little or no academic commentary or international discussion. In India, there is a motto Roti-Kapada-Makkan which means FOOD-CLOTHING-HOUSE and in a nutshell, it may be stated that the Article 11 of ICESCR speaks nothing but 'Roti-Kadapa-Makkan'. In the said Article 11, what is considered 'adequate' has only been discussed in specific contexts, such as refugees, the disabled, the elderly, or workers.

Right to Health

Article 12.1 of the Covenant recognises the right of individuals to 'the enjoyment of the highest attainable standard of physical and mental health.' What is **Health?**. It is not the right of every one to be healthy, but is the right to control one's own health and body (including reproduction), and be free from interference such as torture or medical experimentation. The Covenant requires the States to protect the right by ensuring everyone's access to the underlying determinants of health—say, clean water, sanitation, food, nutrition and housing. There should be a comprehensive system of health care, which is available to everyone without my discrimination what-so-ever and economically accessible to all.

Article 12.2 is about reducing of infant mortality and improving child health etc. It requires States Parties to take special and specific steps to improve their citizens and the steps must include all things taken to reduce child mortality, improving child health, improving environmental and workplace health, preventing and controlling diseases and creating conditions to ensure equal and timely access to medical services for all. They are found to be 'illustrative non-exhaustive examples' rather than a complete statement of States' obligations.

Women have special needs and special rights. Therefore, the right to health is interpreted as requiring States Parties to show special respect to women's reproductive rights and gynecological needs—not by limiting access to contraception or 'censoring, withholding or intentionally misrepresenting' information about sexual health. They must also ensure that women and girls are protected from harmful traditional practices like female genital mutilation. Besides the health care, the right to health extends to the taking care to the underlying determinants of health, namely the access to safe and portable water, adequate supply of safe food, nutrition and housing, healthy occupational and environmental conditions.

Right to Free Education

Article 13.1 of the Covenant is all about the **Right to Free Education.** It recognises the right of everyone to free education—i.e., free for the primary level and ***the progressive introduction of free education*** for the secondary and higher levels. The objective is very clear and specific. It is directed towards 'the full development of the human personality and the sense of its dignity'. It is to be so because it alone can enable all people to participate most effectively in society. Doubtlessly, education is a human right and is an indispensable means for realizing other human rights. That is the reason why the Article is found to be one of the longest and the most important one in the entire Covenant.

What does Article 13.2 say? It lists a number of specific steps the parties are required to pursue for realizing the right of education. They include the provision of 'free, universal and compulsory primary education' generally available and accessible. They also include secondary education in various forms including technical and vocational training-and equally accessible higher education.

These educational rights are available to all persons without any discrimination. The Article requires the parties to develop a school system (Public, Private or Mixed). They must encourage or provide scholarships/study grants for the disadvantaged or handicapped people. The parties are required to make education free at all levels either immediately or progressively. It is clearly shown that the primary education shall be compulsory and available free to all. What about the secondary education? It 'shall be made generally available and accessible to everyone by every appropriate means, and in particular by the prograssive introduction of free education.' How is the higher education? Higher education must be made equally accessible to all, on the basis of capacity by every appropriate means and in particular by the progressive introduction of free education.

Articles 13.3 and 13.4 require parties to respect the educational freedom of parents. The parents have the freedom to choose and establish private educational institutions for their children. This is otherwise called the **Freedom of Education.** Education means not only academic education but also moral and religious education. Hence, the article recognises the right of parents to ensure the religious and moral education of their children in conformity with their own convictions. The public schools ought to respect the freedom of religion and the conscience of the children/students studying there. It is interpreted as requiring public schools as forbidding instructions in a particular religion or belief system unless non-discriminatory exemptions and alternatives are available.

The Committee on Economic, Social and Cultural Rights has the responsibility to interpret the Covenant. The Covenant requires the States to respect the academic freedom of the staff and the students. It considers any type of corporal punishment in schools to be inconsistent with the underlying principles and aims of the Covenant. The dignity of the individual must be respected.

Article 14 of ICESCR is about the initiation of the system of free compulsory primary education. It requires States Parties (which do not have a system of free compulsory primary education) to speedily or rapidly adopt a detailed plan of action for the introduction of a system of free compulsory primary education 'within a reasonable number of years.'

Right to Participation in Cultural Life

Article 15 of the Covenant recognises the right of every person to participate or take part in the cultural life—enjoy the benefit and advantage of scientific progress-and to benefit from the protection of the material and moral rights of any scientific invention/discovery or artistic work created by them. There is the intellectual property and the latter clause is intended to protect such rights. Nevertheless, it is felt that the Committee on Economic, Social and Cultural Rights interprets it as primarily or mainly protecting the moral rights of authors and proclaiming the intrinsically personal character of every creation of human mind and the ensuring durable link between creators and their creations. The Covenant requires States Parties to respect and recognize the authors' rights as they are the creators of their work. The material rights are interpreted as being the right of an adequate standard of living and need not extend over the entire lifespan of the authors. The parties are expected or better, the parties should work to promote the conservation, development and diffusion of science and culture, respect the freedom indispensable for scientific research and creative activity and encourage international contacts and co-operation in these fields.

Part-4 is about the **Measures for Implementation** (Articles 16-25). Implementation of ICESCR consists of a system of reporting. The States Parties have undertaken the obligation to file the reports on the measures adopted by them and the progress made in achieving the general observance of the rights recognised therein (Article 16 para 1). All reports are to be submitted to the Secretary General of United Nations. The U.N. will then transmit the copies to the ECOSOC for their consideration in accordance to the provisions of the Covenant.

The Secretary General on receipt of the reports shall also transmit to the Specilized Agencies the copies of the reports, or any relevant parts therefrom, from the parties to the ICESCR which are also members of these Specialized Agencies in so far as these reports, or parts therefrom, relate to any matters which come within the responsibilities of the said Agencies in accordance with their Constitutional instruments (Article 16, para 2).

Article 17 is about the furnishing of the reports by the States Parties in stages and it is done in accordance with a programme to be established by the Economic and Social Council within one year of the entry into in force of the Covenant after consultation with the parties and concerned Specialized Agencies. Article 19 says about the transmission by ECOSOC to the Commission on Human Rights for study and general recommendations or for information all reports relating to human rights filed by the States and the Specialized Agencies. The Commission on Human Rights makes a general recommendation and thereafter the States Parties to the Covenant and the specialized Agencies submit their comments. Such comments are filed before the ECOSOC (and not to the Commission) [see Article 20].

The Economic and Social Council (ECOSOC) submits from time to time to the General Assembly reports and recommendations of a general nature and a summary of information received from States Parties to the Covenant and the Specialized Agencies on various measures taken and the progress made in achieving the general observance of the rights recognized in the Covenant (Article 21). Thus, one may notice that the system of reporting is the only measure of implementation. That is the only machinery provided by this Covenant.

Articles 22

The Economic and Social Council may bring to the attention of other organs of the United Nations, their subsidiary organs and Specialized Agencies concerned with furnishing technical assistance any matters arising out of the reports referred to in this part of the present Covenant which may assist such bodies in deciding each within its field of competence, on the advisability of international measures likely to contribute to the effective progressive implementation of the present Covenant.

Article 23

The States Parties to the present Covenant agree that international action for the achievement of the rights recognized in the present Covenant includes such methods as the conclusion of conventions, the adoption of recommendations, the furnishing of technical assistance and the holding of regional meeting and technical meeting for the purpose of consultation and study organized in conjunction with the Governments concerned.

Article 24

Nothing in the present Covenant shall be interpreted as impairing the provisions of the Charter of the United Nations and of the Constitutions of the Specialized Agencies which define the respective responsibilities of the various organs of the United Nations and of the Specialized Agencies in regard to the matters dealt with in the present Covenant.

Article 25

Nothing in the present Covenant shall be interpreted as impairing the inherent right of all peoples to enjoy and utilize fully and freely their natural wealth and resources.

It may be clarified that the Committee on Economic, Social and Cultural Rights is a body of human rights experts. The Committee is given the task to monitor the implementation of the Covenant. The Committee consists of 18 independent human rights experts who are elected for a term of 4 years with half the members elected every two years.

The Optional Protocol to the ICESCR is a side agreement to the Covenant. It allows its parties to recognize the competence of the Committee on Economic, Social and Cultural Rights to consider complaints from individuals. The Protocol does not come within the scope of this book. Yet, it may be stated for academic interest that the Optional Protocol was adopted by the U.N. General Assembly on 10, December 2008. It was opened for signature on 24, September, 2009 and as of February, 2013, it has been signed only by 40s States Parties and ratified by 10. Having passed the threshold of the required ratifications, it came into force on 5, May 2013.

Chapter 6
ICESCR: The Complete Revision

UDHR includes civil and political rights. It also includes economic, social, cultural and group rights. In order to transform the **declaration** to a legally binding instrument/document, United Nations adopted two Covenants, namely—

(i) **International Covenant on Civil and Political Rights known as ICCPR**
(ii) **International Covenant on Economic, Social and Cultural Rights—otherwise called ICESCR.**

Why did the United Nations make two separate instruments? There were two streams of arguments—viz., (i) USA and Western allies advocated for two separate documents (ii) USSR (i.e., Former Union of Soviet Socialist Republic) and developing countries pleaded for a single document for both economic and political rights. An agreement on both sides was needed during the period of cold war. US advocated for signature of two separate Covenants. Many feared that a division of the Covenant might prioritize civil and political rights over economic, social and cultural rights. What did it show? It indicated that many countries were totally against proliferation of Covenants. U.S.A. and allies supported the separation. According to them, a single instrument was against the capitalist policy, federalism and US stakeholders' support. U.S.A, therefore moved the motion and the Covenants were proliferated. Resultingly, human rights were classified into three subdivisions—

(i) The first generation rights and they were known as *civil* and political rights.

(ii) The second generation rights and they were called *economic, social and cultural rights.*

(iii) The third generation rights which are otherwise, named *group rights.*

Interestingly enough, the United States of America till now has not incorporated the Covenants in its national law. ICESCR and ICCPR are adumbrated by juxtaposing them with other bill of rights.

International Covenant on Economic, Social and Cultural Rights

ICESCR—this Covenant was adopted by United Nations along side the International Covenant on Civil and Political Rights—ICCPR. Both of them were intended to develop UDHR—Universal Declaration of Human Rights. ICESCR contains second generation rights. Though it was opened for signature in 1966, it came into force only in 1976 with 155 States Parties as at January, 2007. It is a historical fact that the western nations showed preference for civil and political rights during the cold war period. During that period, the socialist States became sponsors of economic, social and cultural rights. Both ICESCR and ICCPR have similar **preamble**—i.e., "founded on the inherent dignity of the human person." Really the rights given in the two Covenants are like a coin with two sides. They are interrelated to the extent that one will be meaningless without the other Covenant.

About the Preamble

The existing **Preamble** of the International Covenant on Economic, Social and Cultural Rights reads—

"The States Parties to the present Covenant.,

Considering that, in accordance with the principles proclaimed in the Charter of the United Nations, recognition of the inherent dignity and of equal and inalienable rights of all members of the human family is the foundation of freedom, justice and peace in the world,

Recognizing that, in a accordance with the Universal Declaration of Human Rights, the ideal of free human beings enjoying freedom from fear and want can only be achieved if conditions are created whereby, everyone may enjoy his economic, social and cultural rights, as well as his civil and political rights,

Considering the obligation of States under the Charter of the United Nations to promote universal respect for, and observance of, human rights and freedoms,

Realizing that the individual, having duties to other individuals and to the community to which he belongs, is under a responsibility to strive for the promotion of and observance of the rights recognized in the present Covenant,

Agree upon the following articles:

The **Preamble** above needs to be amended in the changed and changing context of economic, social and cultural situations throughout the world. It is good to see "...is the foundation of freedom, justice and peace in the world." But, I am of the view that we must add 'good governance' too to the existing **Preamble.** Hence, we may amend the existing one as under:

> *"...is the foundation of freedom, justice, peace and good governance in the world."*

Justice may be of very many kinds and as it stands now, 48 types of justice have been identified by me. Peace means the normal non-warring conditions of a nation, a group of nations or the world at large. In order to have them—freedom, justice and peace—good governance is essential. Governance means the Government; exercise of authority; control etc.

No doubt, conditions must be created whereby everyone may enjoy his economic, social and cultural rights, as well as his civil and political rights. Creation of conditions alone will not be enough. It must be maintained and unfortunately I have seen that many conditions created were not maintained properly. They were damaged, destroyed or torpedoed by vested interests. Hence, the amended version is—

> "...can only be achieved if conditions are created and maintained whereby everyone may enjoy his economic,

> social and cultural rights, as well as his civil and political rights in a conducive environment favourable for sustainable development."

Why do I say "conducive environment? In my Push-Pull-Ego Factor theory of crime causation, I talk of ***Pull Factors*** for the development of an upright ego in the right direction. I mean conducive environment when I speak of **Pull Factors.** Every society has an **Ego** and it should be developed in an upright way in the right direction in a conducive environment. This is needed for the enjoyment of economic, social and cultural rights. Hence, the amended **Preamble** will be

Preamble

The States Parties to the present Covenant,

Considering that, in accordance with the principles proclaimed in the charter of the United Nations, recognition of the inherent dignity and of the equal and inalienable rights of all members of the human family is the foundation of freedom, justice, peace and good governance in the world,

Recognizing that these rights derive from the inherent dignity of the human person,

Recognizing that, in accordance with the Universal Declaration of Human Rights, the ideal of free human beings enjoying freedom from fear and want can only be achieved if conditions are created and maintained whereby everyone may enjoy his economic, social and cultural rights, as well as his civil and political rights in a conducive environment favourable for sustainable development,

Considering the obligation of States under the Charter of the United Nations to promote universal respect for, and observance of, human rights and freedoms,

Realizing that the individual, having duties to other individuals and to the community to which he belongs, is under a responsibility to strive for the promotion and observance of the rights recognized in the present Covenant,

Agree upon the following articles.

PART-1

Part 1 of the existing Covenant is solely on Article 1, which on the right of all people to self-determination with free right to pursue economic, social and cultural development. They have a right to deal freely with their natural resources and wealth. Article I reads:

Article 1

1. "All peoples have the right for self-determination. By virtue of that right, they freely determine their political status and freely pursue their economic, social and cultural development.

2. All peoples may for their own ends, freely dispose their natural wealth and resources without prejudice to any obligations arising out of international economic co-operation, based upon the principle of mutual benefit, and international law. In no case may a people be deprived of its own means of subsistence.

3. The States Parties to the present Covenant, including those having responsibility for the administration of Non-Self-Governing and Trust Territories, shall promote the realization of the right of self-determination and shall respect that right, in conformity with the provisions of the Charter of the United Nations."

Bangladesh, India, Indonesia, Thailand etc. made reservations and interpretative declarations to their application of Article 1 of the Covenant.

(1) Bangladesh interpreted the self-determination clause in Article 1 as applying in the historical context of colonialism.

(2) India interpreted the right of self-determination as applying "only to the peoples under foreign domination" and not to apply to people within nation-states.

(3) Indonesia interpreted the self-determination clause within the context of other international law and as not applying to peoples within a sovereign nation-state.

(4) Thailand interpreted the right to self-determination within the framework of other international law (see, UN Treaty Collection: ICESCR, UN, 3, January 1976).

The reservations and interpretative declarations of Bangladesh, India, Indonesia and Thailand—all in the Eastern hemisphere—are to be seriously considered. Yet, I endorse the self-determination class of Article 1 to be accepted as it is seen in the Covenant.

1. All peoples have the right of self-determination. By virtue of that right they freely determine their political status and freely pursue their economic, social and cultural development.
2. All peoples may, for their own ends, freely dispose of their natural wealth and resources without prejudice to any obligations arising out of international economic co-operation, based upon the principle of mutual benefit, and international law. In no case may a people be deprived of its own means of subsistence.
3. The States Parties to the present Covenant, including those having responsibility for the administration of Non-Self-Governing and Trust Territories, shall promote the realization of the right of self-determination, and shall respect that right, in conformity with the provisions of the charter of the United Nations.

PART II

Article 2

1. "Each party to the present Covenant undertakes to take steps, individually and through international assistance and co-operation, especially economic and technical, to the maximum of its available resources, with a view to achieving progressively the full realization of the rights recognized in the present Covenant by all appropriate means including particularly the adoption of legislative measures.

2. The States Parties to the present Covenant undertake to guarantee that the rights enunciated in the present Covenant

will be exercised without discrimination of any kind as to race, colour, sex, language, religion, political or other opinion, national or social origin, property, birth or other status.

3. Developing countries with due regard to human rights and their national economy, may determine to what extent they would guarantee the economic rights recognized in the present Covenant to non-nationals."

In this context, it may be noted that Bangladesh reserved the right to interpret the non-discrimination clause 2 of the Covenant within the context of its Constitution and domestic law. Egypt accepted the Covenant only to the extent it did not conflict with Islamic Sharia law. For them, Sharia is a primary source of legislation and they did not want to deviate from it. Kuwait interpreted the non-discrimination clauses of Article 2 within its Constitution and laws made thereunder (UN Treaty Collection ICESCR. UN 3, January, 1976)

I have no difficulty to accept Article 2 (1) as it is. About the non-discrimination clause, I want to say that the transgender and hermaphrodites, should be given special emphasis, and I, therefore, add "sex including the transgender and hermaphrodites" to the existing clause. I notice that castes, sub-castes, denomination, sects etc. play an important role in discrimination. They must be included. The aborigines and tribals are important in some countries and they are found to be discriminated. Hence, the amended Article 2(2) will be "The States Parties to the present Covenant undertake to guarantee that the rights enumerated in the present Covenant will be exercised without discrimination of any kind as to race, colour, caste, sub-caste, denomination, sect, sex including transgender and hermaphrodites, language, religion and its various divisions, aborigines and tribals, political or other opinion, national or social origin, property, birth or other status."

Regarding Article 2 (3) I have no objection to accept it as it is. Hence, the amended Article 2 will be as under—

Article 2

1. Each State Party to the present Covenant undertakes to take steps, individually and through international assistance and co-operation, especially economic and technical, to the

maximum of its available resources, with a view to achieving progressively the full realization of the rights recognized in the present Covenant by all appropriate means, including particularly the adoption of legislative measures.

2. The States Parties to the present Covenant undertake to guarantee that the rights enunciated in the present covenant will be exercised without discrimination of any kind as to race, colour, caste, sub-caste, creed, denomination, sect, sex including transgender and hermaphrodites, language, religion and its various divisions, aborigines and tribals, political or other opinion, national or social origin, property birth '*...ologies, ...isms, ...sophies*' or other status

3. Developing countries, with due regard to human rights and their national economy, may determine to what extent they would guarantee the economic rights recognized in the present Covenant to non-nationals.

Article 3 is about equal rights and it reads:

Article 3

"The States Parties to the present Covenant undertake to ensure the equal right of men and women to the enjoyment of all economic, social and cultural rights set forth in the present Covenant."

'Men and Women' means male and female and the division is made on sex which is physical or biological. What about the community of the transgender population and hermaphrodites? The 'equal right' should be made available to them as well. Today, the awareness of the problems faced by the transgender population and hermaphrodites becomes serious issue. They need the rights relating to job, safety, dignity, security and social status etc.

Bangladesh and Kuwait have made reservations and interpretative declarations to their application of the Covenant. Bangladesh interpreted the equal right status of men and women within the context of its Constitution and domestic law. Kuwait too adopted a similar attitude. However, no States Parties have put forward the issue relating to the transgender and hermaphrodites community. The amended article 3 will be—

Article 3

The States Parties to the present Covenant undertake to ensure the equal right of men and women including the transgender and hermaphrodites to the enjoyment of all economic, social and cultural rights set forth in the present Covenant.

What does Article 4 say? It says:

Article 4

"The States Parties to the present Covenant recognize that, in the enjoyment of these rights provided by the State in conformity with the present Covenant, the State may subject such rights only to such limitations, as are determined by law only in so far as this may be compatible with the nature of these rights and solely for the purpose of promoting the general welfare in a democratic society"

"...as are determined by law"—the phrase is not couched in clarity. Today, the laws are of many types—say, social, cultural, moral, ethical, statutory or legal (State-made laws), institutional etc. The ICESCR is concerned only with the economic, social and cultural rights and there is a likelihood that one may misunderstand them to be the laws relating to rights other than the economic, social and cultural matters. There must be clear cut statutes (i.e., an enactment made any a legislature and expressed in a formal document), otherwise, confusions may arise.

Again, what is meant by the phrase "the general welfare in a democratic country" is not clear. What is general in one country may not be general in another country. In other words, the general welfare in African countries may not be the general welfare in European or Asian countries. Hence, there requires clarity in article 4 which I think must be amended as follows:

Article 4

The States Parties to the present Covenant recognize that in the enjoyment of these rights provided by the State in conformity with the present Covenant, the State may subject such rights only to such limitations as are determined by statutes in so far as this may be compatible with the nature of these rights and solely for the purpose of promoting the general as well as the specific welfare in a democratic society.

Article 5 reads:

Article 5

1. "Nothing in the present Covenant may be interpreted as implying for any State, group or person any right to engage in any activity or to perform any act aimed at the destruction of any of the rights or freedoms recognized here in or at their limitation to a greater extent than is provided for in the present Covenant.

2. No restriction upon or derogation from any of the fundamental human rights recognized or existing in any country in virtue of law, conventions, regulation or custom shall be admitted on the pretext that the present Covenant does not recognize such rights or that it recognizes them to a lesser extent."

In Article 5, "...engage in any activity or to perform any act aimed at"—this phrase does not take into account the omissions to do an act. Omissions are as important as commissions and instances are plenty to show that omissions have caused serious rupture in the enjoyment of human rights. Hence, I recommend to put 'omissions' too along with the commissions.

"...destruction of any of the rights or freedoms recognized therein" is indeed fine. Nevertheless, there may be commissions and omissions intended to dilute the enjoyment of human rights. It means that the commissions and omissions will ensure only part—enjoyment of the human rights. Hence, the amended Article 5 (1) will be:

Article 5

1. Nothing in the present Covenant may be interpreted as implying for any State, group or person any right to engage in any activity or to perform any act or to omit to engage/perform any act aimed at the destruction or dilution of any of the rights and freedoms recognized therein or at their limitation to a greater or smaller extent than is provided for in the present

Covenant.

Limitations can be in greater or smaller extent as the limitations may go up or down depending upon many factors. In Article 5 (2), the phrase is "...in virtue of law, conventions, regulations or custom." Here too, I may suggest "statutes" instead of 'law' to avoid confusion and to make more clarity. Again, if custom is accepted, then it goes without saying that 'tradition' too must be recognized. For 'Custom' means a 'habitual practice, the usual way of acting in given circumstances; a practice so long established that it has the force of law. 'Tradition means' the handing down of statements, beliefs, legends, customs etc. from generation to generation esp. by word of mouth or by practice. In law, it means 'delivery, transfer' etc. and sometimes' one sees the traditions put as statutory laws. The source of law can be customs or traditions or both and precisely therefore, customs and traditions are put together to say custom-made laws or tradition—made laws. I wish to amend Article 5(2) as given below:

Article 5(2)

2. There shall be no restriction upon or derogation from or dilution of any of the fundamental human rights recognized or existing in any country in virtue of statutes, conventions, regulations, customs or traditions shall be admitted on the pretext that the present Covenant does not recognize such rights or that it recognizes them to a lesser or greater extent.

Why do I put ***'dilution of'*** along with restriction upon or derogation from in the amended Article 5 (2)? The reason is simple. Restriction and derogation are different from 'dilution' which means reduce the strength, force, or efficiency of by admixture. It is just like making a liquid thinner or weaker by the addition of water or the like. Instances are many that such dilutions take place in the area of human rights enjoyment. If 'lesser' extent is seen on one side, then there will be greater extent on the other side. Hence, lesser and greater must be seen in the Article 5 (2).

PART III

Articles 6, 7 (a-d), 8 (1 & 2), 9,10 (1, 2 & 3), 11 (18-2), 12 (1 and 2), 13 (1-4), 14 and 15 (1-4) are seen in this Part III. They are very important and most of them need amendments to suit to the needs of the hour. Article 6 reads:

Article 6

1. "The States Parties to the present Covenant recognize the right to work, which includes the right of everyone to the opportunity to gain his living by work which he freely chooses or accepts, and will take appropriate steps to safeguard this right.

2. The steps to be taken by a State Party to the present Covenant to achieve the full realization of this right shall include technical and vocational guidance and training programmes, policies and techniques to achieve steady economic, social and cultural development and full and productive employment under conditions safeguarding fundamental political and economic freedoms to the individual."

The above Article 6 (1) needs a lot of amendments, because it was adopted long back when the workers had different working environments. I have seen many workers forced to work for 14-18 hours a day. Some countries pay higher wages to those who work in the IT sectors and extract labour for 16-20 hours a day. There are workers who are compelled to work in abhorring conditions. They do not have even creature comforts and live in loathsome conditions without even any toilet faculties. The wages they are given may be very low and the water/food they get is qualitatively and quantitatively very poor. Hence, the amendment:

Article 6

1. (a) The States Parties to the Covenant recognize the right to work to the free choice of employment to enjoy just, decent, human-friendly and favourable conditions of work and to have access to assistance schemes for the unemployed and to the underemployed.

(b) The right to work includes the right of everyone to the opportunity to gain his living by work which he willingly chooses or accepts and will take appropriate steps to safeguard this right.

(c) The right to work also includes minimum wages for 8 hours of work and extra-wages for extra-time work and the minimum wages prescribed for a particular work should be adequate enough to secure for himself a standard of living that meets the basic requirements of life. It also includes guarantees for his right to comprehensive social security.

(d) Forced labour is prohibited and there shall be equality of opportunity in regard to work as well as a fair wage and equal remuneration for works of equal value.

(e) No child or juvenile shall be employed for any kind of work and those who employ them in any work harmful to their morals or health, dangerous to life or likely to hamper their normal development including their education shall be punished by law. For this, the age limits below which the paid employment of child labour or juvenile work should be set for the purpose of prohibition and punishment.

Assistance schemes for the unemployed-under employed become a necessity. Unemployment becomes a serious problem and some unemployed people go for various kinds of criminal activities for their livelihood. Under-employment too becomes a serious problem as some who are under-employed are seen amidst those who are caught and punished for property crimes. Some studies too prove the fact that unemployment and under-employment are factors which lead some to involve in the commission of crimes. That is the reason why an assistance scheme is suggested by me for them.

Is there any free choice of employment? I do not think that many who live in developing countries have freedom of choice in employment. People study one subject and often take up a job which they get. They do not make use of their studies for the better performance of their job and they do not need it. The European Social Charter in which the economic and social rights were adopted came into force on February 26, 1965. Accordingly, the Charter contained the following rights and principles as well.

1. Everyone shall have the opportunity to earn his living in an occupation freely entered upon.

2. Everyone has the right to appropriate facilities for vocational guidance with a view to helping him choose an occupation suited to his aptitude and interests.

African Charter on Human Rights does not say anything about the free choice of employment. Likewise, the ASEAN Human Rights Declaration too is silent about it. However, the Arab Charter guarantees the right to work to every citizen, to comprehensive social security and **free choice of work** etc. No doubt, there are countries which can afford to provide jobs to the candidates seeking to exercise their freedom for free choice of employment. Let them do so. At the same time, African nations and countries in Asia may find it extremely difficult to implement the provision. Yet, I think that it is a good thing to reach the destination even if it is in a prograssive way. Hence I wish to retain the same.

No doubt, technical and vocational guidance and training programmes-induction, in-service, specialized and orientation—should be given. Any investment on training is an investment on human resources. There should be policies and techniques to achieve steady economic, social and cultural development. Steps taken towards the development will certainly help to achieve the full realization of the right of the people. The Article 6 (2) speaks about the full and productive employment under conditions safeguarding fundamental political and economic freedoms to the individual. I endorse fully the contents in Article 6 (2) and suggest to retain it as it is in the following way.

2. The steps to be taken by a State Party to the present Covenant to achieve the full realization of this right shall include technical and vocational guidance and training programmes, policies and techniques to achieve steady economic, social and cultural development and full and productive employment under conditions safeguarding fundamental political and economic freedoms to the individual.

Article 7 says: "The States Parties to the present Covenant recognize the right of everyone to the enjoyment of just and favourable conditions of work which ensure, in particular:

(a) Remuneration which provides all workers, as a minimum, with:
   (i) Fair and equal remuneration for work of equal value

without distinction of any kind, in particular women being guaranteed conditions of work not inferior to those enjoyed by men, with equal pay for equal work.

(ii) A decent living for themselves and their families in accordance with the provisions of the present Covenant,

(b) Safe and healthy working conditions;

(c) Equal opportunity for everyone to be promoted in his employment to an appropriate higher level, subject to no considerations other than those of seniority and competence;

(d) Rest, leisure and reasonable limitation of working hours and periodic holidays with pay, as well as remuneration for public holidays."

Almost the same rights are recognized by the European Social Charter, 1961 which says that (1) all workers have the right to just conditions of work (2) All workers have the right to safe and healthy working conditions; (3) All workers have the right to a fair remuneration sufficient for a decent standard of living for themselves and their families, etc.

Article 15 of the African Charter on Human and People's Right says: "Every individual has the right to work under equitable and satisfactory conditions, and shall receive equal pay for equal work." What does the Arab Charter on Human Rights speak about it? Articles 30, 31 and 32 are about work and they read:

Article 30: "The State guarantees every citizen's right to work in order to secure for himself a standard of living that meets the basic requirements of life. The State also guarantees every citizen's right to comprehensive social security."

Article 31: "Free choice of work is guaranteed and forced labour is prohibited. Compelling a person to perform work under the terms of a court judgement shall not be deemed to constitute forced labour."

Article 32: "The State shall ensure that its citizens enjoy equality of opportunity in regard to work, as well as a fair wage and equal remuneration for work of equal value."

The Asian Human Rights Charter gives a frightening picture

about workers in Asian countries. According to the Charter, "For the majority of the workers there is little or no protection from unfair labour laws. The fundamental rights to form trade unions and bargain collectively are denied to many. Their wages are grossly inadequate and working conditions are frequently grim and dangerous."

The Charter continues: "Globalization adds to the pressures on workers as many Asian States seek to reduce the cost of production, often in collusion with foreign corporation and international financial institution."

Moreover, the conditions are very horrible. Hence, the Charter says further: "A particularly vulnerable category of workers are migrant workers. Frequently separated from their families, they are exploited in foreign states whose laws they do not understand and are afraid to invoke. They are often denied rights and condition which local workers enjoy. They slog without access to adequate accommodation, health care or legal protection. In many cases, migrants suffer from racism and xenophobia, and domestic helpers are subjected to humiliation and sometimes sexual abuse.

In my view, none of the Declarations, Charters or Conventions mention anything about the transgender community and hermaphrodites. They are many and want to get employed. Often they are ignored and I think that they need special care and protection to enjoy human rights. I find physically handicapped people being ignored in the employment market. The blind, the deaf, the crippled and so on therefore do not and cannot enjoy human rights. Instances are many to show that they go for protests, processions, slogan shouting etc. to get their rights established. Traditionally, the families used to care the physically handicapped people. Increasingly, the values and structures, under the pressure of new forms of economic organizations, have become less tolerant and sympathetic to such differently abled persons. They suffer from enormous discrimination in access to employment. There exist prejudices against them and absence of provisions responding to their demands. They want reservations in appointments to government jobs. They make complaints that their special abilities and capabilities are just ignored by the Government. If at all they are employed they get only low pay and they have hardly any chance of getting promoted. In other words, there exist little or no promotion prospects for them. They feel less in front of others. They cannot live in dignity with respect and to have opportunities for fulfillment of their potential.

Taking everything into consideration, I recommend to amend Article 7 of the ICESER in the following way.

Article 7

The States Parties to the present Covenant recognize the right of everyone to the enjoyment of just and favourable conditions of work which ensure, in particular.

(a) Remuneration which provides all workers, as a minimum, with:

(i) Fair wages and equal remuneration for work of equal value without distinction of any kind, in particular women, physically handicapped or differently abled and transgenders and hermaphrodites being guaranteed conditions of work not inferior to those enjoyed by men, with equal pay for equal work. States where there exists no law for the appointment of transgenders and hermaphrodites, special laws for their appointment should be enacted.

(ii) There shall be a system of equitable remuneration for the work of the inmates in prisons (Center for Personality Development). Every inmate shall be entitled to have provident fund, gratuity and other benefits which employees in similar works are eligible to receive outside the Centre (Prison).

(iii) A decent living for themselves and their families in accordance with the provisions of the present Covenant and their rights include:

(a) The right to adequate and affordable food of nutritional value, freedom from hunger and access to safe and qualitatively good food.

(b) The right to clothing and the right to safe, adequate, clean and affordable housing;

(c) The right to medical care;

(d) The right to clean and safe and pure drinking

water and sanitation, and

(e) The right to a safe, clean and sustainable environment.

(b) Safe and healthy working conditions. They shall include comprehensive social security. Forced labour is prohibited. Compelling a person under the terms of a court judgement shall not be deemed to constitute forced labour.

(c) Equal opportunity for everyone to be promoted in his employment to an appropriate higher level subject to no considerations other than seniority and competence. Special provisions shall be made for the promotion of the physically handicapped or those who are differently abled. If promotion prospects are not available, the workers including the physically handicapped and differently abled must be given grade promotions after a specified period of service to make them live in dignity and respect and to have opportunities for fulfillment of their potential.

(d) Rest, leisure and reasonable limitation of working hours and periodic holidays with pay as well as remuneration for public holidays.

(e) No child or any person shall be subjected to economic and social exploitation. Those who employ children and young people harmful to their morals or health, dangerous to life, or likely to hamper their normal development, including their education should be punished. Special legislations must be enacted for the purpose.

(f) Special protection should be accorded to working mothers during a reasonable period as determined by national laws and regulations before and after child birth. During such period, working mothers should be accorded paid leave or leave with adequate social security benefits. Special protection should be accorded to working mothers during a reasonable period as determined by national laws and regulations after a miscarriage of an unborn child—natural or otherwise. During such period, working women should be accorded paid leave or leave with adequate social security benefits.

(g) To end discrimination against women in the field of employment and right to work, women should be given the right to employment opportunities, free choice of profession, job security, equal remuneration, the right to special protection of health and safe working conditions, especially in safeguarding of the function of reproduction and special protection in times of pregnancy from work that may be harmful. Necessary laws shall be enacted if needed for making reservations for women in certain jobs ensuring full safety, security and protection at work places.

Article 8 of the ICESCR is reproduced as under:

1. "The States Parties to the present Covenant undertake to ensure:

(a) The right of everyone to form trade unions and join the trade union of his choice, subject only to the rules of the organization concerned for the promotion and protection of his economic and social interests. No restrictions may be placed on the exercise of this right other than those prescribed by law and which are necessary in a democratic society in the interests of national security or public order or for the protection of the rights and freedoms of theirs;

(b) The right of trade unions to establish national federations or confederations and the right of the latter to form or join international trade-union organizations;

(c) The right of trade unions to function freely subject to no limitations other than those prescribed by law and which are necessary in a democratic society in the interest of national security or public order or for the protection of the rights and freedoms of others;

(d) The right to strike, provided that it is exercised in conformity with the laws of the particular country.

2. This article shall not prevent the imposition of lawful restrictions on the exercise of these rights by members of the armed forces or of the police or of the administration of the State.

3. Nothing in this Article shall authorize States Parties to the International Labour Organization Convention of 1948 concerning Freedom of Association and Protection of the Right

to Organize to take legislative measures which would prejudice, or apply the law in such a manner as would prejudice, the guarantees provided for in that Convention.

Trade unions are a must, but they should not cause havoc in society. Allegations against the trade union activities and their anti-social activities are reported in the media. It is found that some of them cause terror in society. They rule the workers and many a time threaten the managements with selfish and parochial interests. The leaders of the trade unions at times have unholy nexus with the management. Together they cause irreparable damage to the workers. Cases have been reported that the over activities of some trade unions have resulted in the closure of the industries. The strikes, organized defiance to authority, harsh protests by the trade unions for anything and everything have resulted in causing heavy damages to the industrial growth in some countries. Workers have a right to work just like they have a right not to work. The trade unions pressure the willing to work workers not to work and thereby co-operate with the striking workers. This might cause law and order problems—leading to large scale atrocities against people and property. *Attimary* (i.e., the exorbitant wages extracted from the people for unloading materials) and *Nokkukooli* (i.e., extracting exorbitant amount of money from people for doing nothing—even when the work is done by people who do not belong to any trade unions) in Kerala are notorious ways by which exorbitant money is extracted from people and the workers do so under the cover of the trade union support. Trade unions are politicized and the political godfathers exploit the strength of the workers for their political and personal advantages. Hence, the amendment will be—

Article 8

1. The States Parties to the present Covenant undertake to ensure:
   (i) The right of everyone to form trade unions and join the trade union of his choice for the protection and promotion of social welfare and without jeopardising social interests with national laws and regulations.
   (ii) The right to form trade unions and join the trade union

of his choice will be subject only to the rules of the organization concerned for the promotion and protection of his economic and social interests.

(iii) The right to form trade unions and join the trade union of his choice will mean the right to strike within the limits laid by law.

(iv) No restriction may be placed on the exercise of the rights stated in (a) (b) and (c) other than those prescribed by law and which are necessary in a democratic society in the interest of national security or public order or for the protection of the rights and freedoms of others.

I have deeply studied the working of the trade unions sponsored by political parties. Many a time the activities of the trade unions are politically oriented so much so that they are not concerned generally with the general social welfare. They organize strikes and paralize the social life. Even essential services to the people are denied—essential commodities are made unavailable for the common man. They do not respect the rights of the workers to work as they want them to co-operate with them. The trade union activists, sometimes, cause massive destruction of public properties and involve in the commission of various kinds of crimes. So to conclude, some of the trade unions do not show their commitment to the society. They must recognize the fact that each and every trade union has an individual (trade union) function as well as a social function. Individual benefit along with social welfare must be the motto of trade unions. The mutual rivalry and unhealthy competition among the trade unions cause serious havoc in social life.

Article 8 of ICESCR continues:

(b) The right of trade unions to establish national federations or confederations and the right of the latter to form and join international trade union organizations. This right of national federations or confederations should not be on the basis of political interests or political parties' interests.

What is found today is that the trade unions are abused or misused for making political mileage/advantage. The strength of the trade unions is always a deterrent for the ruling

Government. Precisely therefore, the opposition political parties make use of or misuse or abuse that strength to agitate against the ruling Government. The aim may not be the promotion or protection of the social or economic interests of the labourers. That is the reason why I suggest that the right to strike of the national federations or confederations should not be on the basis of political interests or on political parties' interests. The question does not arise in the case of international trade union organizations.

Article 8 of ICESCR further continues:

(c) The right of trade unions to function freely does not mean that they can do anything without taking into account the social welfare and public interest. The right of trade unions to function freely means that it is subject to no restrictions and limitations other than those prescribed by law and which are necessary in a democratic society in the interests of national security or the integrity of the nation or public order and social welfare or for the protection of the rights and freedoms of others.

What do some of the trade unions do in these days? Allegations are there that they perform their activities fully forgetting their duties to the society. They have rights and concurrently they have duties to the society. They organize strikes denying drinking water to the people, ignoring patients even during epidemics, forgetting the social responsibility during natural calamities etc.

Article 8 of ICESCR says further:

(d) The right to strike, provided that it is exercised in conformity with the laws of the particular country and the laws of the country shall ensure the workers' interest and the interests of the society taking into account the moral values behind.

Today, trade unions are found to involve in a variety of strikes mostly motivated by political interests. The strikes may be: stay-in-strike, hunger strike, token strike, quickie, lightening strike, regulation or work to rule strikes besides the well known 'go slow', 'picketing' and boycott. Most unfortunately, we notice that the leaders of the trade-unions (mostly political leaders, namely Ministers, MPs and MLAs) have, sometimes, clandestine understanding with the management and by that unholy nexus, they torpedo the interests of the workers. Thus, the leaders cash on the workers making huge fortunes. As they are political leaders, very often, their objective or motive is political or at least, predominantly political. Stay in strikes (refusal to do work when the employees are present in the office or factory) and its various forms like sit-down strikes, pen-down strikes, tool-down strikes etc. are in existence. No doubt, such types of strikes organized by trade unions are illegal. In 'Go slow', there is no stoppage of work, but work at the normal pace is conspicuously absent. Doubtlessly, it is a misconduct on the part of trade unions to declare 'go slow'. Lightening strikes are staged suddenly without any prior notice to the authorities and public. It is illegal to do so. 'Regulation or work to rule' strikes may be declared by public utility services. It consists of 'meticulous adherence to regulations not normally observed.' A 'regulation strike' is probably no strike at all, for, it consists of refusal to do the work which the employer cannot in law insist on.

Not all strikes result in violence, but most of them may manifest a potential for it. The violence erupts when (i) bitterness exists between a large number of strikers and the struck employer. (ii) violence is deliberately employed (encouraged) either as a direct strike weapon or as a basis to justify counterforce or restraint and (iii) an incident or misunderstanding which may momentarily influence the persons then and there involved (see V.P. Arya, *Strikes, Lock-outs and Gheraos,* Oxford, Calcutta, 1967). The trade union's right to strike must be exercised honestly and sincerely with twin objectives—namely, the protection of the workers' interest and the protection of social welfare. There should be moral values behind any strikes by trade unions.

The amended version of Article 8 (2) ICESCR will be:

2. This article shall not prevent the imposition of lawful restrictions on the exercise of these rights by members of the armed forces or of para-military forces or of the civil police or of the administration of the State.

Why do I put "Para-military forces" in the Article? Sometimes, the para-military forces have resorted to strikes to get their demands accepted by the Government. Many countries do not allow the formation of unions or associations for the armed forces and para-military forces. Nevertheless, recently some countries allow Union or Association for the civil police under strict restrictions. Here too, I notice politicisation of police associations by political parties and certainly it affects the working of the police system in an undesirable way. While I am not in favour of forming associations by armed forces, I am not totally against such forming of associations for the civil police and there should be special laws for imposing lawful restrictions on the exercise of these rights. The para-military forces too should be brought under the purview of the Article 8 (2)

I have no objection to accept Article 8 (3) of the Covenant which reads:

Article 8 (3)

Nothing in this Article shall authorize States Parties to the International Labour Organization Convention of 1948 concerning Freedom of Association and Protection of the Right to organize to take legislative measures which would prejudice, or apply the law in such a manner as would prejudice, the guarantees provided for in that Convention. The Article 8 (3) is accepted as it is in the amended text.

What does Article 9 of the Covenant say?

Article 9

"The States Parties to the present covenant recognize the right of everyone to social security including social insurance."

This Article needs amendments in the following ways.

Article 9

(1) The States Parties to the present Covenant recognize the right of everyone to social security including social insurance which assists him or her to secure the means for a dignified and decent existence.

(2) Motherhood, infancy, childhood and old age are entitled to special care and protection. Every child, whether born in or out of wedlock shall enjoy the same social protection.

(3) People or group of persons who, through civil conflict, Government policies, economic hardships are displaced from their homes and seek refuge in other places internally or in foreign land. Likewise there are minorities and indigenous

people, whose most basic rights are frequently violated live in society. Gays, lesbians, transgender and hermaphrodites are discriminated. Their identity is denied. The peasants, the suppressed, the oppressed, the landless, the homeless, the nomads and so on deserve special protection and social security. Each State Party shall enact special legislations to the amelioration of their social and economic conditions.

(4) Those affected by HIV or AIDS, those suffering from mental disorders, those who are mentally retarded, those who are paralysed, those who are incapacitated by old age diseases become victims of gross discrimination. All of them have a right to live and die with dignity. The States Parties shall provide to them facilities for enjoying their right to adequate medical care and they shall be protected from prejudice, discrimination, neglect and persecution.

(5) Each State Party recognizes the rights of the migrant workers to join and take part in meetings of trade unions and the rights to receive the same social security benefits and medical as nationals of the country/state of employment.

Article 10 of ICESCR is:

"The States Parties to the present Covenant recognize that:

1. The widest possible protection and assistance should be accorded to the family, which is the natural and fundamental group unit of society particularly for its establishment and while it is responsible for the care and education of dependent children. Marriage must be entered into with the free consent of the intending spouses.

2. Special protection should be accorded to mothers during a reasonable period before and after child birth. During such period, working mothers should be accorded paid leave and leave with adequate social security benefits.

3. Special measures of protection and assistance should be taken on behalf of all children and young persons without any discrimination for reasons of parentage or other conditions. Children and young persons should be protected from economic and social exploitation. Their employment in work harmful to their morals or health or dangerous to life or likely to hamper their normal development should be punishable by law. States should also set age limits below which the paid employment of child labour should be prohibited and punishable by law."

Family means a lot. In current parlance, it is parents and their children, whether dwelling together or not. It may be a joint family where people in more than one generation may stay together or siblings and their wives and children stay together. It may be a nuclear family where there will be only parents and their children, or children of one person or one couple collectively. It can be a group of persons closely related by blood, as parents, children, uncles, aunts and cousins (joint family). A family may be the father/mother and their children or a couple without children or a couple with children of earlier marriage of one of them/both of them. Thus, the types of family are many. It may be a disorganized family, broken family, separated family, divorced family etc. A family is the place of abode whereas a home is not. It is often said that the difference between the 'house' (family) and the 'home' is that the former is built by bricks and the latter by pleasant emotions. Whatever that be, as seen in Article 10 (1), the widest possible protection and assistance should be accorded to the 'home'—the place in which one's domestic affections are centered and shared. Family for me means a 'home'. Hence the amendment is:

Article 10

The States Parties to the present Covenant recognize that:

(i) The widest and deepest protection and assistance should be accorded to the family (meaning home and not house) which is the natural, basic and fundamental group unit of the society, particularly for its establishment and maintenance. It is responsible for the care and protection of the children, the old/older parents and dependants and education of dependent children and their upbringing in an upright way in the right direction.

(ii) Marriages must be entered into with the free and willing consent of the intending spouses.

Family, to repeat, here means 'home' and the States Parties must provide widest protection and assistance. Also, the protection and assistance should be deepest—meaning thereby that they must be full and large. Family (Home) is the basic unit of a society and should be responsible not only for the care and protection of the children, but also for the same to the old/older parents, dependents and so on. The children must be brought up in an upright way in the right direction meaning thereby that they should be provided with an environment pregnant with moral values. The home is the first school and the mother is the first teacher. It is the first play ground and the first church/temple/mosque/gurudwara as well as the first hospital and the members at home share their affection and emotions lavishly among them. No amendment is recommended to the right for marriage. Article 10 (2) is deleted as the same is given elsewhere in the Covenant.

African Charter on Human and People's Right gives great importance to family. Under Article 18(2), it is laid down that "The State shall have the duty to assist the family which is the custodian of morals and traditional values recognized by the community". Again Article 18(4) says: "The aged and the disabled shall have the right to special measures of protection in keeping with their physical or moral needs." Clubbing them together, I suggest the following provision to be added to the existing Article 10 of the Covenant as under:

(iii) The family (home) is the custodian of morals and traditional values recognized by the community. The aged, the sick and the disabled shall have the right to special measures of protection in keeping with their physical or moral needs.

I find that the women suffer a lot in their family and it may be because of the patriarchal system prevailing in some societies. There is discrimination and refusal to recognize the rights of women in the family atmosphere. Sometimes, they are treated only as an instrument of sexual satisfaction for men. Moreover, the girl child suffers a lot and she is victimized in many ways including sexual abuse by the dear and near living with them. Hence, the following amendment:

(iv) The family shall be the place where there should be no discrimination against women and girl children. Girl child shall be specially protected from sexual abuses by the dear and near ones including the father, step-father and those related by blood or otherwise.

Article 10 (3) is retained with minor amendments as follows:

3. Special measures of protection and assistance should be taken on behalf of all children and young persons without any

discrimination for reasons of parentage or other conditions. Children and young persons should be protected from economic, social and sexual exploitations. Their employment in work harmful to their morals or dignity or health or dangerous to life or likely to hamper their normal development should be punishable by law. States should also set age limits below which the paid employment of child labour should be prohibited and made punishable by law.

Here, I put "...morals or dignity". Why? Reports are seen in the media and cases are registered by police on account of child pornography, the sale and trafficking of girl children for prostitution, kidnapping of children for beggary, conscription into drug trafficking and misuse of male children for sexual abuses etc.

Article 11, ICESCR reads:

Article 11

1. "The States Parties to the present Covenant recognize the right of everyone to an adequate standard of living for himself and his family, including adequate food, clothing and housing, and to the continuous improvement of living conditions. The States Parties will take appropriate steps to ensure the realization of this right, recognizing to this effect the essential importance of international co-operation based on free consent.

2. The States Parties to the present Covenant recognizing the fundamental right of everyone to be free from hunger, shall take, individually and through international co-operation, the measures, including specific programmes, which are needed.

(a) To improve methods of production, conservation and distribution of food by making full use of technical and scientific knowledge, by disseminating knowledge of the principles of nutrition and by developing or reforming agrarian systems in such a way as to achieve the most efficient development and utilization of natural resources.

(b) Taking into account the problems of both food-importing and food-exporting countries to ensure an equitable distribution of world food supplies in relation to need."

Really, the rights given under Article 11 are great. As stated earlier, India has a slogan: **Roti-Kapada-Makkan**—meaning, food-clothing-housing. Many people in many countries are street sleepers, nomadics and homeless without any latrines to cater to nature's call. I have seen many answering their nature's call in public—at the visibility of many. This Article gives a lot of consolation for them. Almost the same rights are seen in the **ASEAN** Human Rights Declaration and it reads:

"Every person has the right to an adequate standard of living for himself or herself and his or her family including:

a. The right to adequate and affordable food, freedom from hunger and access to safe and nutritious food;
b. The right to clothing;
c. The right to adequate and affordable housing;
d. The right to medical care and necessary social services;
e. The right to safe, drinking water and sanitation;
f. The right to a safe, clean and sustainable environment."

Asian Human Rights Charter emphatically says: "...It signifies the right to live with basic human dignity, the right to livelihood, the right to a habitat or home."

Noting the needs and demands of the people around the world, I wish to amend Article 11 as under:

Article 11

1. The States Parties to the present Covenant recognize the right of everyone to an adequate standard of living with basic human dignity and it includes:

(a) adequate and affordable food, freedom from hunger, access to safe, pure drinking water and sanitation;
(b) adequate and affordable housing with latrine and bathing facilities in a clean and sustainable environment;
(c) Continuous improvement of living conditions with medical care and social services.

(2) The States Parties to the present Covenant, recognizing the fundamental right of everyone to be free from hunger shall

take, individually and through international co-operation, the measures, including specific programmes for pregnant women, the aged and the infirm, to children and other vulnerable groups, which are needed.

There are countries where free food of nutritional value is given to school children. Special arrangements for the free supply of food in hospitals, old age homes etc. are made. Again the pregnant women are specially considered for such a scheme. Subsidised food-materials are given to people who live under the poverty line. So long as man has a **Moral Ego** in him (see, **PUSH-PULL-EGO FACTOR** Theory of Dr. James Vadackumchery), the free supply of food for the needy will be considered as the responsibility of the State and the right of the disabled people. Asian Human Rights Charter says: "The State must also take all possible measures to prevent infant morality, elimination of malnutrition and epidemics and increase life expectancy through clean and healthy environment and adequate preventive as well as curative medical facilities." This responsibility is in addition to the State's responsibility over the programmes for the free supply of food for the poor and the needy.

Article 11.2 (a & b) may be retained as there are—i.e.,

(a) To improve methods of production, conservation and distribution of food by making full use of technical and scientific knowledge, by disseminating knowledge of the principles of nutrition and by developing or reforming agrarian systems in such a way as to achieve the most efficient development and utilization of natural resources;

(b) Taking into account the problems of, both food-importing and food-exporting countries, to ensure an equitable distribution of world food supplies in relation to need.

What does Article 12, ICESCR say? It reads:

Article 12

1. "The States Parties to the present Covenant recognize the right of everyone to the enjoyment of the highest attainable standard of physical and mental health.

2. The steps to be taken by the States Parties to the present Covenant to achieve the full realization of this right shall include those necessary for:

(a) The provision for the reduction of the still birth-rate of infant mortality and for the healthy development of the child;
(b) The improvement of all aspects of environmental and industrial hygiene;
(c) The prevention, treatment and control of epidemic, endemic, occupational and other diseases;
(d) The creation of conditions which would assure to all medical service and medical attention in the event of sickness."

In my view, poverty, even in States which are industrially developed or have attained a high rate of financial stability and economic growth, is a cause of the violation of human rights. Poverty is found to be a causative factor for many crimes like dacoity, theft, prostitution, child labour, slavery, sale of human organ, mutilation of body for the purpose of begging etc. A life of dignity is not possible amidst poverty and their physical or material needs are unattended then.

Like the physical health of the people, the mental health too is important. We witness some countries where extremism, fundamentalism, fanaticism, terrorism etc. are rampant and one of the etiologial factors is the poverty and lack of facilities to the enjoyment of the mental health. Along with the mental health, the moral health is important. There must be moral values in every society. In short, everyone has a right for the enjoyment of his physical, mental and moral health and the States should recognize this right as a human right. The amended Article 12 will be as under:

Article 12

1. The States Parties to the present Covenant recognize the right of everyone to the full enjoyment of the highest allainable standard of physical, psychological and moral health. States where religious freedom is permitted, everyone should have the right for the enjoyment of spiritual health.

In my view, part enjoyment is not what is envisaged. It must be full because, the physical and psychological health is enjoyed along with moral health which is uprightly formed in the right direction. In countries where there exists religious freedom, spiritual health must be enjoyed fully by people.

Article 12.2 (a) (b) (c) and (d) is amended as:

Article 12

2. The time-bound and effective-short term and long term-steps to be taken for implementation by the States Parties to the present Covenant to achieve the full realization of this right shall include those necessary for:

(a) The provision for the control and reduction of the still birth rate and of infant mortality and for the healthy development of the child and its morality in an upright way in the right direction;

(b) The improvement of every aspect of environmental and industrial hygiene;

(c) The control, reduction, prevention, diagnosis, treatment and prognosis of epidemic, occupational and other diseases;

(d) The creation, maintenance and continuation of conditions and environments which would assure to all medical service and medical attention in the event of sickness.

It is not enough that the States Parties may take steps. The steps taken should be effective and meaningful. The steps taken must be time-bound. There is no meaning in taking steps which prolong indefinitely and we have any number of such experiences in the past. There is a saying: "Government business is Government business" which means that there is no time-limits for the fulfillment of Government business. The effective and time bound steps may be long term or short term and we want both.

Still birth means the birth of a dead child or a fetus dead at birth. In rural areas and among the tribal population, the problem is very severe. Why? No one seems to be concerned about it. Therefore it is necessary to implement steps for control as well as reduction of still birth rate and infant mortality.

Infants dying between 2-6 years of age is incredibly high in some countries. The video pictures telecasted, at times, show the deplorable conditions of children in some parts of the world. They are human skeletons moving around. They should not grow in such an unhealthy environment. They must grow in a healthy atmosphere with moral values uprightly formed in the right direction. There must be the diagnosis, prognosis etc. for the control, reduction and prevention of communicable and other diseases. Creation of conditions alone is not enough. The conditions must be properly maintained and continued for short and long term medical attention.

Article 13 of the Covenant is about education and allied matters:

Article 13

1. "The States Parties to the present Covenant recognize the right of everyone to education. They agree that education shall be directed to the full development of the human personality and the sense of its dignity and shall strengthen the respect for human rights and fundamental freedoms. They further agree that education shall enable all persons to participate effectively in a free society, promote understanding, tolerance and friendship among all nations and all racial, ethnic or religious groups, and further the activities of the United Nations for the maintenance of peace.

2. The States Parties to the present Covenant recognize that, with a view to achieving the full realization of this right:

(a) Primary education shall be compulsory and available free to all,

(b) Secondary education in its different forms, including technical and vocational secondary education, shall be made generally available and accessible to all by every appropriate means and in particular by the progressive introduction of free education;

(c) Higher education shall be made equally accessible to all, on the basis of capacity, by every appropriate means, and in particular by the progressive introduction of free education;

(d) Fundamental education shall be encouraged or intensified as far as possible for those persons who have not received or completed the whole period of their primary education;

(e) The development of a system of schools at all levels shall be actively pursued, an adequate fellowship system shall be established, and the material conditions of teaching staff shall be continuously improved.

3. The States Parties to the present Covenant undertake to have respect for the liberty of parents and, when applicable, legal guardians to choose for their children schools, other than those established by the public authorities, which conform to such minimum educational standards as may be laid down or approved by the State and to ensure the religious and moral education of their children in conformity with their own convictions.

4. No part of this article shall be construed so as to interfere with the liberty of individuals and bodies to establish and direct educational institutions, subject always to the observance of the principles set forth in paragraph 1 of this article and to the requirement that the education given in such institutions shall conform to such minimum standards as may be laid down by the State."

Education does not mean and include 'training' and therefore, I suggest 'training' too in the amended article 13. Education means the act or process of imparting or acquiring general knowledge and of developing the powers of reasoning and judgement. Thus, we may have academic education, moral education, religious education (in countries where it is permitted), cultural education etc. Training, in my view, is instruction or discipline of a person who is being trained. There is toilet training-Countries where latrines and urinals are not provided or people who answer the nature's call in public need special toilet training. They should have special training for personal hygiene and social hygiene. Their clothing must be washed regularly and the environment must be protected without being polluted. One sees wastes including human wastes, wastes of animals on roads, public places, rivers, rivulets and everywhere showing that the people in general do not have adequate education and training. The States have a responsibility in this regard.

Personality is defined in different ways by scholars in psychology. Among the many descriptions given for personality, I may subscribe to 'the sum total of the physical, mental, emotional and social characteristics of an individual'. In common parlance, it is 'the visible aspect of one's character as it impresses others. In my view, it is necessary to form the conscience of man in an upright way in the right direction by education and training given to him. For, conscience is nothing but a sense of what is right or wrong in one's conduct or motives, impelling one toward right action.' No doubt, the ethical and moral principles written in human conscience do control or inhibit one's actions or thoughts (see, Push-Pull-Ego Factor theory of crime causation). Therefore the education and training imparted to a person should be aimed and directed to the full and total development of human personality, conscience etc. The amended Article 13 will be:

Article 13

1. The States Parties to the present Covenant recognize the right of everyone to education and training. They agree that education and training shall be aimed and directed to the full and total development of the human personality and conscience and the sense of its dignity and shall strengthen the respect for human rights and fundamental freedoms. They further agree that education and training shall enable all persons to participate meaningfully and effectively in a free society, promote and propagate understanding, tolerance, appreciation and friendship among all nations and all racial, ethnic or religious groups, and further, the activities of the United Nations for the maintenance of peace for a new world order.

Effective participation does not mean a 'meaningful' participation. Meaningful here means 'with a subtime purpose'. No doubt, there should be wide propaganda via media and otherwise so that the promotion of understanding, tolerance etc. become easy. Otherwise, there will be strong protests. A new world order is what is aimed at.

Article 13.2 (a) is about compulsory and free primary

education for all. It is praise-worthy to have such a system. Primary education, in my view, means a lot. It should contain academic, moral, religious (where permitted), cultural and social education pregnant with meaning and values. Today, we see the students studying in pre-primary/primary schools at unrest as they go for paralysing the working of schools with boycotting of classes and organizing strikes etc. They shout slogans, destroy public property, attack fellow students, agitate against teachers and authorities, involve in various types of criminal activities. Hence, the amended version is.

2. The States Parties to the present Covenant recognize that with a view to achieving the full and total realization of this right.

(a) Primary education shall be academic and value-oriented. It shall be compulsory and available free to all.

No doubt, the eradication of illiteracy is a binding obligation of every State and precisely therefore, every citizen has the right to education and the States should provide such facilities. Eradication of illiteracy is just an initial step and does not have any meaning if facilities for secondary and higher education are denied to the citizens and therefore, no amendment is proposed to Article 13.2 (b) which reads:

(b) (i) Secondary education in its different forms, including technical and vocational secondary education, shall be made generally available and accessible to all by every appropriate means, and in particular by the progressive introduction of free education.

Of course, primary education is compulsory for all. What happens in some countries is that the girls are not allowed to study higher. They are denied of secondary education. People are not prepared to transcend the traditional concepts about girls and women based on patriarchal traditions and precisely because of it, the girls and women are generally not permitted to go for secondary/higher education. No doubt, we must reinterpret our cultural, traditional, religious thinkings which support gender inequality in education. We must eliminate discrimination based on caste, ethnic origins, colour, creed, occupation, place of origin, religion and others as far as the access to secondary and higher education is concerned. The following amendment may be put along with Article 13.2 (b)

(ii) Girls and women shall be encouraged by means and methods to make use of the facility offered for secondary education in different forms as gender inequality is noted in this sphere of education of girls and women.

(iii) Children born and brought up in tribal areas or suffering discrimination owing to race, colour, caste/sub-caste, ethnic origin, creed, religion, place of origin, occupation shall be encouraged by means and methods to make use of the facilities offered for secondary education in its various forms.

The above provision becomes necessary as the tribal children generally do not go for higher education. Children born to parents who have traditional occupation (e.g., carpentry, smithy etc.) in India are discouraged to go for higher education. 'A cobbler's son needs to do cobbler's job' is the attitude and it must be changed.

Article 13.2 (c) is about the accessibility to higher education. What is the meaning of 'on the basis of capacity.?' The situation is that the richer people go to better schools and they get special coaching and specilized tuition during the period of their higher education. Resultingly, they score high marks in examinations. What about the poor? They usually go to schools which are rated to be poor in everything and such students do not score much in examinations. In my opinion, there should be reservation of seats for admissions to higher education on the basis of the income of their family. Even among those who have poor income, there must be reservations for children who come from the tribal communities or who are socially handicapped owing to their birth or other social conditions. If such reservations are not offered, they will never come up in education. Resultingly, their vertical and horizontal mobility will be thwarted. The amended Article 13.2 (c) will be:

(c) Higher education shall be made equally accessible to all, subject to certain percentage of reservations for those who are economically poor or socially weaker, on the basis of their merit and capability, by every appropriate means, and in particular by the progressive introduction of free education.

This is a period of adult education, continuing education, distance education etc. There is also provision for studies for those who have no basic or fundamental education. The amended Article 13.2 (d) will be:

(d) Fundamental education must be encouraged, promoted or intensified as far as possible for those persons who have not received or completed the whole period of their primary education. Adult education, continuing education, distance education or education via correspondence and contact classes must be encouraged or intensified by means and methods made easily accessible to those who are interested in fundamental education. Facilities for fundamental education for those who have completed certain age should be provided even when they do not have any basic or primary education.

As given above, the Article 13.2 (e) is as follows: "The development of a system of schools at all level shall be actively pursued, an adequate fellowship system shall be established and the material conditions of teaching staff shall be continuously improved."

Amendments for Article 13.2 (e) is as under:

(e) The development of a system of schools at all levels shall be actively pursued, an adequate fellowship system shall be established and the material conditions of teaching staff shall be continuously improved for faculty development which will include special professional courses, orientation courses and specialized courses. The teachers must be regularly monitored to know their academic excellence and professional competence to continue as the members of the faculty. If found unsuitable, they shall be terminated from service.

Article 13.3 needs an amendment in the following way.

3. The States Parties to the present Covenant undertake to have regard and respect for the liberty of parents and when applicable, to legal guardians to choose for their children schools, other than those established by the public authorities, which conform to such minimum educational standards as may be laid down or approved by the State and to ensure the religious (if permitted) and/or moral education of their children in conformity with their own convictions. The desire of the children too may be taken into account when decisions are made.

The Article 13.3 is fine. Nevertheless, cases have been reported that children who get admitted in schools as per the interests of their parents suffer from severe tension, stress and frustrations to cope with the school environments. Resultingly, problems come up and such problems include adjustment difficulties including delinquent behaviour. However, in my opinion, the desire of the children too must be taken into account when decisions are made.

I do not recommend any amendment to Article 13.4 of the Covenant. Accordingly—

4. No part of this article shall be construed so as to interfere with the liberty of individuals and bodies to establish and direct educational institutions, subject always to the observance of the principles set forth in paragraph 1 of this article and to the requirement that the education given in such institutions shall conform to such minimum standards as may be laid down by the State.

The above article is fine and intended to the establishment of more educational institutions. But, the experience so far is not very encouraging. Education and educational institutions have become a business—a lucrative enterprise to extract money from the students and their parents seeking admission. There is the capitation fee which is exorbitant. In addition, there exists visible and clandestine methods of collecting money under various heads. Education *Mafia* is very notorious and one may notice corruption everywhere. The self-financing institutions are blamed as some of them are found to thrive and flourish on crime and corruption.

No amendment is suggested to Article 14, ICESCR and it is:

Article 14

Each State Party to the present Covenant which at the time of becoming a party has not been able to secure in its metropolitan territory or other territories under its jurisdiction compulsory primary education free of change, undertakes, within two years, to work out and adopt a detailed plan of action for the progressive implementation within a reasonable number of years, to be fixed in the plan of the principle of compulsory education free of charge for all.

1. Article 15 ICESCR confers rights on many counts. It reads:

   "The States Parties to the present Covenant recognize the right of everyone:

(a) To take part in cultural life;
(b) To enjoy the benefits of scientific progress and its applications.
(c) To benefit from the protection of the moral and material interests resulting from any scientific, literary or artistic production of which he is the author.

2. The steps to be taken by the States Parties to the present Covenant to achieve the full realization of this right shall include those necessary for the conservation, the development and the diffusion of science and culture.
3. The States Parties to the present Covenant undertake to respect the freedom indispensable for scientific research and creative activity.
4. The States Parties to the present Covenant recognize the benefits to be derived from the encouragement and development of international contacts and co-operation in the scientific and cultural fields."

Right to life also means sharing of life with other human beings. There will be cultural identities and they help individuals and communities to cope with the pressures of economic and social changes. They give meaning to life in a period of rapid transformation—says Asian Human Rights Charter. No doubt people should respect and recognize the cultures and traditions of all communities. It is argued by human rights activists that people in one community or people living in one part of the world must eliminate those features (in their cultures) which go contrary to the universal principles of human rights. Is it possible to do so? Arab Charter on Human Rights, under Articles 35 and 36 speak about the cultural life. Under article 35, it is stated:

"Citizens have a right to live in an intellectual and cultural environment in which Arab nationalism is a source of pride in which human rights are sacrificed and in which racial, religious and other forms of discrimination are rejected and international co-operation and cause of world peace are supported." Under Article 36, it is seen: "Everyone has the right to participate in cultural life, as well as the right to enjoy literary and artistic works and to be given opportunities to develop his artistic, intellectual and creative talents."

African Charter on Human and People's Rights, under Article 17 says: "(1) Every individual shall have the right to education; (2) Every individual may freely take part in cultural life of his communities; (3) The promotion and protection of morals and traditional values recognized by the community shall be the duty of the State." Under Article 18, it is further laid down that "the State shall have the duty to assist the family which is the custodian of morals and traditional values recognized by the community." Article 11.2 of the European Convention of Human Rights tells about the protection of morals. According to the ASEAN Human Rights Declaration; "Every person has the right, individually or in association with others to freely take part in cultural life, to enjoy the arts and the benefits of scientific progress and its applications and to benefit from the protection of the moral and material interests resulting from any scientific, literary or appropriate artistic production of which one is the author." Taking everything said above together, I am suggesting the amendment as fellows:

Article 15

1. The States Parties to the present Covenant recognize the right of everyone:

(a) To take part in cultural life as well as the right to enjoy literary and artistic works and to be given opportunities to develop his artistic, intellectual and creative talents; to promote and protect the morals and traditional values recognized by the community.

Science is rapidly progressing and in today's IT world of communication, the scientific progress reaches everyone quickly with lightening speed. The transport facilities are superb so much so that the scientific progress and development have become incredible in the space era where satellites control the world. The amendment is:

(b) To enjoy the benefits of scientific progress and its application for the maintenance of peace and harmony, security and stability, neutrality and freedom, such that the rights set forth in this Covenant can be fully realised. Towards this end, the States Parties shall continue to enhance friendship and co-operation in the furtherance to peace, harmony and stability for establishing a new world order.

I have no suggestion for an amendment to Article 15.1 (c) and it reads:

(c) To benefit from the protection of the moral and material interests resulting from any scientific, literary or artistic production of which he is the author.

Before I make any further recommendation for an amendment, I want to clarify certain words—

1. Preservation—means *to keep alive.*
2. Conservation—means *to keep from loss, decay, waste or injury.*
3. Maintenance—means *to keep in existence or continuance.*
4. Development—means *the act or process of progressing.*
5. Dissemination—means *to scatter or spread widely.*
6. Diffusion—means *to scatter or spread widely or thinly.*

The amended Article 15.2 will be—

2. The steps to be taken by the States Parties to the present Covenant to achieve the full and total realization of this right shall include those necessary for the preservation, conservation, maintenance, development and the diffusion or dissemination of science and culture.

The freedom is inevitable and indispensable not only for research but also for extension. Creativity with intuitive analysis will be the best. Therefore, the amendment of Article 15.2 will be:

3. The States Parties to the present Covenant undertake to respect the inevitable freedom indispensable for scientific research, extension and creative activity with intuitive analysis.

Research without extension is meaningless and creative activity without intuitive analysis will be purposeless. Finally, Article 15.4 is accepted without any amendment—i.e.,

4. The States Parties to the present Covenant recognize the benefits to be derived from the encouragement and development of international contacts and co-operation in the scientific and cultural fields.

A number of States Parties have signed the Covenant and more countries are likely to come soon. United States of America has signed the Covenant, but not ratified so far. Many States Parties have made reservations and interpretative declaration to their application of the Covenant. Examples are:

1. Algeria (signed on 10, December 1968 and ratified on 12, September 1989) interprets parts of Article 13, protecting the liberty of parents to freely choose and establish suitable educational institutions so as not to "impair its rights freely to organize its educational system."

2. France (ratified on 4, November 1980) reserves the right to govern the access of aliens to employment, social security and other benefits.

3. Ireland reserves the right to promote Irish language.

4. Norway reserves the right to strike so as to allow for compulsory arbitration of some labour disputes.

The reservations made by States Parties show that there exist differences of opinion on many counts in the Covenant.

I find a lot of areas not included in the Covenant. Perhaps, it is because the framers were not aware of such areas when the draft was prepared and accepted. They are:

1. After 1966, the social commitments of many States Parties have increased manifold and as such a number of legislations have been enacted covering various aspects of social life existing in many countries. Social legislations are the channels through which human rights in liberal and developing societies are ensured. Special legislations for safeguarding of civil rights, human rights, victim's right etc. are comparatively recent enactments in many countries towards social changes and recognition of people's rights. Of course, mass education and widespread propaganda are a *sine qua non* for the creation of an awareness of human rights among the people in any country. The new Article 16 is:

Article 16

The States Parties to the present Covenant recognize the right of everyone to have protection through the enactment of legislations in areas of—

1. Abuse and neglect of the old and the older—especially of the older women;
2. Abuse and neglect of children of both sexes and the same of transgender community.

3. Abuse and neglect of the marginalized sections of the society—widows, extremely poor, minorities, sex-workers, hermaphrodites, people suffering from disabilities, tribals, gays and lesbians and so on
4. Bonded labour, employment of children, refusal to pay minimum wages, compensation to the victims of crime and anti-social acts, divorcees, adoption, inheritance, begging, vagrancy, consumption of intoxicating drinks and of drugs injurious to health, drug trafficking, human trafficking etc.
5. Prohibiting or regulating certain pastimes like gambling, horse-racing, lotteries, cross-world puzzles etc. as they operate to the detriment of poor families resulting in the drain of their meagre financial resources, anti-social activities leading to student disputes, communal riots, racial or ethnic conflicts, religious bigotry or agrarian unrest and fights in the name of *'...isms, ...ologies and ...sophies'*, and finally leading to extremism, fundamentalism, fanaticism, terrorism and insurgency.

United Nations have formulated some principles for the older people and those principles were adopted by the General Assembly Resolution 46/91 of 16, December 1991. In my view, they must have an important place in the ICESCR itself as an Article because the older (60+) in some countries outnumber children now. The number of people over 65 years of age will triple by 2050. Now, the 21st century is known as the 'century of the elderly persons' and 22nd century will be called the century of the 'aging of the aged.' Hence, the Article proposed in ICESCR is:

Article 17

The States Parties to the present Covenant recognize the rights of the old and the older namely:

a. Independence

(1) Their right to have access to adequate food, water, shelter, clothing and health care through provisions of income, family and community support and self-help;

(2) Their right to have the opportunity to work or to have access to other income generating opportunities;

(3) Their right to participate in determining when and at what pace withdrawal from labour force takes place;

(4) Their right to have access to appropriate educational and training programmes;

(5) Their right to live in environments that are safe and adaptable to personal preferences and changing capacities;

(6) Their right to reside at for as long as possible.

b. Participation

(1) Their right to remain integrated in society, participate actively in the formulation and implementation of policies that directly affect their well-being and share their knowledge and skills with younger generations;

(2) Their right to seek and develop opportunities for service to the community and to serve as volunteers to their interests and capabilities;

(3) Their right to form movements and associations of older persons.

c. Care

(1) Their right to benefit from family and community care and protection in accordance with each society's system of cultural values;

(2) Their right to have access to health care to keep them to maintain or regain the optimum level of physical, mental and emotional well-being and to prevent or delay the onset of illness;

(3) Their right to have access to social and legal services to enhance their autonomy, protection and care;

(4) Their right to utilize appropriate levels of institutional care providing protection, rehabilitation and social and mental stimulation in a humane and secure environment;

(5) Their right to enjoy human rights and fundamental freedoms when residing in any shelter, care or treatment facility including full respect for their

dignity, beliefs, needs and privacy and make decisions about their care and quality of lives.

d. Self-Fulfillment

(1) Their right to pursue opportunities for the full development of their potential;

(2) Their right to have access to the educational, cultural, spiritual and recreational resources of society.

e. Dignity

(1) Their right to live in dignity and security and be free from exploitation and physical or mental abuse;

(2) Their right to be treated fairly regardless of age, gender, racial or ethnic or religious background, disability, or other status and be valued independently of their economic contributions.

Necessary legislations incorporating the principle set forth on each area stated above shall be enacted by the States Parties to the present Covenant.

Crimes of many descriptions are on the increase now all over the world. Out of them, economic and financial crimes are very important. There are many crimes which are committed as a result of the unholy nexus among political leaders, bureaucrats and businessmen of all decriptions. White collar crimes, consensus crimes, corruption and bribery, contractual crimes may be seen. All of them and many others of similar nature affect adversely the economic growth and development of any country. Hence, the Article 18:

Article 18

The States Parties to the present Covenant recognize the right of everyone to be protected against all kinds of crimes coming under—

1. Economic Crimes—Say, Hoarding, black marketing, adulteration, investment frauds, money chain & multi-marketing etc.
2. Financial Crimes—Say, Tax evasion, loan sharking, labour racketeering, securities frauds etc.

3. Nexus Crimes—Say, Bankruptcy frauds, sweet heart contracts, charity and religious frauds, commodities feud etc.
4. Bureaucratic Crimes—Say, Abuse of power, misuse of authority, non-use of power and authority, exercise of pseudo-authority, hoarding of files etc.
5. JEL Crimes—Say, Judgements resulting out of an unholy nexus among the legislators, executives and judicial officers.
6. Consensus Crimes—Say, corruption, bribery and adjustment frauds etc.
7. White Collar Crimes—Say, Commercial bribery and kickbacks, insurance adjustment, credit card frauds and various con-games etc.
8. Organized Crimes—Say, real estate, liquor, drug trafficking, food product adulterations etc.
9. Extremist Crimes—Say, Fundamentalism, fanaticism, terrorism, insurgency etc.
10. Corruption and malpractices etc.

Special legislations shall be enacted to control, reduce and prevent crimes stated above in their various forms.

Chapter 7
International Covenant on Economic, Social and Cultural Rights (ICESCR): The Draft

Human beings have social, cultural and economic rights. People live in different parts of the world and certainly there will be differences among them. For example, poverty deprives individuals, families and communities of their rights and promotes many undesirable situations like child labour, sale of human organs, prostitution etc. A life of dignity is just not possible in the midst of poverty. The ICESER was drafted by experts with their notions and concepts about the economic, social and cultural rights. No amendment is seen after its adoption and precisely therefore, this is an attempt to make a full and total revision of the said international instrument to suit to the needs and aspirations of the people living in various parts of the world. The draft is prepared and placed before the international community for debates and discussions.

INTERNATIONAL COVENANT ON ECONOMIC, SOCIAL AND CULTURAL RIGHTS

Preamble

The States Parties to the present Covenant,

Considering that, in accordance with the principles proclaimed in the Charter of the United Nations, recognition of the inherent dignity and of equal and inalienable rights of all members of the human family is the foundation of freedom, justice, peace and good governance.

Recognizing that these rights derive from the inherent dignity of human person.

Recognizing that, in accordance with the Universal Declaration of Human Rights, the ideal of free human beings enjoying civil and political freedom and freedom from fear and want can only be achieved if favourable conditions are created and maintained whereby everyone may enjoy his civil and political rights, as well as his economic, social and cultural rights in a conducive environment for development.

PART-I

Article 1

1. All peoples have the right of self-determination. By virtue of that right they freely determine their political status and freely pursue their economic, social and cultural development.

2. All peoples may, for their own ends, freely dispose of their natural wealth and resources without prejudice to any obligations arising out of international economic co-operation, based upon the principle of mutual benefit, and international law. In no case may a people be deprived of its own means of subsistence.

3. The States Parties to the present Covenant, including those having responsibility for the administration of Non-Self-Governing and Trust Territories, shall promote the realization of the right of self-determination, and shall respect that right, in conformity with the provisions of the Charter of the United Nations.

PART-II

Article 2

1. Each State Party to the present Covenant undertakes to respect and to ensure to all individuals within its territory and subject to its jurisdiction the rights recognized in the present Covenant, without distinction of anykind, such as race, colour, sex including transgender, hermaphrodites, language, religion, sect, caste, subcaste, denomination, creed, political or other opinion, national or social origin, aborigines and tribals, property, birth, '*...ologies, ...isms, ...sophies*' or other status.

2. Where not already provided by existing legislative or other measures, each State Party to the present Covenant undertakes to take the necessary, effective and time bound steps, in accordance with its Constitutional processes and with the provisions of the present Covenant, to adopt such laws or other measures as may be necessary to give effect to the rights recognized in the present Covenant and to get them legally enforced in case violations take place.

3. Each State Party to the present Covenant undertakes:

(a) to ensure that any person whose rights or freedoms as hereinafter recognized are violated shall have an effective remedy within a time-frame not withstanding that the violation has been committed by person/s acting in an official capacity in which case, it shall be free of cost to the victim/s.

(b) To ensure that any person claiming such a remedy shall have his right thereto determined by competent judicial, administrative or legislative authorities or by any other competent authority provided for by the legal system of the State, and to develop the possibilities of judicial remedy;

(c) To ensure that the competent authorities shall enforce such remedies when granted along with victim compensation/restitution or both.

Article 3

The States Parties to the present Covenant undertake to ensure the equal right of men and women including transgender and hermaphrodites to the enjoyment of all civil and political rights set forth in the present Covenant.

Article 4

1. In time of public emergency—internal, external or both—which threatens the life of the nation and the existence of which is officially proclaimed, the States Parties to the present Covenant may take measures and stratagems derogating from their obligations under the present Covenant to the extent strictly required by the exigencies of the situation, provided that

such measures are not inconsistent with their other obligations under international law and do not involve discrimination solely on the ground of race, colour, creed, sex including transgender or hermaphrodites, languages, religion, caste or subcaste, sect, denomination, political or other opinions, national or social origin, aborigines and tribals, property, birth, '*...ologies ,...isms, ...sophies'*, or other status.

2. No derogation from articles 6, 7, 8 (paragraphs 1 and 2), 11, 15, 16 and 18 shall be made under this provision.

3. Any State Party to the present Covenant availing itself of the right of derogation shall immediately inform the other States Parties to the present Covenant, through the intermediary of the Secretary General of the United Nations, of the provisions from which it has derogated and of the reasons, measures and stratagems by which it was actuated. A further communication shall be made through the same intermediary on the date of which it terminates such derogation.

Article 5

1. Nothing in the present Covenant may be interpreted as implying for any State, group or persons any rights or freedoms to engage in any activity or omit to engage in an activity or perform any act or omit to perform an act aimed at the dilution or at the destruction of the rights and freedoms recognized herein or at their limitation or to a greater extent than is provided for in the present Covenant.

2. There shall be no restriction upon or derogation from or dilution of any of the fundamental human rights and freedoms recognized or existing in any State Party to the present Covenant pursuant to law, Conventions, regulations, rules, precedents, customs or traditions on the pretext that the present Covenant does not recognize such rights and freedoms or that it recognizes them to a lesser extent.

PART III

Article 6

1. (a) The States Parties to the Covenant recognize the right to work to the free choice of employment to enjoy just, decent,

human-friendly and favourable conditions of work and to have access to assistance schemes for the unemployed and to the underemployed.

(b) The right to work includes the right of everyone to the opportunity to gain his living by work which he willingly chooses or accepts and will take appropriate steps to safeguard this right.

(c) The right to work also includes minimum wages for 8 hours of work and extra-wages for extra-time work and the minimum wages prescribed for a particular work should be adequate enough to secure for himself a standard of living that meets the basic requirements of life. It also includes guarantees for his right to comprehensive social security.

(d) Forced labour is prohibited and there shall be equality of opportunity in regard to work as well as a fair wage and equal remuneration for works of equal value.

(e) No child or juvenile shall be employed for any kind of work and those who employ them in any work harmful to their morals or health, dangerous to life or likely to hamper their normal development including their education shall be punished by law. For this, the age limits below which the paid employment of child labour or juvenile work should be set for the purpose of prohibition and punishment.

2. The steps to be taken by a State Party to the present Covenant to achieve the full realization of this right shall include technical and vocational guidance and training programmes, policies and techniques to achieve steady economic, social and cultural development and full and productive employment under conditions safeguarding fundamental political and economic freedoms to the individual.

Article 7

The States Parties to the present Covenant recognize the right of everyone to the enjoyment of just and favourable conditions of work which ensure, in particular.

(a) Remuneration which provides all workers, as a minimum, with:

(i) Fair wages and equal remuneration for work of

equal value without distinction of any kind, in particular women, physically handicapped or differently abled and transgenders and hermaphrodites being guaranteed conditions of work not inferior to those enjoyed by men, with equal pay for equal work. States where there exists no law for the appointment of transgenders and hermaphrodites, special laws for their appointment should be enacted.

(ii) There shall be a system of equitable remuneration for the work of the inmates in prisons (Center for Personality Development). Every inmate shall be entitled to have provident fund, gratuity and other benefits which employees in similar works are eligible to receive outside the Centre (Prison).

(iii) A decent living for themselves and their families in accordance with the provisions of the present Covenant and their rights include:

(a) The right to adequate and affordable food of nutritional value, freedom from hunger and access to safe and qualitatively good food.

(b) The right to clothing and the right to safe, adequate, clean and affordable housing;

(c) The right to medical care;

(d) The right to clean and safe and pure drinking water and sanitation and

(e) The right to a safe, clean and sustainable environment.

(b) Safe and healthy working conditions. They shall include comprehensive social security. Forced labour is prohibited. Compelling a person under the terms of a court judgement shall not be deemed to constitute forced labour.

(c) Equal opportunity for everyone to be promoted in his employment to an appropriate higher level subject to no considerations other than seniority and competence. Special provisions shall be made for the promotion of the physically handicapped or those who are differently abled. If promotion prospects are not available, the workers including the physically handicapped and differently abled must be given grade promotions after a specified period of service to make them live in dignity and respect and to have opportunities for fulfillment of their potential.

(d) Rest, leisure and reasonable limitation of working hours and periodic holidays with pay as well as remuneration for public holidays.

(e) No child or any person shall be subjected to economic and social exploitation. Those who employ children and young people harmful to their morals or health, dangerous to life, or likely to hamper their normal development, including their education should be punished. Special legislations must be enacted for the purpose.

(f) Special protection should be accorded to working mothers during a reasonable period as determined by national laws and regulations before and after child birth. During such period, working mothers should be accorded paid leave or leave with adequate social security benefits. Special protection should be accorded to working mothers during a reasonable period as determined by national laws and regulations after a miscarriage of an unborn child—natural or otherwise. During such period, working women should be accorded paid leave or leave with adequate social security benefits.

(g) To end discrimination against women in the field of employment and right to work, women should be given the right to employment opportunities, free choice of profession, job security, equal remuneration, the right to special protection of health and safe working conditions, especially in safeguarding of the function of reproduction and special protection in times of pregnancy from work that may be harmful. Necessary laws shall be enacted if needed for making reservations for women in certain jobs ensuring full safety, security and protection at work places.

Article 8

1. The States Parties to the present Covenant undertake to ensure:

(i) The right of everyone to form trade unions and join the trade union of his choice for the protection and promotion of social welfare and without jeopardising social interests with national laws and regulations.
(ii) The right to form trade unions and join the trade union of his choice will be subject only to the rules of the organization concerned for the promotion and protection of his economic and social interests.
(iii) The right to form trade unions and join the trade union of his choice will mean the right to strike within the limits laid by law.
(iv) No restriction may be placed on the exercise of the rights stated in (a) (b) and (c) other than those prescribed by law and which are necessary in a democratic society in the interest of national security or public order or for the protection of the rights and freedoms of others.

(b) The right of trade unions to establish national federations or confederations and the right of the latter to form and join international trade union organizations. This right of national federations or confederations should not be on the basis of political interests or political parties' interests.

(c) The right of trade unions to function freely does not mean that they can do anything without taking into account the social welfare and public interest. The right of trade unions to function freely means that it is subject to no restrictions and limitations other than those prescribed by law and which are necessary in a democratic society in the interests of national security or the integrity of the nation or public order and social welfare or for the protection of the rights and freedoms of others.

(d) The right to strike, provided that it is exercised in conformity with the laws of the particular country and the laws of the country shall ensure the workers' interest and the interests of the society taking into account the moral values behind.

2. This article shall not prevent the imposition of lawful

restrictions on the exercise of these rights by members of the armed forces or of para-military forces or of the civil police or of the administration of the State.

Article 8(3)

Nothing in this Article shall authorize States Parties to the International Labour Organization Convention of 1948 concerning Freedom of Association and Protection of the Right to organize to take legislative measures which would prejudice, or apply the law in such a manner as would prejudice, the guarantees provided for in that Convention.

Article 9

(1) The States Parties to the present Covenant recognize the right of everyone to social security including social insurance which assists him or her to secure the means for a dignified and decent existence.

(2) Motherhood, infancy, childhood and old age are entitled to special care and protection. Every child, whether born in or out of wedlock shall enjoy the same social protection.

(3) People or group of persons who, through civil conflict, Government policies, economic hardships are displaced from their homes and seek refuge in other places internally or in foreign land. Likewise there are minorities and indigenous people, whose most basic rights are frequently violated live in society. Gays, lesbians, transgender and hermaphrodites are discriminated. Their identity is denied. The peasants, the suppressed, the oppressed, the landless, the homeless, the nomads and so on deserve special protection and social security. Each State Party shall enact special legislations to the amelioration of their social and economic conditions.

(4) Those affected by HIV or AIDS, those suffering from mental disorders, those who are mentally retarded, those who are paralysed, those who are incapacitated by old age diseases become victims of gross discrimination. All of them have a right to live and die with dignity. The States Parties shall provide to them facilities for enjoying their right to adequate medical care and they shall be protected from prejudice, discrimination,

neglect and persecution.

(5) Each State Party recognizes the rights of the migrant workers to join and take part in meetings of trade unions and the rights to receive the same social security benefits and medical as nationals of the country/state of employment.

Article 10

The States Parties to the present Covenant recognize that:

(i) The widest and deepest protection and assistance should be accorded to the family (meaning home and not house) which is the natural, basic and fundamental group unit of the society, particularly for its establishment and maintenance. It is responsible for the care and protection of the children, the old/older parents and dependants and education of dependent children and their upbringing in an upright way in the right direction.

(ii) Marriages must be entered into with the free and willing consent of the intending spouses.

(iii) The family (home) is the custodian of morals and traditional values recognized by the community. The aged, the sick and the disabled shall have the right to special measures of protection in keeping with their physical or moral needs.

(iv) The family shall be the place where there should be no discrimination against women and girl children. Girl child shall be specially protected from sexual abuses by the dear and near ones including the father, step-father and those related by blood or otherwise.

3. Special measures of protection and assistance should be taken on behalf of all children and young persons without any discrimination for reasons of parentage or other conditions. Children and young persons should be protected from economic, social and sexual exploitations. Their employment in work harmful to their morals or dignity or health or dangerous to life or likely to hamper their normal development should be punishable by law. States should also set age limits below which the paid employment of child labour should be prohibited and

made punishable by law.

Article 11

1. The States Parties to the present Covenant recognize the right of everyone to an adequate standard of living with basic human dignity and it includes:

(a) adequate and affordable food, freedom from hunger, access to safe, pure drinking water and sanitation;
(b) adequate and affordable housing with latrine and bathing facilities in a clean and sustainable environment;
(c) Continuous improvement of living conditions with medical care and social services.

(2) The States Parties to the present Covenant, recognizing the fundamental right of everyone to be free from hunger shall take, individually and through international co-operation, the measures, including specific programmes for pregnant women, the aged and the infirm, to children and other vulnerable groups, which are needed.

(a) To improve methods of production, conservation and distribution of food by making full use of technical and scientific knowledge, by disseminating knowledge of the principles of nutrition and by developing or reforming agrarian systems in such a way as to achieve the most efficient development and utilization of natural resources;
(b) Taking into account the problems of, both food-importing and food-exporting countries, to ensure an equitable distribution of worla food supplies in relation to need.

Article 12

1. The States Parties to the present Covenant recognize the right of everyone to the full enjoyment of the highest allainable standard of physical psychological and moral health. States where religious freedom is permitted, everyone should have the right for the enjoyment of spiritual health.

Article 12

2. The time-bound and effective-short term and long term-steps to be taken for implementation by the States Parties to the present Covenant to achieve the full realization of this right shall include those necessary for:

(a) The provision for the control and reduction of the still birth rate and of infant mortality and for the healthy development of the child and its morality in an upright way in the right direction;
(b) The improvement of every aspect of environmental and industrial hygiene;
(c) The control, reduction, prevention, diagnosis, treatment and prognosis of epidemic, occupational and other diseases;
(d) The creation, maintenance and continuation of conditions and environments which would assure to all medical service and medical attention in the event of sickness.

Article 13

1. The States Parties to the present Covenant recognize the right of everyone to education and training. They agree that education and training shall be aimed and directed to the full and total development of the human personality and conscience and the sense of its dignity and shall strengthen the respect for human rights and fundamental freedoms. They further agree that education and training shall enable all persons to participate meaningfully and effectively in a free society, promote and propagate understanding, tolerance, appreciation and friendship among all nations and all racial, ethnic or religious groups, and further, the activities of the United Nations for the maintenance of peace for a new world order.

2. The States Parties to the present Covenant recognize that with a view to achieving the full and total realization of this right.

(a) Primary education shall be academic and value-oriented. It shall be compulsory and available free to all.

(b) (i) Secondary education in its different forms, including technical and vocational secondary education, shall be made generally available and accessible to all by every appropriate means, and in particular by the progressive introduction of free education.

(ii) Girls and women shall be encouraged by means and methods to make use of the facility offered for secondary education in different forms as gender inequality is noted in this sphere of education of girls and women.

(iii) Children born and brought up in tribal areas or suffering discrimination owing to race, colour, caste/sub-caste, ethnic origins, creed, religion, place of origin, occupation shall be encouraged by means and methods to make use of the facilities offered for secondary education in its various forms.

(c) Higher education shall be made equally accessible to all, subject to certain percentage of reservations for those who are economically poor or socially weaker, on the basis of their merit and capability, by every appropriate means, and in particular by the progressive introduction of free education.

(d) Fundamental education must be encouraged, promoted or intensified as far as possible for those persons who have not received or completed the whole period of their primary education. Adult education, continuing education, distance education or education via correspondence and contact classes must be encouraged or intensified by means and methods made easily accessible to those who are interested in fundamental education. Facilities for fundamental education for those who have completed certain age should be provided even when they do not have any basic or primary education.

(e) The development of a system of schools at all levels shall be actively pursued, an adequate fellowship system shall be established and the material conditions of teaching staff shall be continuously improved for faculty development which will include special professional courses, orientation courses and specialized courses. The teachers must be regularly monitored to know their academic excellence and professional competence to continue as the members of the faculty. If found unsuitable, they shall be terminated from service.

3. The States Parties to the present Covenant undertake to have regard and respect for the liberty of parents and when applicable, to legal guardians to choose for their children schools, other than those established by the public authorities, which conform to such minimum educational standards as may be laid down or approved by the State and to ensure the religious (if permitted) and/or moral education of their children in conformity with their own convictions. The desire of the children too may be taken into account when decisions are made.

4. No part of this article shall be construed so as to interfere with the liberty of individuals and bodies to establish and direct educational institutions, subject always to the observance of the principles set forth in paragraph 1 of this Article and to the requirement that the education given in such institutions shall conform to such minimum standards as may be laid down by the State.

Article 14

Each State Party to the present Covenant which at the time of becoming a party has not been able to secure in its metropolitan territory or other territories under its jurisdiction compulsory primary education free of change, undertakes, within two years, to work out and adopt a detailed plan of action for the progressive implementation within a reasonable number of years, to be fixed in the plan of the principle of compulsory education free of charge for all.

Article 15

1. The States Parties to the present Covenant recognize the right of everyone:

(a) To take part in cultural life as well as the right to enjoy literary and artistic works and to be given opportunities to develop his artistic, intellectual and creative talents; to promote and protect the morals and traditional values recognized by the community.

(b) To enjoy the benefits of scientific progress and its application for the maintenance of peace and harmony, security and stability, neutrality and freedom, such that the rights set forth in this Covenant can be fully realised. Towards this end, the States Parties shall continue to enhance friendship and co-operation in the furtherance to peace, harmony and stability for establishing a new world order.

(c) To benefit from the protection of the moral and material interests resulting from any scientific, literary or artistic production of which he is the author.

2. The steps to be taken by the States Parties to the present Covenant to achieve the full and total realization of this right shall include those necessary for the preservation, conservation, maintenance, development and the diffusion or dissemination of science and culture.

3. The States Parties to the present Covenant undertake to respect the inevitable freedom indispensable for scientific research, extension and creative activity with intuitive analysis.

4. The States Parties to the present Covenant recognize the benefits to be derived from the encouragement and development of international contacts and co-operation in the scientific and cultural fields.

Article 16

The States Parties to the present Covenant recognize the right of everyone to have protection through the enactment of legislations in areas of—

1. Abuse and neglect of the old and the older—especially of the older women;
2. Abuse and neglect of children of both sexes and the same of transgender community.
3. Abuse and neglect of the marginalized sections of the society—widows, extremely poor, minorities, sex-workers, hermaphrodites, people suffering from disabilities, tribals, gays and lesbians and so on.
4. Bonded labour, employment of children, refusal to pay

minimum wages, compensation to the victims of crime and anti-social acts, divorcees, adoption, inheritance, begging, vagrancy, consumption of intoxicating drinks and of drugs injurious to health, drug trafficking, human trafficking etc.

5. Prohibiting or regulating certain pastimes like gambling, horse-racing, lotteries, cross-world puzzles etc. as they operate to the detriment of poor families resulting in the drain of their meagre financial resources, anti-social activities leading to student disputes, communal riots, racial or ethnic conflicts, religious bigotry or agrarian unrest and fights in the name of *'...isms, ...ologies and ...sophies'*, and finally leading to extremism, fundamentalism, fanaticism, terrorism and insurgency.

Article 17

The States Parties to the present Covenant recognize the rights of the old and the older namely:

a. Independence

(1) Their right to have access to adequate food, water, shelter, clothing and health care through provisions of income, family and community support and self-help;
(2) Their right to have the opportunity to work or to have access to other income generating opportunities;
(3) Their right to participate in determining when and at what pace withdrawal from labour force takes place;
(4) Their right to have access to appropriate educational and training programmes;
(5) Their right to live in environments that are safe and adaptable to personal preferences and changing capacities;
(6) Their right to reside at for as long as possible.

b. Participation

(1) Their right to remain integrated in society, participate actively in the formulation and

implementation of policies that directly affect their well-being and share their knowledge and skills with younger generations;

(2) Their right to seek and develop opportunities for service to the community and to serve as volunteers to their interests and capabilities;

(3) Their right to form movements and associations of older persons.

c. Care

(1) Their right to benefit from family and community care and protection in accordance with each society's system of cultural values;

(2) Their right to have access to health care to keep them to maintain or regain the optimum level of physical, mental and emotional well-being and to prevent or delay the onset of illness;

(3) Their right to have access to social and legal services to enhance their autonomy, protection and care;

(4) Their right to utilize appropriate levels of institutional care providing protection, rehabilitation and social and mental stimulation in a humane and secure environment;

(5) Their right to enjoy human rights and fundamental freedoms when residing in any shelter, care or treatment facility including full respect for their dignity, beliefs, needs and privacy and make decisions about their care and quality of lives.

d. Self-Fulfillment

(1) Their right to pursue opportunities for the full development of their potential;

(2) Their right to have access to the educational, cultural, spiritual and recreational resources of society.

e. Dignity

(1) Their right to live in dignity and security and be free from exploitation and physical or mental abuse;

(2) Their right to be treated fairly regardless of age, gender, racial or ethnic or religious background, disability, or other status and be valued independently of their economic contributions.

Necessary legislations incorporating the principle set forth on each area stated above shall be enacted by the States Parties to the present Covenant.

Article 18

The States Parties to the present Covenant recognize the right of everyone to be protected against all kinds of crimes coming under—

1. Economic Crimes—Say, Hoarding, black marketing, adulteration, investment frauds, money chain & multi-marketing etc.
2. Financial Crimes—Say, Tax evasion, loan sharking, labour racketeering, securities frauds etc.
3. Nexus Crimes—Say, Bankruptcy frauds, sweet heart contracts, charity and religious frauds, commodities feud etc.
4. Bureaucratic Crimes—Say, Abuse of power, misuse of authority, non-use of power and authority, exercise of pseudo-authority, hoarding of files etc.
5. JEL Crimes—Say, Judgements resulting out of an unholy nexus among the legislators, executives and judicial officers.
6. Consensus Crimes—Say, corruption, bribery and adjustment frauds etc.
7. White Collar Crimes—Say, Commercial bribery and kickbacks, insurance adjustment, credit card frauds and various con-games etc.
8. Organized Crimes—Say, real estate, liquor, drug trafficking, food product adulterations etc.
9. Extremist Crimes—Say, Fundamentalism, fanaticism, terrorism, insurgency etc.
10. Corruption and malpractices etc.

Special legislations shall be enacted to control, reduce and prevent crimes stated above in their various forms.

PART-4

Appendices

1. Universal Declaration of Human Rights
2. The European Convention on Human Rights
3. African Charter on Human and Peoples' Rights
4. Arab Charter on Human Rights
5. ASEAN Human Rights Declaration
6. ASIAN Human Rights Charter
7. American Convention on Human Rights
8. International Covenant on Civil and Political Rights
9. International Covenant on Economic, Social and Cultural Rights

Appendix-1
Universal Declaration of Human Rights

Preamble

Whereas recognition of the inherent dignity and of the equal and inalienable rights of all members of the human family is the foundation of freedom, justice and peace in the world,

Whereas disregard and contempt for human rights have resulted in barbarous acts which have outraged the conscience of mankind, and the advent of a world in which human beings shall enjoy freedom of speech and belief and freedom from fear and want has been proclaimed as the highest aspiration of the common people,

Whereas it is essential, if man is not to be compelled to have recourse, as a last resort, to rebellion against tyranny and oppression, that human rights should be protected by the rule of law,

Whereas it is essential to promote the development of friendly relations between nations,

Whereas the peoples of the United Nations have in the Charter reaffirmed their faith in fundamental human rights, in the dignity and worth of the human person and in the equal rights of men and women and have determined to promote social progress and better standards of life in larger freedom,

Whereas Member States have pledged themselves to achieve, in co-operation with the United Nations, the promotion of universal respect for and observance of human rights and fundamental freedoms,

Whereas a common understanding of these rights and freedoms is of the greatest importance for the full realization of this pledge,

Now, Therefore THE GENERAL ASSEMBLY proclaims THIS UNIVERSAL DECLARATION OF HUMAN RIGHTS as a common standard of achievement for all peoples and all nations, to the end that every individual and every organ of society, keeping this Declaration constantly in mind, shall strive by teaching and education to promote respect for these rights and freedoms and by progressive measures, national and international, to secure their universal and effective recognition and observance, both among the peoples of Member States themselves and among the peoples of territories under their jurisdiction.

Article 1

All human beings are born free and equal in dignity and rights. They are endowed with reason and conscience and should act towards one another in a spirit of brotherhood.

Article 2

Everyone is entitled to all the rights and freedoms set forth in this Declaration, without distinction of any kind, such as race, colour, sex, language, religion, political or other opinion, national or social origin, property, birth or other status. Furthermore, no distinction shall be made on the basis of the political, jurisdictional or international status of the country or territory to which a person belongs, whether it be independent, trust, non-self-governing or under any other limitation of sovereignty.

Article 3

Everyone has the right to life, liberty and security of person.

Article 4

No one shall be held in slavery or servitude; slavery and the slave trade shall be prohibited in all their forms.

Article 5

No one shall be subjected to torture or to cruel, inhuman or degrading treatment or punishment.

Article 6

Everyone has the right to recognition everywhere as a person before the law.

Article 7

All are equal before the law and are entitled without any discrimination to equal protection of the law. All are entitled to equal protection against any discrimination in violation of this Declaration and against any incitement to such discrimination.

Article 8

Everyone has the right to an effective remedy by the competent national tribunals for acts violating the fundamental rights granted him by the constitution or by law.

Article 9

No one shall be subjected to arbitrary arrest, detention or exile.

Article 10

Everyone is entitled in full equality to a fair and public hearing by an independent and impartial tribunal, in the determination of his rights and obligations and of any criminal charge against him.

Article 11

(1) Everyone charged with a penal offence has the right to be presumed innocent until proved guilty according to law in a public trial at which he has had all the guarantees necessary for his defence.

(2) No one shall be held guilty of any penal offence on account of any act or omission which did not constitute a penal offence, under national or international law, at the time when it was committed. Nor shall a heavier penalty be imposed than the one that was applicable at the time the penal offence was committed.

Article 12

No one shall be subjected to arbitrary interference with his privacy, family, home or correspondence, nor to attacks upon his honour and reputation. Everyone has the right to the protection of the law against such interference or attacks.

Article 13

(1) Everyone has the right to freedom of movement and residence within the borders of each state.
(2) Everyone has the right to leave any country, including his own, and to return to his country.

Article 14

(1) Everyone has the right to seek and to enjoy in other countries asylum from persecution.
(2) This right may not be invoked in the case of prosecutions genuinely arising from non-political crimes or from acts contrary to the purposes and principles of the United Nations.

Article 15

(1) Everyone has the right to a nationality.
(2) No one shall be arbitrarily deprived of his nationality nor denied the right to change his nationality.

Article 16

(1) Men and women of full age, without any limitation due to race, nationality or religion, have the right to marry

and to found a family. They are entitled to equal rights as to marriage, during marriage and at its dissolution.

(2) Marriage shall be entered into only with the free and full consent of the intending spouses.

(3) The family is the natural and fundamental group unit of society and is entitled to protection by society and the State.

Article 17

(1) Everyone has the right to own property alone as well as in association with others.

(2) No one shall be arbitrarily deprived of his property.

Article 18

Everyone has the right to freedom of thought, conscience and religion; this right includes freedom to change his religion or belief, and freedom, either alone or in community with others and in public or private, to manifest his religion or belief in teaching, practice, worship and observance.

Article 19

Everyone has the right to freedom of opinion and expression; this right includes freedom to hold opinions without interference and to seek, receive and impart information and ideas through any media and regardless of frontiers.

Article 20

(1) Everyone has the right to freedom of peaceful assembly and association.

(2) No one may be compelled to belong to an association.

Article 21

(1) Everyone has the right to take part in the government of his country, directly or through freely chosen representatives.

(2) Everyone has the right of equal access to public service in his country.
(3) The will of the people shall be the basis of the authority of government; this will shall be expressed in periodic and genuine elections which shall be by universal and equal suffrage and shall be held by secret vote or by equivalent free voting procedures.

Article 22

Everyone, as a member of society, has the right to social security and is entitled to realization, through national effort and international co-operation and in accordance with the organization and resources of each State, of the economic, social and cultural rights indispensable for his dignity and the free development of his personality.

Article 23

(1) Everyone has the right to work, to free choice of employment, to just and favourable conditions of work and to protection against unemployment.
(2) Everyone, without any discrimination, has the right to equal pay for equal work.
(3) Everyone who works has the right to just and favourable remuneration ensuring for himself and his family an existence worthy of human dignity, and supplemented, if necessary, by other means of social protection.
(4) Everyone has the right to form and to join trade unions for the protection of his interests.

Article 24

Everyone has the right to rest and leisure, including reasonable limitation of working hours and periodic holidays with pay.

Article 25

(1) Everyone has the right to a standard of living adequate for the health and well-being of himself and of his

family, including food, clothing, housing and medical care and necessary social services, and the right to security in the event of unemployment, sickness, disability, widowhood, old age or other lack of livelihood in circumstances beyond his control.

(2) Motherhood and childhood are entitled to special care and assistance. All children, whether born in or out of wedlock, shall enjoy the same social protection.

Article 26

(1) Everyone has the right to education. Education shall be free, at least in the elementary and fundamental stages. Elementary education shall be compulsory. Technical and professional education shall be made generally available and higher education shall be equally accessible to all on the basis of merit.

(2) Education shall be directed to the full development of the human personality and to the strengthening of respect for human rights and fundamental freedoms. It shall promote understanding, tolerance and friendship among all nations, racial or religious groups, and shall further the activities of the United Nations for the maintenance of peace.

(3) Parents have a prior right to choose the kind of education that shall be given to their children.

Article 27

(1) Everyone has the right freely to participate in the cultural life of the community, to enjoy the arts and to share in scientific advancement and its benefits.

(2) Everyone has the right to the protection of the moral and material interests resulting from any scientific, literary or artistic production of which he is the author.

Article 28

Everyone is entitled to a social and international order in which the rights and freedoms set forth in this Declaration can be fully realized.

Article 29

(1) Everyone has duties to the community in which alone the free and full development of his personality is possible.
(2) In the exercise of his rights and freedoms, everyone shall be subject only to such limitations as are determined by law solely for the purpose of securing due recognition and respect for the rights and freedoms of others and of meeting the just requirements of morality, public order and the general welfare in a democratic society.
(3) These rights and freedoms may in no case be exercised contrary to the purposes and principles of the United Nations.

Article 30

Nothing in this Declaration may be interpreted as implying for any State, group or person any right to engage in any activity or to perform any act aimed at the destruction of any of the rights and freedoms set forth herein.

Appendix-2
The European Convention on Human Rights

The Governments signatory hereto, being Members of the Council of Europe,

Considering the Universal Declaration of Human Rights proclaimed by the General Assembly of the United Nations on 10 December 1948;

Considering that this Declaration aims at securing the universal and effective recognition and observance of the Rights therein declared;

Considering that the aim of the Council of Europe is the achievement of greater unity between its Members and that one of the methods by which the aim is to be pursued is the maintenance and further realization of Human Rights and Fundamental Freedoms;

Reaffirming their profound belief in those Fundamental Freedoms which are the foundation of justice and peace in the world and are best maintained on the one hand by an effective political democracy and on the other by a common understanding and observance of the Human Rights upon which they depend;

Being resolved, as the Governments of European countries which are like-minded and have a common heritage of political traditions, ideals, freedom and the rule of law to take the first steps for the collective enforcement of certain of the Rights stated in the Universal Declaration;

Have agreed as follows:

Article 1

The High Contracting Parties shall secure to everyone within their jurisdiction the rights and freedoms defined in Section I of this Convention.

SECTION I

Article 2

1. Everyone's right to life shall be protected by law. No one shall be deprived of his life intentionally save in the execution of a sentence of a court following his conviction of a crime for which this penalty is provided by law.
2. Deprivation of life shall not be regarded as inflicted in contravention of this article when it results from the use of force which is no more than absolutely necessary:
   (a) in defence of any person from unlawful violence;
   (b) in order to effect a lawful arrest or to prevent escape of a person lawfully detained;
   (c) in action lawfully taken for the purpose of quelling a riot or insurrection.

Article 3

No one shall be subjected to torture or to inhuman or degrading treatment or punishment.

Article 4

1. No one shall be held in slavery or servitude.
2. No one shall be required to perform forced or compulsory labour.
3. For the purpose of this article the term forced or compulsory labour' shall not include:
   (a) any work required to be done in the ordinary course of detention imposed according to the provisions of Article 5 of this Convention or during conditional release from such detention;
   (b) any service of a military character or, in case of conscientious objectors in countries where they are recognized, service exacted instead of compulsory

military service;

(c) any service exacted in case of an emergency or calamity threatening the life or well-being of the community;

(d) any work or service which forms part of normal civic obligations.

Article 5

1. Everyone has the right to liberty and security of person. No one shall be deprived of his liberty save in the following cases and in accordance with a procedure prescribed by law:

   (a) the lawful detention of a person after conviction by a competent court;

   (b) the lawful arrest or detention of a person for non-compliance with the lawful order of a court or in order to secure the fulfillment of any obligation prescribed by law;

   (c) the lawful arrest or detention of a person effected for the purpose of bringing him before the competent legal authority of reasonable suspicion of having committed and offence or when it is reasonably considered necessary to prevent his committing an offence or fleeing after having done so;

   (d) the detention of a minor by lawful order for the purpose of educational supervision or his lawful detention for the purpose of bringing him before the competent legal authority;

   (e) the lawful detention of persons for the prevention of the spreading of infectious diseases, of persons of unsound mind, alcoholics or drug addicts, or vagrants;

   (f) the lawful arrest or detention of a person to prevent his effecting an unauthorized entry into the country or of a person against whom action is being taken with a view to deportation or extradition.

2. Everyone who is arrested shall be informed promptly, in a language which he understands, of the reasons for his arrest and the charge against him.

3. Everyone arrested or detained in accordance with the provisions of paragraph 1(c) of this article shall be brought promptly before a judge or other officer authorized by law to exercise judicial power and shall be entitled to trial within a reasonable time or to release pending trial. Release may be conditioned by guarantees to appear for trial.
4. Everyone who is deprived of his liberty by arrest or detention shall be entitled to take proceedings by which the lawfulness of his detention shall be decided speedily by a court and his release ordered if the detention is not lawful.
5. Everyone who has been the victim of arrest or detention in contravention of the provisions of this article shall have an enforceable right to compensation.

Article 6

1. In the determination of his civil rights and obligations or of any criminal charge against him, everyone is entitled to a fair and public hearing within a reasonable time by an independent and impartial tribunal established by law. Judgement shall be pronounced publicly by the press and public may be excluded from all or part of the trial in the interest of morals, public order or national security in a democratic society, where the interests of juveniles or the protection of the private life of the parties so require, or the extent strictly necessary in the opinion of the court in special circumstances where publicity would prejudice the interests of justice.

2. Everyone charged with a criminal offence shall be presumed innocent until proved guilty according to law.

3. Everyone charged with a criminal offence has the following minimum rights:

(a) to be informed promptly, in a language which he understands and in detail, of the nature and cause of the accusation against him;
(b) to have adequate time and the facilities for the preparation of his defence;
(c) to defend himself in person or through legal assistance of his own choosing or, if he has not sufficient means to

pay for legal assistance, to be given it free when the interests of justice so require;

(d) to examine or have examined witnesses against him and to obtain the attendance and examination of witnesses on his behalf under the same conditions as witnesses against him;

(e) to have the free assistance of an interpreter if he cannot understand or speak the language used in court.

Article 7

1. No one shall be held guilty of any criminal offence on account of any act or omission which did not constitute a criminal offence under national or international law at the time when it was committed. Nor shall a heavier penalty be imposed than the one that was applicable at the time the criminal offence was committed.

2. This article shall not prejudice the trial and punishment of any person for any act or omission which, at the time when it was committed, was criminal according the general principles of law recognized by civilized nations.

Article 8

1. Everyone has the right to respect for his private and family life, his home and his correspondence.

2. There shall be no interference by a public authority with the exercise of this right except such as is in accordance with the law and is necessary in a democratic society in the interests of national security, public safety or the economic well-being of the country, for the prevention of disorder or crime, for the protection of health or morals, or for the protection of the rights and freedoms of others.

Article 9

1. Everyone has the right to freedom of thought, conscience and religion; this right includes freedom to change his religion or belief, and freedom, either alone or in community with others and in public or private, to manifest his religion or belief, in

worship, teaching, practice and observance.

2. Freedom to manifest one's religion or beliefs shall be subject only to such limitations as are prescribed by law and are necessary in a democratic society in the interests of public safety, for the protection of public order, health or morals, or the protection of the rights and freedoms of others.

Article 10

1. Everyone has the right to freedom of expression. This right shall include freedom to hold opinions and to receive and impart information and ideas without interference by public authority and regardless of frontiers. This article shall not prevent States from requiring the licensing of broadcasting, television or cinema enterprises.

2. The exercise of these freedoms, since it carries with it duties and responsibilities, may be subject to such formalities, conditions, restrictions or penalties as are prescribed by law and are necessary in a democratic society, in the interests of national security, territorial integrity or public safety, for the prevention of disorder or crime, for the protection of health or morals, for the protection of the reputation or the rights of others, for preventing the disclosure of information received in confidence, or for maintaining the authority and impartiality of the judiciary.

Article 11

1. Everyone has the right to freedom of peaceful assembly and to freedom of association with others, including the right to form and to join trade unions for the protection of his interests.

2. No restrictions shall be placed on the exercise of these rights other than such as are prescribed by law and are necessary in a democratic society in the interests of national security or public safety, for the prevention of disorder or crime, for the protection of health or morals or for the protection of the rights and freedoms of others. This article shall not prevent the imposition of lawful restrictions on the exercise of these rights by members of the armed forces, of the police or of the administration of the State.

Article 12

Men and women of marriageable age have the right to marry and to found a family, according to the national laws governing the exercise of this right.

Article 13

Everyone whose rights and freedoms as set forth in this Convention are violated shall have an effective remedy before a national authority notwithstanding that the violation has been committed by persons acting in an official capacity.

Article 14

The enjoyment of the rights and freedoms set forth in this Convention shall be secured without discrimination on any ground such as sex, race, colour, language, religion, political or other opinion, national or social origin, association with a national minority, property, birth or other status.

Article 15

1. In time of war or other public emergency threatening the life of the nation any High Contracting Party may take measures derogating from its obligations under this Convention to the extent strictly required by the exigencies of the situation, provided that such measures are not inconsistent with its other obligations under international law.

2. No derogation from Article 2, except in respect of deaths resulting from lawful acts of war, or from Articles 3, 4 (paragraph 1) and 7 shall be made under this provision.

3. Any High Contracting Party availing itself of this right of derogation shall keep the Secretary-General of the Council of Europe fully informed of the measures which it has taken and the reasons therefore. It shall also inform the Secretary-General of the Council of Europe when such measures have ceased to operate and the provisions of the Convention are again being fully executed.

Article 16

Nothing in Articles 10, 11, and 14 shall be regarded as preventing the High Contracting Parties from imposing restrictions on the political activity of aliens.

Article 17

Nothing in this Convention may be interpreted as implying for any State, group or person any right to engage in any activity or perform any act aimed at the destruction on any of the rights and freedoms set forth herein or at their limitation to a greater extent than is provided for in the Convention.

Article 18

The restrictions permitted under this Convention to the said rights and freedoms shall not be applied for any purpose other than those for which they have been prescribed.

Appendix-3
African Charter on Human and Peoples' Rights

Preamble

The African States members of the Organisation of African Unity, parties to the present Convention entitled "African Charter on Human and Peoples' Rights;

Recalling Decision 115 (XVI) of the Assembly of Heads of State and Government at its Sixteenth Ordinary Session held in Monrovia, Liberia, from 17 to 20 July 1979 on the preparation of "a preliminary draft on an African Charter on Human and Peoples' Rights, providing inter alia for the establishment of bodies to promote and protect human and peoples' rights";

Considering the Charter of the Organisation of African Unity, which stipulates that "freedom, equality, justice and dignity are essential objectives for the achievement of the legitimate aspirations of the African peoples";

Reaffirming the pledge they solemnly made in Article 2 of the said Charter to eradicate all forms of colonialism from Africa, to coordinate and intensify their cooperation and efforts to achieve a better life for the peoples of Africa and to promote international cooperation having due regard to the Charter of the United Nations and the Universal Declaration of Human Rights;

Taking into consideration the virtues of their historical tradition and the values of African civilization which should inspire and characterize their reflection on the concept of human and peoples' rights;

Recognizing on the one hand, that fundamental human rights stem from the attitudes of human beings, which justifies their international protection and on the other hand that the reality and respect of peoples' rights should necessarily guarantee human rights;

Considering that the enjoyment of rights and freedoms also implies the performance of duties on the part of everyone;

Convinced that it is henceforth essential to pay particular attention to the right to development and that civil and political rights cannot be dissociated from economic, social and cultural rights in their conception as well as universality and that the satisfaction of economic, social and cultural rights is a guarantee for the enjoyment of civil and political rights;

Conscious of their duty to achieve the total liberation of Africa, the peoples of which are still struggling for their dignity and genuine independence, and undertaking to eliminate colonialism, neo-colonialism, apartheid, Zionism and to dismantle aggressive foreign military bases and all forms of discrimination, language, religion or political opinions;

Reaffirming their adherence to the principles of human and peoples' rights and freedoms contained in the declarations, conventions and other instruments adopted by the Organisation of African Unity, the Movement of Non-Aligned Countries and the United Nations;

Firmly convinced of their duty to promote and protect human and peoples' rights and freedoms and taking into account the importance traditionally attached to these rights and freedoms in Africa;

Have agreed as follows:

PART I: RIGHTS AND DUTIES

CHAPTER I: HUMAN AND PEOPLES' RIGHTS

Article 1

The Member States of the Organisation of African Unity, parties to the present Charter shall recognise the rights, duties and freedoms enshrined in the Charter and shall undertake to adopt legislative or other measures to give effect to them.

Article 2

Every individual shall be entitled to the enjoyment of the rights and freedoms recognised and guaranteed in the present Charter without distinction of any kind such as race, ethnic group, colour, sex, language, religion, political or any other opinion, national and social origin, fortune, birth or any status.

Article 3

1. Every individual shall be equal before the law.
2. Every individual shall be entitled to equal protection of the law.

Article 4

Human beings are inviolable. Every human being shall be entitled to respect for his life and the integrity of his person. No one may be arbitrarily deprived of this right.

Article 5

Every individual shall have the right to the respect of the dignity inherent in a human being and to the recognition of his legal status. All forms of exploitation and degradation of man, particularly slavery, slave trade, torture, cruel, inhuman or degrading punishment and treatment shall be prohibited.

Article 6

Every individual shall have the right to liberty and to the security of his person. No one may be deprived of his freedom except for reasons and conditions previously laid down by law. In particular, no one may be arbitrarily arrested or detained.

Article 7

1. Every individual shall have the right to have his cause heard. This comprises:

(a) The right to an appeal to competent national organs

against acts of violating his fundamental rights as recognized and guaranteed by conventions, laws, regulations and customs in force;

(b) The right to be presumed innocent until proved guilty by a competent court or tribunal;

(c) The right to defence, including the right to be defended by counsel of his choice;

(d) The right to be tried within a reasonable time by an impartial court or tribunal.

2. No one may be condemned for an act or omission which did not constitute a legally punishable offence at the time it was committed. No penalty may be inflicted for an offence for which no provision was made at the time it was committed. Punishment is personal and can be imposed only on the offender.

Article 8

Freedom of conscience, the profession and free practice of religion shall be guaranteed. No one may, subject to law and order, be submitted to measures restricting the exercise of these freedoms.

Article 9

1. Every individual shall have the right to receive information.
2. Every individual shall have the right to express and disseminate his opinions within the law.

Article 10

1. Every individual shall have the right to free association provided that he abides by the law.
2. Subject to the obligation of solidarity provided for in Article 29, no one may be compelled to join an association.

Article 11

Every individual shall have the right to assemble freely with others. The exercise of this right shall be subject only to necessary restrictions provided for by law, in particular those enacted in the interest of national security, the safety, health, ethics and rights and freedoms of others.

Article 12

1. Every individual shall have the right to freedom of movement and residence within the borders of a State provided he abides by the law.
2. Every individual shall have the right to leave any country including his own, and to return to his country. This right may only be subject to restrictions, provided for by law for the protection of national security, law and order, public health or morality.
3. Every individual shall have the right, when persecuted, to seek and obtain asylum in other countries in accordance with the law of those countries and international conventions.
4. A non-national legally admitted in a territory of a State Party to the present Charter, may only be expelled from it by virtue of a decision taken in accordance with the law.
5. The mass expulsion of non-nationals shall be prohibited. Mass expulsion shall be that which is aimed at national, racial, ethnic or religious groups.

Article 13

1. Every citizen shall have the right to participate freely in the government of his country, either directly or through freely chosen representatives in accordance with the provisions of the law.
2. Every citizen shall have the right of equal access to the public service of the country.
3. Every individual shall have the right of access to public property and services in strict equality of all persons before the law.

Article 14

The right to property shall be guaranteed. It may only be encroached upon in the interest of public need or in the general interest of the community and in accordance with the provisions of appropriate laws.

Article 15

Every individual shall have the right to work under equitable and satisfactory conditions, and shall receive equal pay for equal work.

Article 16

1. Every individual shall have the right to enjoy the best attainable state of physical and mental health.
2. States Parties to the present Charter shall take the necessary measures to protect the health of their people and to ensure that they receive medical attention when they are sick.

Article 17

1. Every individual shall have the right to education.
2. Every individual may freely take part in the cultural life of his community.
3. The promotion and protection of morals and traditional values recognized by the community shall be the duty of the State.

Article 18

1. The family shall be the natural unit and basis of society. It shall be protected by the State which shall take care of its physical health and moral.
2. The State shall have the duty to assist the family which is the custodian of morals and traditional values recognized by the community.
3. The State shall ensure the elimination of every

discrimination against women and also ensure the protection of the rights of women and the child as stipulated in international declarations and conventions.

4. The aged and the disabled shall also have the right to special measures of protection in keeping with their physical or moral needs.

Article 19

All peoples shall be equal; they shall enjoy the same respect and shall have the same rights. Nothing shall justify the domination of a people by another.

Article 20

1. All peoples shall have the right to existence. They shall have the unquestionable and inalienable right to self-determination. They shall freely determine their political status and shall pursue their economic and social development according to the policy they have freely chosen.
2. Colonized or oppressed peoples shall have the right to free themselves from the bonds of domination by resorting to any means recognized by the international community.
3. All peoples shall have the right to the assistance of the States Parties to the present Charter in their liberation struggle against foreign domination, be it political, economic or cultural.

Article 21

1. All peoples shall freely dispose of their wealth and natural resources. This right shall be exercised in the exclusive interest of the people. In no case shall a people be deprived of it.
2. In case of spoliation, the dispossessed people shall have the right to the lawful recovery of its property as well as to an adequate compensation.
3. The free disposal of wealth and natural resources shall

be exercised without prejudice to the obligation of promoting international economic cooperation based on mutual respect, equitable exchange and the principles of international law.

4. States Parties to the present Charter shall individually and collectively exercise the right to free disposal of their wealth and natural resources with a view to strengthening African Unity and solidarity.
5. States Parties to the present Charter shall undertake to eliminate all forms of foreign exploitation particularly that practised by international monopolies so as to enable their peoples to fully benefit from the advantages derived from their national resources.

Article 22

1. All peoples shall have the right to their economic, social and cultural development with due regard to their freedom and identity and in the equal enjoyment of the common heritage of mankind.
2. States shall have the duty, individually or collectively, to ensure the exercise of the right to development.

Article 23

1. All peoples shall have the right to national and international peace and security. The principles of solidarity and friendly relations implicitly affirmed by the Charter of the United Nations and reaffirmed by that of the Organisation of African Unity shall govern relations between States.

2. For the purpose of strengthening peace, solidarity and friendly relations, States Parties to the present Charter shall ensure that:

(a) any individual enjoying the right of asylum under Article 12 of the present Charter shall not engage in subversive activities against his country of origin or any other State Party to the present Charter;

(b) their territories shall not be used as bases for subversive or terrorist activities against the people of any other State Party to the present Charter.

Article 24

All peoples shall have the right to a general satisfactory environment favourable to their development.

Article 25

States Parties to the present Charter shall have the duty to promote and ensure through teaching, education and publication, the respect of the rights and freedoms contained in the present Charter and to see to it that these freedoms and rights as well as corresponding obligations and duties are understood.

Article 26

States Parties to the present Charter shall have the duty to guarantee the independence of the Courts and shall allow the establishment and improvement of appropriate national institutions entrusted with the promotion and protection of the rights and freedoms guaranteed by the present Charter.

CHAPTER II: DUTIES

Article 27

1. Every individual shall have duties towards his family and society, the State and other legally recognised communities and the international community.
2. The rights and freedoms of each individual shall be exercised with due regard to the rights of others, collective security, morality and common interest.

Article 28

Every individual shall have the duty to respect and consider his fellow beings without discrimination, and to maintain relations aimed at promoting, safeguarding and reinforcing mutual respect and tolerance.

Article 29

The individual shall also have the duty:

1. To preserve the harmonious development of the family and to work for the cohesion and respect of the family; to respect his parents at all times, to maintain them in case of need.
2. To serve his national community by placing his physical and intellectual abilities at its service;
3. Not to compromise the security of the State whose national or resident he is;
4. To preserve and strengthen social and national solidarity, particularly when the latter is strengthened;
5. To preserve and strengthen the national independence and the territorial integrity of his country and to contribute to his defence in accordance with the law;
6. To work to the best of his abilities and competence, and to pay taxes imposed by law in the interest of the society;
7. To preserve and strengthen positive African cultural values in his relations with other members of the society, in the spirit of tolerance, dialogue and consultation and, in general, to contribute to the promotion of the moral well being of society;
8. To contribute to the best of his abilities, at all times and at all levels, to the promotion and achievement of African unity.

Appendix-4
Arab Charter on Human Rights

The Governments of the member States of the League of Arab States.

Preamble

Given the Arab nation's belief in human dignity since God honoured it by making the Arab World the cradle of religions and the birthplace of civilizations which confirmed its right to a life of dignity based on freedom, justice and peace,

Pursuant to the eternal principles of brotherhood and equality among all human beings which were firmly established by the Islamic Sharia and the other divinely-revealed religions,

Being proud of the humanitarian values and principles which it firmly established in the course of its long history and which played a major role in disseminating centres of learning between the East and the West, thereby making it an international focal point for seekers of knowledge, culture and wisdom.

Conscious of the fact that the entire Arab World has always worked together to preserve its faith, believing in its unity, struggling to protect its freedom, defending the right of nations to self-determination and to safeguard their resources, believing in the rule of law and that every individual's enjoyment of freedom, justice and equality of opportunity is the yardstick by which the merits of any society are gauged,

Rejecting racism and zionism, which constitute a violation of human rights and pose a threat to world peace,

Acknowledging the close interrelationship between human rights and world peace,

Reaffirming the principles of the Charter of the United Nations and the Universal Declaration of Human Rights, as well as the provisions of the United Nations International Covenants on Civil and Political Rights and Economic, Social and Cultural Rights and the Cairo Declaration on Human Rights in Islam.

In confirmation of all the above, have agreed as follows:

PART I

Article 1

(a) All peoples have the right of self-determination and control over their natural wealth and resources and, accordingly, have the right to freely determine the form of their political structure and to freely pursue their economic, social and cultural development.

(b) Racism, zionism, occupation and foreign domination pose a challenge to human dignity and constitute a fundamental obstacle to the realization of the basic rights of peoples. There is a need to condemn and endeavour to eliminate all such practices.

PART II

Article 2

Each State Party to the present Charter undertakes to ensure to all individuals within its territory and subject to its jurisdiction the right to enjoy all the rights and freedoms recognized herein, without any distinction on grounds of race, colour, sex, language, religion, political opinion, national or social origin, property, birth or other status and without any discrimination between men and women.

Article 3

(a) No restriction upon or derogation from any of the fundamental human rights recognized or existing in any State Party to the present Charter in virtue of law, conventions or custom shall be admitted on the pretext that the present Charter does not recognize such rights or that it recognizes them to a lesser extent.

(b) No State Party to the present Charter shall derogate from the fundamental freedoms recognized herein and which are enjoyed by the nationals of another State that shows less respect for those freedoms.

Article 4

(a) No restrictions shall be placed on the rights and freedoms recognized in the present Charter except where such is provided by law and deemed necessary to protect the national security and economy, public order, health or morals or the rights and freedoms of others.

(b) In time of public emergency which threatens the life of the nation, the States Parties may take measures derogating from their obligations under the present Charter to the extent strictly required by the exigencies of the situation.

(c) Such measures or derogations shall under no circumstances affect or apply to the rights and special guarantees concerning the prohibition of torture and degrading treatment, return to one's country, political asylum, trial, the inadmissibility of retrial for the same act, and the legal status of crime and punishment.

Article 5

Every individual has the right to life, liberty and security of person. These rights shall be protected by law.

Article 6

There shall be no crime or punishment except as provided by law and there shall be no punishment in respect of an act preceding the promulgation of that provision. The accused shall benefit from subsequent legislation if it is in his favour.

Article 7

The accused shall be presumed innocent until proved guilty at a lawful trial in which he has enjoyed the guarantees necessary for his defence.

Article 8

Everyone has the right to liberty and security of person and no one shall be arrested, held in custody or detained without a legal warrant and without being brought promptly before a judge.

Article 9

All persons are equal before the law and everyone within the territory of the State has a guaranteed right to legal remedy.

Article 10

The death penalty may be imposed only for the most serious crimes and anyone sentenced to death shall have the right to seek pardon or commutation of the sentence.

Article 11

The death penalty shall under no circumstances be imposed for a political offence.

Article 12

The death penalty shall not be inflicted on a person under 18 years of age, on a pregnant woman prior to her delivery or on a nursing mother within two years from the date on which she gave birth.

Article 13

(a) The States Parties shall protect every person in their territory from being subjected to physical or mental torture or cruel, inhuman or degrading treatment. They shall take effective measures to prevent such acts and shall regard the practice thereof, or participation therein, as a punishable offence.

(b) No medical or scientific experimentation shall be carried out on any person without his free consent.

Article 14

No one shall be imprisoned on the ground of his proven inability to meet a debt or fulfil any civil obligation.

Article 15

Persons sentenced to a penalty of deprivation of liberty shall be treated with humanity.

Article 16

No one shall be tried twice for the same offence.

Anyone against whom such proceedings are brought shall have the right to challenge their legality and to demand his release.

Anyone who is the victim of unlawful arrest or detention shall be entitled to compensation.

Article 17

Privacy shall be inviolable and any infringement thereof shall constitute an offence.

This privacy includes private family affairs, the inviolability of the home and the confidentiality of correspondence and other private means of communication.

Article 18

Everyone shall have the inherent right to recognition as a person before the law.

Article 19

The people are the source of authority and every citizen of full legal age shall have the right of political participation, which he shall exercise in accordance with the law.

Article 20

Every individual residing within the territory of a State shall have the right to liberty of movement and freedom to choose his place of residence in any part of the said territory, within the limits of the law.

Article 21

No citizen shall be arbitrarily or unlawfully prevented from leaving any Arab country, including his own, nor prohibited from residing, or compelled to reside, in any part of his country.

Article 22

No citizen shall be expelled from his country or prevented from returning thereto.

Article 23

Every citizen shall have the right to seek political asylum in other countries in order to escape persecution. This right shall not be enjoyed by persons facing prosecution for an offence under the ordinary law. Political refugees shall not be extraditable.

Article 24

No citizen shall be arbitrarily deprived of his original nationality, nor shall his right to acquire another nationality be denied without a legally valid reason.

Article 25

Every citizen has a guaranteed right to own private property. No citizen shall under any circumstances be divested of all or any part of his property in an arbitrary or unlawful manner.

Article 26

Everyone has a guaranteed right to freedom of belief, thought and opinion.

Article 27

Adherents of every religion have the right to practise their religious observances and to manifest their views through expression, practice or teaching, without prejudice to the rights of others. No restrictions shall be imposed on the exercise of freedom of belief, thought and opinion except as provided by law.

Article 28

All citizens have the right to freedom of peaceful assembly and association. No restrictions shall be placed on the exercise of this right unless so required by the exigencies of national security, public safety or the need to protect the rights and freedoms of others.

Article 29

The State guarantees the right to form trade unions and the right to strike within the limits laid down by law.

Article 30

The State guarantees every citizen's right to work in order to secure for himself a standard of living that meets the basic requirements of life. The State also guarantees every citizen's right to comprehensive social security.

Article 31

Free choice of work is guaranteed and forced labour is prohibited. Compelling a person to perform work under the terms of a court judgement shall not be deemed to constitute forced labour.

Article 32

The State shall ensure that its citizens enjoy equality of opportunity in regard to work, as well as a fair wage and equal remuneration for work of equal value.

Article 33

Every citizen shall have the right of access to public office in his country.

Article 34

The eradication of illiteracy is a binding obligation and every citizen has a right to education. Primary education, at the very least, shall be compulsory and free and both secondary and university education shall be made easily accessible to all.

Article 35

Citizens have a right to live in an intellectual and cultural environment in which Arab nationalism is a source of pride, in which human rights are sanctified and in which racial, religious and other forms of discrimination are rejected and international cooperation and the cause of world peace are supported.

Article 36

Everyone has the right to participate in cultural life, as well as the right to enjoy literary and artistic works and to be given opportunities to develop his artistic, intellectual and creative talents.

Article 37

Minorities shall not be deprived of their right to enjoy their culture or to follow the teachings of their religions.

Article 38

(a) The family is the basic unit of society, whose protection it shall enjoy.
(b) The State undertakes to provide outstanding care and special protection for the family, mothers, children and the aged.

Article 39

Young persons have the right to be afforded the most ample opportunities for physical and mental development.

Appendix-5
ASEAN Human Rights Declaration

WE, the Heads of State/Government of the Member States of the Association of Southeast Asian Nations (hereinafter referred to as "ASEAN"), namely Brunei Darussalam, the Kingdom of Cambodia, the Republic of Indonesia, the Lao People's Democratic Republic, Malaysia, the Republic of the Union of Myanmar, the Republic of the Philippines, the Republic of Singapore, the Kingdom of Thailand and the Socialist Republic of Viet Nam, on the occasion of the 21st ASEAN Summit in Phnom Penh, Cambodia.

REAFFIRMING our adherence to the purposes and principles of ASEAN as enshrined in the ASEAN Charter, in particular the respect for and promotion and protection of human rights and fundamental freedoms, as well as the principles of democracy, the rule of law and good governance;

REAFFIRMING FURTHER our commitment to the Universal Declaration of Human Rights, the Charter of the United Nations, the Vienna Declaration and Programme of Action, and other international human rights instruments to which ASEAN Member States are parties;

REAFFIRMING ALSO the importance of ASEAN's efforts in promoting human rights, including the Declaration of the Advancement of Women in the ASEAN Region and the Declaration on the Elimination of Violence against Women in the ASEAN Region;

CONVINCED that this Declaration will help establish a framework for human rights cooperation in the region and contribute to the ASEAN community building process;

Hereby Declare as Follows:

General Principles

1. All persons are born free and equal in dignity and rights. They are endowed with reason and conscience and should act towards one another in a spirit of humanity.

2. Every person is entitled to the rights and freedoms set forth herein, without distinction of any kind, such as race, gender, age, language, religion, political or other opinion, national or social origin, economic status, birth, disability or other status.

3. Every person has the right of recognition everywhere as a person before the law. Every person is equal before the law. Every person is entitled without discrimination to equal protection of the law.

4. The rights of women, children, the elderly, persons with disabilities, migrant workers, and vulnerable and marginalised groups are an inalienable, integral and indivisible part of human rights and fundamental freedoms.

5. Every person has the right to an effective and enforceable remedy, to be determined by a court or other competent authorities, for acts violating the rights granted to that person by the constitution or by law.

6. The enjoyment of human rights and fundamental freedoms must be balanced with the performance of corresponding duties as every person has responsibilities to all other individuals, the community and the society where one lives. It is ultimately the primary responsibility of all ASEAN Member States to promote and protect all human rights and fundamental freedoms.

7. All human rights are universal, indivisible, interdependent and interrelated. All human rights and fundamental freedoms in this Declaration must be treated in a fair and equal manner, on the same footing and with the same emphasis. At the same time, the realisation of human rights must be considered in the regional and national context bearing in mind different political, economic, legal, social, cultural, historical and religious backgrounds.

8. The human rights and fundamental freedoms of every person shall be exercised with due regard to the human rights and fundamental freedoms of others. The exercise of human

rights and fundamental freedoms shall be subject only to such limitations as are determined by law solely for the purpose of securing due recognition for the human rights and fundamental freedoms of others, and to meet the just requirements of national security, public order, public health, public safety, public morality, as well as the general welfare of the peoples in a democratic society.

9. In the realisation of the human rights and freedoms contained in this Declaration, the principles of impartiality, objectivity, non-selectivity, non-discrimination, non-confrontation and avoidance of double standards and politicisation, should always be upheld. The process of such realisation shall take into account peoples' participation, inclusively and the need for accountability.

Civil and Political Rights

10. ASEAN Member States affirm all the civil and political rights in the Universal Declaration of Human Rights. Specifically, ASEAN Member States affirm the following rights and fundamental freedoms:

11. Every person has an inherent right to life which shall be protected by law. No person shall be deprived of life save in accordance with law.

12. Every person has the right to personal liberty and security. No person shall be subject to arbitrary arrest, search, detention, abduction or any other form of deprivation of liberty.

13. No person shall be held in servitude or slavery in any of its forms, or be subject to human smuggling or trafficking in persons, including for the purpose of trafficking in human organs.

14. No person shall be subject to torture or to cruel, inhuman or degrading treatment or punishment.

15. Every person has the right to freedom of movement and residence within the borders of each State. Every person has the right to leave any country including his or her own, and to return to his or her country.

16. Every person has the right to seek and receive asylum in another State in accordance with the laws of such State and applicable international agreements.

17. Every person has the right to own, use, dispose of and give that person's lawfully acquired possessions alone or in association with others. No person shall be arbitrarily deprived of such property.

18. Every person has the right to a nationality as prescribed by law. No person shall be arbitrarily deprived of such nationality nor denied the right to change that nationality.

19. The family as the natural and fundamental unit of society is entitled to protection by society and each ASEAN Member State. Men and women of full age have the right to marry on the basis of their free and full consent, to found a family and to dissolve a marriage, as prescribed by law.

20. (1) Every person charged with a criminal offence shall be presumed innocent until proved guilty according to law in a fair and public trial, by a competent, independent and impartial tribunal, at which the accused is guaranteed the right to defence.

(2) No person shall be held guilty of any criminal offence on account of any act or omission which did not constitute a criminal offence, under national or international law, at the time when it was committed and no person shall suffer greater punishment for an offence than was prescribed by law at the time it was committed.

(3) No person shall be liable to be tried or punished again for an offence for which he or she has already been finally convicted or acquitted in accordance with the law and penal procedure of each ASEAN Member State.

21. Every person has the right to be free from arbitrary interference with his or her privacy, family, home or correspondence including personal data, or to attacks upon that person's honour and reputation. Every person has the right to the protection of the law against such interference or attacks.

22. Every person has the right to freedom of thought, conscience and religion. All forms of intolerance, discrimination and incitement of hatred based on religion and beliefs shall be eliminated.

23. Every person has the right to freedom of opinion and expression, including freedom to hold opinions without

interference and to seek, receive and impart information, whether orally, in writing or through any other medium of that person's choice.

24. Every person has the right to freedom of peaceful assembly.

25. (1) Every person who is a citizen of his or her country has the right to participate in the government of his or her country, either directly or indirectly through democratically elected representatives, in accordance with national law.

(2) Every citizen has the right to vote in periodic and genuine elections, which should be by universal and equal suffrage and by secret ballot, guaranteeing the free expression of the will of the electors, in accordance with national law.

Economic, Social and Cultural Rights

26. ASEAN Member States affirm all the economic, social and cultural rights in the Universal Declaration of Human Rights. Specifically, ASEAN Member States affirm the following:

27. (1) Every person has the right to work, to the free choice of employment, to enjoy just, decent and favourable conditions of work and to have access to assistance schemes for the unemployed.

(2) Every person has the right to form trade unions and join the trade union of his or her choice for the protection of his or her interests, in accordance with national laws and regulations.

(3) No child or any young person shall be subjected to economic and social exploitation. Those who employ children and young people in work harmful to their morals or health, dangerous to life, or likely to hamper their normal development, including their education should be punished by law. ASEAN Member States should also set age limits below which the paid employment of child labour should be prohibited and punished by law.

28. Every person has the right to an adequate standard of living for himself or herself and his or her family including:

a. The right to adequate and affordable food, freedom from hunger and access to safe and nutritious food;
b. The right to clothing;
c. The right to adequate and affordable housing;
d. The right to medical care and necessary social services;
e. The right to safe drinking water and sanitation;
f. The right to a safe, clean and sustainable environment.

29. (1) Every person has the right to the enjoyment of the highest attainable standard of physical, mental and reproductive health, to basic and affordable health-care services, and to have access to medical facilities.
(2) The ASEAN Member States shall create a positive environment in overcoming stigma, silence, denial and discrimination in the prevention, treatment, care and support of people suffering from communicable diseases, including HIV/AIDS.

30. (1) Every person shall have the right to social security, including social insurance where available, which assists him or her to secure the means for a dignified and decent existence.
(2) Special protection should be accorded to mothers during a reasonable period as determined by national laws and regulations before and after childbirth. During such period, working mothers should be accorded paid leave or leave with adequate social security benefits.
(3) Motherhood and childhood are entitled to special care and assistance. Every child, whether born in or out of wedlock, shall enjoy the same social protection.

31. (1) Every person has the right to education.
(2) Primary education shall be compulsory and made available free to all. Secondary education in its different forms shall be available and accessible to all through every appropriate means. Technical and vocational education shall be made generally available. Higher education shall be equally accessible to all on the basis of merit.
(3) Education shall be directed to the full development

of the human personality and the sense of his or her dignity. Education shall strengthen the respect for human rights and fundamental freedoms in ASEAN' Member States. Furthermore, education shall enable all persons to participate effectively in their respective societies, promote understanding, tolerance and friendship among all nations, racial and religious groups, and enhance the activities of ASEAN for the maintenance of peace.

32. Every person has the right, individually or in association with others, to freely take part in cultural life, to enjoy the arts and the benefits of scientific progress and its applications and to benefit from the protection of the moral and material interests resulting from any scientific, literary or appropriate artistic production of which one is the author.

33. ASEAN Member States should take steps, individually and through regional and international assistance and cooperation, especially economic and technical, to the maximum of its available resources, with a view to achieving progressively the full realisation of economic, social and cultural rights recognised in this Declaration.

34. ASEAN Member States may determine the extent to which they would guarantee the economic and social rights found in this Declaration to non-nationals, with due regard to human rights and the organisation and resources of their respective national economies.

Right to Development

35. The right to development is an inalienable human right by virtue of which every human person and the peoples of ASEAN are entitled to participate in, contribute to, enjoy and benefit equitably and sustainably from economic, social, cultural and political development. The right to development should be fulfilled so as to meet equitably the developmental and environmental needs of present and future generations. While development facilitates and is necessary for the enjoyment of all human rights, the lack of development may not be invoked to justify the violations of internationally recognised human rights.

36. ASEAN Member States should adopt meaningful people-

oriented and gender responsive development programmes aimed at poverty alleviation, the creation of conditions including the protection and sustainability of the environment for the peoples of ASEAN to enjoy all human rights recognised in this Declaration on an equitable basis, and the progressive narrowing of the development gap within ASEAN.

37. ASEAN Member States recognise that the implementation of the right to development requires effective development policies at the national level as well as equitable economic relations, international cooperation and a favourable international economic environment. ASEAN Member States should mainstream the multidimensional aspects of the right to development into the relevant areas of ASEAN community building and beyond, and shall work with the international community to promote equitable and sustainable development, fair trade practices and effective international cooperation.

Right to Peace

38. Every person and the peoples of ASEAN have the right to enjoy peace within an ASEAN framework of security and stability, neutrality and freedom, such that the rights set forth in this Declaration can be fully realised. To this end, ASEAN Member States should continue to enhance friendship and cooperation in the furtherance of peace, harmony and stability in the region.

Cooperation in the Promotion and Protection of Human Rights

39. ASEAN Member States share a common interest in and commitment to the promotion and protection of human rights and fundamental freedoms which shall be achieved through, inter alia, cooperation with one another as well as with relevant national, regional and international institutions/organisations, in accordance with the ASEAN Charter.

40. Nothing in this Declaration may be interpreted as implying for any State, group or person any right to perform any act aimed at undermining the purposes and principles of ASEAN, or at the destruction of any of the rights and fundamental freedoms set forth in this Declaration and

international human rights instruments to which ASEAN Member States are parties.

Adopted by the Heads of State/Government of ASEAN Member States at Phnom Penh, Cambodia, this Eighteenth Day of November in the Year Two Thousand and Twelve, in one single original copy in the English Language.

Appendix-6
Asian Human Rights Charter

*Preamble

For long, especially during the colonial period, the peoples of Asia suffered from gross violations of their rights and freedoms. Today large sections of our people continue to be exploited and oppressed and many of our societies are torn apart by hatred and intolerance. Increasingly the people realize that peace and dignity are possible only when the equal and inalienable rights of all persons and groups are recognised and protected. They are determined to secure peace and justice for themselves and the coming generations through the struggle for human rights and freedoms. Towards that end they adopt this Charter as an affirmation of the desire and aspirations of the peoples of Asia to live in peace and dignity.

Background to the Charter

1.1 The Asian struggle for rights and freedoms has deep historical roots, in the fight against oppression in civil society and the political oppression of colonialism, and subsequently for the establishment or restoration of democracy. The reaffirmation of rights is necessary now more than ever before. Asia is passing through a period of rapid change, which affects social structures,

---

* The final version of the Charter was written by Prof. Yash Ghai under the direction of a Committee of which he was a Member consisting of Justices Krishna Iyer, P.N. Bhagwati and so on from AHRC (Asian Human Rights Commission, Asian Human Rights Charter was declared in KWANGJU, South Korea on 17, May, 1998.

political institutions and the economy. Traditional values are under threat from new forms of development and technologies, as well as political authorities and economic organizations that manage these changes.

1.2 In particular the marketization and globalization of economies are changing the balance between the private and the public, the state and the international community, and worsening the situation of the poor and the disadvantaged. These changes threaten many valued aspects of life, the result of the dehumanizing effects of technology, the material orientation of the market, and the destruction of the community. People have decreasing control over their lives and environment, and some communities do not have protection even against eviction from their traditional homes and grounds. There is a massive exploitation of workers, with wages that are frequently inadequate for even bare subsistence and low safety standards that put the lives of workers in constant danger. Even the most elementary of labour rights and laws are seldom enforced.

1.3 Asian development is full of contradictions. There is massive and deepening poverty in the midst of growing affluence of some sections of the people. Levels of health, nutrition and education of large numbers of our people are appalling, denying the dignity of human life. At the same time valuable resources are wasted on armaments, Asia being the largest purchaser of arms of all regions. Our governments claim to be pursuing development directed at increasing levels of production and welfare but our natural resources are being depleted most irresponsibly and the environment is so degraded that the quality of life has worsened immeasurably, even for the better off among us. Building of golf courses has a higher priority than the care of the poor and the disadvantaged.

1.4 Asians have in recent decades suffered from various forms of conflict and violence, arising from ultra-nationalism, perverted ideologies, ethnic differences, and fundamentalism of all religions. Violence emanates from both the state and sections of civil society. For large masses, there is little security of person, property or community. There is massive displacement of communities and there are an increasing number of refugees.

1.5 Governments have arrogated enormous powers to themselves. They have enacted legislation to suppress people's rights and freedoms and colluded with foreign firms and groups in the plunder of national resources. Corruption and nepotism are rampant and there is little accountability of those holding public or private power. Authoritarianism has in many states been raised to the level of national ideology, with the deprivation of the rights and freedoms of their citizens, which are denounced as foreign ideas inappropriate to the religious and cultural traditions of Asia. Instead there is the exhortation of spurious theories of Asian Values which are a thin disguise for their authoritarianism. Not surprisingly, Asia, of all the major regions of the world, is without a regional official charter or other regional arrangements for the protection of rights and freedoms.

1.6 In contrast to the official disregard or contempt of human rights in many Asian states, there is increasing awareness among their peoples of the importance of rights and freedoms. They realize the connections between their poverty and political powerlessness and the denial to them of these rights and freedoms. They believe that political and economic systems have to operate within a framework of human rights and freedoms to ensure economic justice, political participation and accountability, and social peace. There are many social movements that have taken up the fight to secure for the people their rights and freedoms.

1.7 Our commitment to rights is not due to any abstract ideological reasons. We believe that respect for human rights provides the basis for a just, humane and caring society. A regime of rights is premised on the belief that we are all inherently equal and have an equal right to live in dignity. It is based on our right to determine our destiny through participation in policy making and administration. It enables us to develop and enjoy our culture and to give expression to our artistic impulses. It respects diversity. It recognizes our obligations to future generations and the environment they will inherit. It establishes standards for assessing the worth and legitimacy of our institutions and policies.

General Principles

2.1 It is possible from specific rights and the institutions and procedures for their protection to draw some general principles which underlie these rights and whose acceptance and implementation facilitates their full enjoyment. The principles, which are discussed below, should provide the broad framework for public policies within which we believe rights would be promoted.

Universality and Indivisibility of Rights

2.2 We endorse the Universal Declaration of Human Rights, the International Covenant on Economic, Social and Cultural Rights, the International Covenant on Civil and Political Rights, and other international instruments for the protection of rights and freedoms. We believe that rights are universal, every person being entitled to them by virtue of being a human being. Cultural traditions affect the way in which a society organizes relationships within itself, but they do not detract from the universalism of rights which are primarily concerned with the relationship of citizens with the state and the inherent dignity of persons and groups. We also believe that rights and freedoms are indivisible and it is a fallacy to suppose that some types of rights can be suppressed in the name of other rights. Human beings have social, cultural and economic needs and aspirations that cannot be fragmented or compartmentalised, but are mutually dependent. Civil, political and cultural rights have little meaning unless there are the economic resources to exercise and enjoy them. Equally, the pursuit and acquisition of material wealth is sterile and self-defeating without political freedoms, the opportunity to develop and express one's personality and to engage in cultural and other discourses.

2.3 Notwithstanding their universality and indivisibility, the enjoyment and the salience of rights depend on social, economic and cultural contexts. Rights are not abstractions, but foundations for action and policy. Consequently we must move from abstract formulations of rights to their concretization in the Asian context by examining the circumstances of specific groups whose situation is defined by massive violations of their rights. It is only by relating rights and their implementation to the specificity of the Asian situation that the enjoyment of rights will be possible. Only in this way will Asia be able to contribute to the world-wide movement for the protection of rights.

2.4 Widespread poverty, even in states which have achieved a high rate of economic development, is a principal cause of the violation of rights. Poverty deprives individuals, families, and communities of their rights and promotes prostitution, child labour, slavery, sale of human organs, and the mutilation of the body to enhance the capacity to beg. A life of dignity is impossible in the midst of poverty. Asian states must direct their development policies towards the elimination of poverty through more equitable forms of development.

The Responsibility for the Protection of Human Rights

2.5 The responsibility for the protection of rights is both international and domestic. The international community has agreed upon norms and institutions that should govern the practice of human rights. The peoples of Asia support international measures for the protection of rights. State sovereignty cannot be used as an excuse to evade international norms or ignore international institutions. The claim of state sovereignty is justified only when a state fully protects the rights of its citizens.

2.6 On the other hand, international responsibility cannot be used for the selective chastisement or punishment of particular states; or for the privileging of one set of rights over others. Some fundamental causes of the violation of human rights lie in the inequities of the international world economic and political order. The radical transformation and democratization of the world order is a necessary condition for the global enjoyment of human rights. The logic of the universalism and equality of rights is the responsibility of the international community for the social and economic welfare of all people throughout the world, and consequently the obligation to ensure a more equitable distribution of resources and opportunities across the world.

2.7 The primary responsibility for the promotion of human rights rests with states. The rights of states and peoples to just economic, social, political and cultural development must not be negated by global processes. States must establish open political processes in which rights and obligations of different groups are acknowledged and the balance between the interests of individuals and the community is achieved. Democratic and accountable governments are the key to the promotion and protection of rights.

2.8 The capacity of the international community and states to promote and protect rights has been weakened by processes of globalization as more and more power over economic and social policy and activities has moved from states to business corporations. States are increasingly held hostage by financial and other corporations to implement narrow and short sighted economic policies which cause so much misery to so many people, while increasing the wealth of the few. Business corporations are responsible for numerous violations of rights, particularly those of workers, women and indigenous peoples. It is necessary to strengthen the regime of rights by making corporations liable for the violation of rights.

Sustainable Development and the Protection of the Environment

2.9 Economic development must be sustainable. We must protect the environment against the avarice and depredations of commercial enterprises to ensure that the quality of life does not decline just as the gross national product increases. Technology must liberate, not enslave human beings. Natural resources must be used in a manner consistent with our obligation to future generations. We must never forget that we are merely temporary custodians of the resources of nature. Nor should we forget that these resources are given to all human kind, and consequently we have a joint responsibility for their responsible, fair and equitable use.

Rights

3.1 We endorse all the rights that are contained in international instruments. It is unnecessary to restate them here. We believe that these rights need to be seen in a holistic manner and that individual rights are best pursued through a broader conceptualization which forms the basis of the following section.

The Right to Life

3.2 Foremost among rights is the right to life, from which flow other rights and freedoms. The right to life is not confined to mere physical or animal existence but includes the right to every limb or faculty through which life is enjoyed. It signifies the right to live with basic human dignity, the right to livelihood, the right to a habitat or home, the right to education and the right to a clean and healthy environment for without these there can be no real and effective exercise or enjoyment of the right to life. The state must also take all possible measures to prevent infant mortality, eliminate malnutrition and epidemics, and increase life expectancy through a clean and healthy environment and adequate preventative as well as curative medical facilities. It must make primary education free and compulsory.

3.3 Yet in many parts of Asia, wars, ethnic conflicts, cultural and religious oppression, corruption of politics, environmental pollution, disappearances, torture, state or private terrorism, violence against women, and other acts of mass violence continue to be a scourge to humanity resulting in the loss of thousands of innocent human lives.

3.4 To ensure the right to life, propagation of war or ethnic conflict or incitement to hatred and violence in all spheres of individual or societal or national or international life should be prohibited.

3.5 The state has the responsibility to thoroughly investigate cases of torture, disappearances and custodial deaths, rapes and sexual abuses and to bring culprits to justice.

3.6 There must be no arbitrary deprivation of life. States should take measures not only to prevent and mete out punish for the deprivation of life by criminal acts and terrorist acts but also prevent arbitrary disappearances and killings by their own security forces. The law must strictly control and limit the circumstances in which a person may be deprived of his or her life by state authorities or officials.

3.7 All states must abolish the death penalty. Where it exists, it may be imposed only rarely for the most serious crimes. Before a person can be deprived of life by the imposition of the death penalty, he or she must be ensured a fair trial before an independent and impartial tribunal with full opportunity of legal representation of his or her choice, adequate time for preparation of defence, presumption of innocence and the right to review by a higher tribunal. Execution should never be carried out in public or otherwise exhibited in public.

The Right to Peace

4.1 All persons have the right to live in peace so that they can fully develop all their capacities, physical, intellectual, moral and spiritual, without being the target of any kind of violence. The peoples of Asia have suffered great hardships and tragedies due to wars and civil conflicts which have caused many deaths, mutilation of bodies, external or internal displacement of persons, break up of families, and in general the denial of any prospects of a civilized or peaceful existence. Both the state and civil society have in many countries become heavily militarized in which all scores are settled by force and citizens have no protection against the intimidation and terror of state or private armies.

4.2 The duty of the state to maintain law and order should be conducted under strict restraint on the use of force in accordance with standards established by the international community, including humanitarian law. Every individual and group is entitled to protection against all forms of state violence, including violence perpetrated by its police and military forces.

4.3 The right to live in peace requires that political, economic or social activities of the state, the corporate sector and the civil society should respect the security of all peoples, especially of vulnerable groups. People must be ensured security in relation to the natural environment they live in, the political, economic and social conditions which permit them to satisfy their needs and aspirations without recourse to oppression, exploitation, violence, and without detracting from all that is of value in their society.

4.4 In fighting fascist invasion, colonialism, and neo-colonialism, Asian states played a crucial role in creating conditions for their peoples to live in peace. In this fight, they had justifiably stressed the importance of national integrity and nonintervention by hegemonic powers. However, the demands of national integrity or protection against the threats of foreign domination cannot now be used as a pretext for refusing to the people their right to personal security and peaceful existence any more than the suppression of people's rights can be justified as an excuse to attract foreign investments. Neither can they justify any refusal to inform the international community about the individual security of its people. The right of persons to live in peace can be guaranteed only if the states are accountable to the international community.

4.5 The international community of states has been deeply implicated in wars and civil conflicts in Asia. Foreign states have used Asian groups as surrogates to wage wars and have armed groups and governments engaged in internal conflicts. They have made huge profits out of the sale of armaments. The enormous expenditures on arms have diverted public revenues from programmes for the development of the country or the well-being of the people. Military bases and other establishments (often of foreign powers) have threatened the social and physical security of the people who live in their vicinity.

The Right to Democracy

5.1 Colonialism and other modern developments significantly changed the nature of Asian political societies. The traditional systems of accountability and public participation in affairs of state as well as the relationship of citizens to the government were altered fundamentally. Citizens became subjects, while the government became more pervasive and powerful. Colonial laws and authoritarian habits and style of administration persisted after independence. The state has become the source of corruption and the oppression of the people. The democratization and humanization of the state is a pre-condition for the respect for and the protection of rights.

5.2 The state, which claims to have the primary responsibility for the development and well-being of the people, should be humane, open and accountable. The corollary of the respect for human rights is a tolerant and pluralistic system, in which people are free to express their views and to seek to persuade others and in which the rights of minorities are respected. People must participate in public affairs, through the electoral and other decision-making and implementing processes, free from racial, religious or gender discriminations.

The Right to Cultural Identity and The Freedom of Conscience

6.1 The right to life involves not only material but also the moral conditions which permit a person to lead a meaningful existence. This meaning is not only individually determined but is also based on shared living with other human beings. The Asian traditions stress the importance of common cultural identities. Cultural identities help individuals and communities to cope with the pressures of economic and social change; they give meaning to life in a period of rapid transformation. They are the source of pride and security. There are many vulnerable communities in Asia as elsewhere whose cultures are threatened or derided. Asian peoples and governments must respect the cultures and traditions of its diverse communities.

6.2 The plurality of cultural identities in Asia is not contrary to the universality of human rights but rather as so many cultural manifestations of human dignity enriching universal norms. At the same time we Asian peoples must eliminate those features in our cultures which are contrary to the universal principles of human rights. We must transcend the traditional concept of the family based on patriarchal traditions so as to retrieve in each of our cultural traditions, the diversity of family norms which guarantee women's human rights. We must be bold in reinterpreting our religious beliefs which support gender inequality. We must also eliminate discriminations based on caste, ethnic origins, occupation, place of origin and others, while enhancing in our respective cultures all values related to mutual tolerance and mutual support. We must stop practices which sacrifice the individual to the collectivity or to the powerful, and thus renew our communal and national solidarity.

6.3 The freedom of religion and conscience is particularly important in Asia where most people are deeply religious. Religion is a source of comfort and solace in the midst of poverty and oppression. Many find their primary identity in religion. However religious fundamentalism is also a cause of divisions and conflict. Religious tolerance is essential for the enjoyment of the right of conscience of others, which includes the right to change one's belief.

The Right to Development and Social Justice

7.1 Every individual has the right to the basic necessities of life and to protection against abuse and exploitation. We all have the right to literacy and knowledge, to food and clean water, shelter and to medical facilities for a healthy existence. All individuals and human groups are entitled to share the benefits of the progress of technology and of the growth of the world economy.

7.2 Development, for individuals and states, does not mean merely economic development. It means the realization of the full potential of the human person. Consequently they have the right to artistic freedom, freedom of expression and the cultivation of their cultural and spiritual capacities. It means the right to participate in the affairs of the state and the community. It implies that states have the right to determine their own economic, social and cultural policies free from hegemonic pressures and influences.

Rights of Vulnerable Groups

8.1 Asian states should formulate and implement public policies within the above general framework of rights. We believe that in this way we will establish fair and humane conditions for our individual and corporate lives and ensure social justice. However, there are particular groups who for historical or other reasons are weak and vulnerable and consequently require special protection for the equal and effective enjoyment of their human rights. We discuss the situation of several such groups, but we recognize that there are also other groups who suffer from discrimination and oppression. They include people who through civil conflict, government policies or economic hardships are displaced from their homes and seek refuge in other places internally or in foreign lands. Our states and societies have become less tolerant of minorities and indigenous people, whose most basic rights are frequently violated. Many of our societies still discriminate against gays and lesbians, denying them their identity and causing them great anguish and misery. Various economic groups, like peasants and fishing communities, suffer from great deprivation and live in constant fear of threats to their livelihood from landlords and capitalist enterprises. All these groups deserve special attention. We urge states and communities to give the highest priority to the amelioration of their social and economic conditions.

Women

9.1 In most Asian societies women suffer from discrimination and oppression. The cause of their oppression lies in both history and contemporary social and economic systems.

9.2 The roots of patriarchy are systemic and its structures dominate all institutions, attitudes, social norms and customary laws, religions and values in Asian societies, crossing the boundaries of class, culture, caste and ethnicity. Oppression takes many forms, but is most evident in sexual slavery, domestic violence, trafficking in women and rape. They suffer discrimination in both public and private spheres. The increasing militarization of many societies in Asia has led to the increase of violence against women in situations of armed conflict, including mass rape, forced labour, racism, kidnapping and displacement from their homes. As female victims of armed conflict are often denied justice, rehabilitation, compensation and reparation of the war crimes committed against them, it is important to emphacise that systematic rape is a war crime and a crime against humanity.

9.3 To end discrimination against women in the field of employment and the right to work, women should be given the right to employment opportunities, the free choice of profession, job security, equal remuneration, the right to compensation in respect of domestic work, the right to protection of health and safe working conditions, especially in safeguarding of the function of reproduction and special protection in times of pregnancy from work that may be harmful. Women should be given the full right to control their sexual and reproductive health, free from discrimination or coercion, and be given access to information about sexual and reproductive health care and safe reproductive technology.

9.4 There are few legal provisions to protect women against violations of their rights within the domestic and patriarchal realm. Their rights in public law are seldom observed. Affirmative measures should be taken to ensure full and equal participation of women in the political and public life of the society. A considerable increase in the presence of women in the various institutions of state power and in the fields of business, agriculture and land ownership must be provided for by way of affirmative action. The political, social and economic empowerment of women is essential for the defence of their legal rights.

Children

10.1 As with women, their oppression takes many forms, the most pervasive of which are child labour; sexual slavery; child pornography; the sale and trafficking of children; prostitution; sale of organs; conscription into drug trafficking; the physical, sexual and psychological abuse of children within families; discrimination against children with HIV/AIDS; forced religious conversion of children; the displacement of children with and without their families by armed conflicts; discrimination; and environmental degradation. An increasing number of children are forced to live on the streets of Asian cities and are deprived of the social and economic support of families and communities.

10.2 Widespread poverty, lack of access to education and social dislocation in rural areas are among the causes of the trends which increase the vulnerability of children. Long-established forms of exploitation and abuse, such as bonded labour or the use of children for begging or sexual gratification are rampant. Female infanticide due to patriarchal gender preference and female genital mutilation are widely practised in some Asian countries.

10.3 Asian states have failed dismally to look after children and provide them with even the bare means of subsistence or shelter. We call on Asian states to ratify and implement the Convention on the Rights of the Child. We also call on communities to take the responsibility for monitoring violations of children's rights and to press for the implementation of the UN Convention in appropriate ways in their own social contexts.

Differently Abled Persons

11.1 Traditionally Asian societies cared for those who were physically or mentally handicapped. Increasingly our communal values and structures, under the pressure of new forms of economic organizations, have become less tolerant of such persons. They suffer enormous discrimination in access to education, employment and housing. They are unable to enjoy many of their human rights due to prejudice against them and the absence of provisions responding to their special demands. Their considerable abilities are not properly recognized and they are forced into jobs which offer low pay and little prospects of promotion. They have the right to provisions which enable them to live in dignity, with security and respect, and to have opportunities to realize their full potential.

11.2 The need to treat such persons with respect for their human rights is apparent in the dismal way Asian states treat those with HIV or AIDS. They are the victims of gross discrimination. A civilized society which respects human rights would recognize their right to live and die with dignity. It would secure to them the right to adequate medical care and to be protected from prejudice, discrimination or persecution.

Workers

12.1 The rapid industrialization of Asian societies has undermined traditional forms of the subsistence economy and has destroyed possibilities of the livelihood of large sections of the rural people. Increasingly they and other groups are forced into wage employment, often in industry, working under appalling conditions. For the majority of the workers there is little or no protection from unfair labour laws. The fundamental rights to form trade unions and bargain collectively are denied to many. Their wages are grossly inadequate and working conditions are frequently grim and dangerous. Globalization adds to the pressures on workers as many Asian states seek to reduce the costs of production, often in collusion with foreign corporations and international financial institutions.

12.2 A particularly vulnerable category of workers are migrant workers. Frequently separated from their families, they are exploited in foreign states whose laws they do not understand and are afraid to invoke. They are often denied rights and conditions which local workers enjoy. They slog without access to adequate accommodation, health care, or legal protection. In many cases migrants suffer racism and xenophobia, and domestic helpers are subjected to humiliation and sometimes, sexual abuse.

Students

13.1 Students in Asia struggled against colonialism and fought for democratization and social justice. As a result of their fearless commitment to social transformation they have often suffered from state violence and repression and remain as one of the key targets for counter-insurgency operations and internal security laws and operations. Students are frequently denied the right to academic freedom and to the freedoms of expression and association.

Prisoners and Political Detainees

14.1 In few areas is there such a massive violation of internationally recognized norms as in relation to prisoners and political detainees.

14.2 Arbitrary arrests, detention, imprisonment, ill-treatment, torture, cruel and inhuman punishment are common occurrences in many parts of Asia. Detainees and prisoners are often forced to live in unhygienic conditions, are denied adequate food and health care and are prevented from having communication with, and support from, their families. Different kinds of prisoners are frequently mixed in one cell, with men, women and children kept in proximity. Prison cells are normally overcrowded. Deaths in custody are common. Prisoners are frequently denied access to lawyers and the right to fair and speedy trials.

14.3 Asian governments often use executive powers of detention without trial. They use national security legislation to arrest and detain political opponents. It is notable that, in many countries in Asia, freedom of thought, belief and conscience have been restricted by administrative limits on freedom of speech and association.

The Enforcement of Rights

15.1 Many Asian states have guarantees of human rights in their constitutions, and many of them have ratified international instruments on human rights. However, there continues to be a wide gap between rights enshrined in these documents and the abject reality that denies people their rights. Asian states must take urgent action to implement the human rights of their citizens and residents.

Principles for Enforcement

15.2 We believe that systems for the protection of rights should be based on the following principles.

15.2a Human rights are violated by the state, civil society and business corporations. The legal protection for rights has to be extended against violations by all these groups. It is also necessary to reform these groups by strengthening their ethical foundations and values and inculcating in them a sense of their responsibility towards the disadvantaged and the oppressed.

15.2b The promotion and enforcement of rights is the responsibility of all groups in society, although the primary responsibility is that of the state. The enjoyment of many rights, especially social and economic, requires a positive and proactive role of governments. There is a clear and legitimate role for NGOs in raising consciousness of rights, formulating standards, and ensuring their protection by governments and other groups. Professional groups like lawyers and doctors have special responsibilities connected with the nature of their work to promote the enforcement of rights and prevent abuses of power.

15.2c Since rights are seriously violated in situations of civil strife and are strengthened if there is peace, it is the duty of the state and other organizations to find peaceful ways to resolve social and ethnic conflicts and to promote tolerance and harmony. For the same reasons no state should seek to dominate other states and states should settle their differences peacefully.

15.2d Rights are enhanced if democratic and consensual practices are followed and it is therefore the responsibility of all states and other organisations to promote these practices in their work and in their dealings with others.

15.2e Many individuals and groups in Asia are unable to exercise their rights due to restrictive or oppressive social customs and practices, particularly those related to caste, gender, or religion. Therefore the immediate reform of these customs and practices is necessary for the protection of rights. The reforms must be enforced with vigour and determination.

15.2f A humane and vigorous civil society is necessary for the promotion and protection of human rights and freedoms, for securing rights within civil society and to act as a check on state institutions. Freedoms of expression and association are necessary for the establishment and functioning of institutions of civil society.

15.2g It is necessary to curb the exploitative practices of business corporations and to ensure that they do not violate rights of workers, consumers and the public.

Strengthening the Framework for Rights

15.3a It is essential to secure the legal framework for rights. All states should include guarantees of rights in their constitutions, which should be constitutionally protected against erosion by legislative amendments. They should also ratify international human rights instruments. They should review their legislation and administrative practices against national and international standards with the aim of repealing provisions which contravene these standards, particularly legislation carried over from the colonial period.

15.3b Knowledge and consciousness of rights should be raised among the general public, and state and civil society institutions. Awareness of the national and international regime of rights should be promoted. Individuals and groups should be acquainted with legal and administrative procedures whereby they can secure their rights and prevent abuse of authority. NGOs should be encouraged to become familiar with and deploy mechanisms, both national and inter-national, for monitoring and review of rights. Judicial and administrative decisions on the protection of rights should be widely disseminated, nationally and in the Asian region. Governments, NGOs and educational institutions should co-operate in disseminating information about the importance and content of human rights.

15.3c Numerous violations of rights occur while people are in custody and through other activities of security forces. Sometimes these violations take place because the security forces do not respect the permissible scope of their powers or do not realise that the orders under which they are acting are unlawful. Members of the police, prison services and the armed forces should be provided training in human rights norms.

The Machinery for the Enforcement of Rights

15.4a The judiciary is a major means for the protection of rights. It has the power to receive complaints of the violation of rights, to hear evidence, and to provide redress for violations, including punishment for violators. The judiciary can only perform this function if the legal system is strong and well-organized. The members of the judiciary should be competent, experienced and have a commitment to human rights, dignity and justice. They should be independent of the legislature and the executive by vesting the power of their appointment in a judicial service commission and by constitutional safeguards of their tenure. Judicial institutions should fairly reflect the character of the different sections of the people by religion, region, gender and social class. This means that there must be a restructuring of the judiciary and the investigative machinery. More women, more underprivileged categories and more of the Pariahs of society must by deliberate State action be lifted out of the mire and instilled in judicial positions with necessary training. Only such a measure will command the confidence of the weaker sector whose human rights are ordinarily ignored in the traditional societies of Asia.

15.4.b The legal profession should be independent. Legal aid should be provided for those who are unable to afford the services of lawyers or have access to courts, for the protection of their rights. Rules which unduly restrict access to courts should be reformed to provide a broad access. Social and welfare organizations should be authorised to bring legal action on behalf of individuals and groups who are unable to utilize the courts.

15.4c All states should establish Human Rights Commissions and specialized institutions for the protection of rights, particularly of vulnerable members of society. They can provide easy, friendly and inexpensive access to justice for victims of human rights violations. These bodies can supplement the role of the judiciary. They enjoy special advantages: they can help establish standards for the implementation of human rights norms; they can disseminate information about human rights; they can investigate allegations of violation of rights; they can promote conciliation and mediation; and they can seek to enforce human rights through administrative or judicial means. They can act on their own initiative as well on complaints from members of the public.

15.4d Civil society institutions can help to enforce rights through the organization of People's Tribunals, which can touch the conscience of the government and the public. The establishment of People's Tribunals emphasizes that the responsibility for the protection of rights is wide, and not a preserve of the state. They are not confined to legal rules in their adjudication and can consequently help to uncover the moral and spiritual foundations of human rights.

Regional Institutions for the Protection of Rights

16.1 The protection of human rights should be pursued at all levels, local, national, regional and international. Institutions at each level have their special advantages and skills. The primary responsibility for the protection of rights is that of states, therefore priority should be given to the enhancement of state capacity to fulfil this obligation.

16.2 Asian states should adopt regional or sub-regional institutions for the promotion and protection of rights. There should be an inter-state Convention on Human Rights, formulated in regional forums with the collaboration of national and regional NGOs. The Convention must address the realities of Asia, particularly the obstacles that impede the enjoyment of rights. At the same time it must be fully consistent with international norms and standards. It should cover violations of rights by groups and corporations in addition to state institutions. An independent commission or a court must be established to enforce the Convention. Access to the commission or the court must be open to NGOs and other social organizations.

Appendics-7
American Convention on Human Rights "Pact of San Jose, Costa Rica"

Preamble

The American states signatory to the present Convention,

Reaffirming their intention to consolidate in this hemisphere, within the framework of democratic institutions, a system of personal liberty and social justice based on respect for the essential rights of man;

Recognizing that the essential rights of man are not derived from one's being a national of a certain state, but are based upon attributes of the human personality, and that they therefore justify international protection in the form of a convention reinforcing or complementing the protection provided by the domestic law of the American states;

Considering that these principles have been set forth in the Charter of the Organization of American States, in the American Declaration of the Rights and Duties of Man, and in the Universal Declaration of Human Rights, and that they have been reaffirmed and refined in other international instruments, worldwide as well as regional in scope;

Reiterating that, in accordance with the Universal Declaration of Human Rights, the ideal of free men enjoying freedom from fear and want can be achieved only if conditions are created whereby everyone may enjoy his economic, social, and cultural rights, as well as his civil and political rights; and Considering that the Third Special Inter-American Conference (Buenos Aires, 1967) approved the incorporation into the Charter of the Organization itself of broader standards with respect to economic, social, and educational rights and resolved that an inter-American convention on human rights should determine the structure, competence, and procedure of the organs responsible for these matters,

Have agreed upon the following:

PART I—STATE OBLIGATIONS AND RIGHTS PROTECTED

CHAPTER I—GENERAL OBLIGATIONS

Article 1. Obligation to Respect Rights

1. The States Parties to this Convention undertake to respect the rights and freedoms recognized herein and to ensure to all persons' opinion, national or social origin, economic status, birth, or any other social condition.
2. For the purposes of this Convention, 'person' means every human being.

Article 2. Domestic Legal Effects

Where the exercise of any of the rights or freedoms referred to in Article 1 is not already ensured by legislative or other provisions, the States Parties undertake to adopt, in accordance with their constitutional processes and the provisions of this Convention, such legislative or other measures as may be necessary to give effect to those rights or freedoms.

CHAPTER II—CIVIL AND POLITICAL RIGHTS

Article 3. Right to Juridical Personality

Every person has the right to recognition as a person before the law.

Article 4. Right to Life

1. Every person has the right to have his life respected. This right shall be protected by law and, in general, from

the moment of conception. No one shall be arbitrarily deprived of his life.

2. In countries that have not abolished the death penalty, it may be imposed only for the most serious crimes and pursuant to a final judgment rendered by a competent court and in accordance with a law establishing such punishment, enacted prior to the commission of the crime. The application of such punishment shall not be extended to crimes to which it does not presently apply.
3. The death penalty shall not be reestablished in states that have abolished it.
4. In no case shall capital punishment be inflicted for political offenses or related common crimes.
5. Capital punishment shall not be imposed upon persons who, at the time the crime was committed, were under 18 years of age or over 70 years of age; nor shall it be applied to pregnant women.
6. Every person condemned to death shall have the right to apply for amnesty, pardon, or commutation of sentence, which may be granted in all cases. Capital punishment shall not be imposed while such a petition is pending decision by the competent authority.

Article 5. Right to Humane Treatment

1. Every person has the right to have his physical, mental, and moral integrity respected.
2. No one shall be subjected to torture or to cruel, inhuman, or degrading punishment or treatment. All persons deprived of their liberty shall be treated with respect for the inherent dignity of the human person.
3. Punishment shall not be extended to any person other than the criminal.
4. Accused persons shall, save in exceptional circumstances, be segregated from convicted persons, and shall be subject to separate treatment appropriate to their status as unconvicted persons.
5. Minors while subject to criminal proceedings shall be separated from adults and brought before specialized tribunals, as speedily as possible, so that they may be

treated in accordance with their status as minors.

6. Punishments consisting of deprivation of liberty shall have as an essential aim the reform and social readaptation of the prisoners.

Article 6. Freedom from Slavery

1. No one shall be subject to slavery or to involuntary servitude, which are prohibited in all their forms, as are the slave trade and traffic in women.
2. No one shall be required to perform forced or compulsory labor. This provision shall not be interpreted to mean that, in those countries in which the penalty established for certain crimes is deprivation of liberty at forced labor, the carrying out of such a sentence imposed by a competent court is prohibited. Forced labor shall not adversely affect the dignity or the physical or intellectual capacity of the prisoner.
3. For the purposes of this article, the following do not constitute forced or compulsory labor:
   a. Work or service normally required of a person imprisoned in execution of a sentence or formal decision passed by the competent judicial authority. Such work or service shall be carried out under the supervision and control of public authorities, and any persons performing such work or service shall not be placed at the disposal of any private party, company, or juridical person;
   b. Military service and, in countries in which conscientious objectors are recognized, national service that the law may provide for in lieu of military service;
   c. Service exacted in time of danger or calamity that threatens the existence or the well-being of the community; or
   d. Work or service that forms part of normal civic obligations.

Article 7. Right to Personal Liberty

1. Every person has the right to personal liberty and security.
2. No one shall be deprived of his physical liberty except for the reasons and under the conditions established beforehand by the constitution of the State Party concerned or by a law established pursuant thereto.
3. No one shall be subject to arbitrary arrest or imprisonment.
4. Anyone who is detained shall be informed of the reasons for his detention and shall be promptly notified of the charge or charges against him.
5. Any person detained shall be brought promptly before a judge or other officer authorized by law to exercise judicial power and shall be entitled to trial within a reasonable time or to be released without prejudice to the continuation of the proceedings. His release may be subject to guarantees to assure his appearance for trial.
6. Anyone who is deprived of his liberty shall be entitled to recourse to a competent court, in order that the court may decide without delay on the lawfulness of his arrest or detention and order his release if the arrest or detention is unlawful. In States Parties whose laws provide that anyone who believes himself to be threatened with deprivation of his liberty is entitled to recourse to a competent court in order that it may decide on the lawfulness of such threat, this remedy may not be restricted or abolished. The interested party or another person in his behalf is entitled to seek these remedies.
7. No one shall be detained for debt. This principle shall not limit the orders of a competent judicial authority issued for nonfulfillment of duties of support.

Article 8. Right to a Fair Trial

1. Every person has the right to a hearing, with due guarantees and within a reasonable time, by a competent, independent, and impartial tribunal, previously established by law, in the substantiation of any accusation of a criminal nature

made against him or for the determination of his rights and obligations of a civil, labor, fiscal, or any other nature.

2. Every person accused of a criminal offense has the right to be presumed innocent so long as his guilt has not been proven according to law. During the proceedings, every person is entitled, with full equality, to the following minimum guarantees:

a. The right of the accused to be assisted without charge by a translator or interpreter, if he does not understand or does not speak the language of the tribunal or court;
b. Prior notification in detail to the accused of the charges against him;
c. Adequate time and means for the preparation of his defense;
d. The right of the accused to defend himself personally or to be assisted by legal counsel of his own choosing, and to communicate freely and privately with his counsel;
e. The inalienable right to be assisted by counsel provided by the state, paid or not as the domestic law provides, if the accused does not defend himself personally or engage his own counsel within the time period established by law;
f. The right of the defense to examine witnesses present in the court and to obtain the appearance, as witnesses, of experts or other persons who may throw light on the facts;
g. The right not to be compelled to be a witness against himself or to plead guilty; and
h. The right to appeal the judgment to a higher court.

3. A confession of guilt by the accused shall be valid only if it is made without coercion of any kind.

4. An accused person acquitted by a nonappealable judgment shall not be subjected to a new trial for the same cause.

5. Criminal proceedings shall be public, except insofar as may be necessary to protect the interests of justice.

Article 9. Freedom from *Ex Post Facto* Laws

No one shall be convicted of any act or omission that did not constitute a criminal offense, under the applicable law, at the time it was committed. A heavier penalty shall not be imposed than the one that was applicable at the time the criminal offense was committed. If subsequent to the commission of the offense the law provides for the imposition of a lighter punishment, the guilty person shall benefit therefrom.

Article 10. Right to Compensation

Every person has the right to be compensated in accordance with the law in the event he has been sentenced by a final judgment through a miscarriage of justice.

Article 11. Right to Privacy

1. Everyone has the right to have his honour respected and his dignity recognized.
2. No one may be the object of arbitrary or abusive interference with his private life, his family, his home, or his correspondence, or of unlawful attacks on his honour or reputation.
3. Everyone has the right to the protection of the law against such interference or attacks.

Article 12. Freedom of Conscience and Religion

1. Everyone has the right to freedom of conscience and of religion. This right includes freedom to maintain or to change one's religion or beliefs, and freedom to profess or disseminate one's religion or beliefs, either individually or together with others, in public or in private.

2. No one shall be subject to restrictions that might impair his freedom to maintain or to change his religion or beliefs.

3. Freedom to manifest one's religion and beliefs may be subject only to the limitations prescribed by law that are necessary to protect public safety, order, health, or morals, or the rights or freedoms of others.

4. Parents or guardians, as the case may be, have the right to provide for the religious and moral education of their children or wards that is in accord with their own convictions.

Article 13. Freedom of Thought and Expression

1. Everyone has the right to freedom of thought and expression. This right includes freedom to seek, receive, and impart information and ideas of all kinds, regardless of frontiers, either orally, in writing, in print, in the form of art, or through any other medium of one's choice.

2. The exercise of the right provided for in the foregoing paragraph shall not be subject to prior censorship but shall be subject to subsequent imposition of liability, which shall be expressly established by law to the extent necessary to ensure:

a. Respect for the rights or reputation of others; or
b. The protection of national security, public order, or public health or morals.

3. The right of expression may not be restricted by indirect methods or means, such as the abuse of government or private controls over newsprint, radio broadcasting frequencies, or equipment used in the dissemination of information, or by any other means tending to impede the communication and circulation of ideas and opinions.

4. Notwithstanding the provisions of paragraph 2 above, public entertainments may be subject by law to prior censorship for the sole purpose of regulating access to them for the moral protection of childhood and adolescence.

5. Any propaganda for war and any advocacy of national, racial, or religious hatred that constitute incitements to lawless violence or to any other similar action against any person or group of persons on any grounds including those of race, color, religion, language, or national origin shall be considered as offenses punishable by law.

Article 14. Right of Reply

1. Anyone injured by inaccurate or offensive statements or

ideas disseminated to the public in general by a legally regulated medium of communication has the right to reply or to make a correction using the same communications outlet, under such conditions as the law may establish.

2. The correction or reply shall not in any case remit other legal liabilities that may have been incurred.

3. For the effective protection of honour and reputation, every publisher, and every newspaper, motion picture, radio, and television company, shall have a person responsible who is not protected by immunities or special privileges.

Article 15. Right of Assembly

The right of peaceful assembly, without arms, is recognized. No restrictions may be placed on the exercise of this right other than those imposed in conformity with the law and necessary in a democratic society in the interest of national security, public safety or public order, or to protect public health or morals or the rights or freedom of others.

Article 16. Freedom of Association

1. Everyone has the right to associate freely for ideological, religious, political, economic, labor, social, cultural, sports, or other purposes.
2. The exercise of this right shall be subject only to such restrictions established by law as may be necessary in a democratic society, in the interest of national security, public safety or public order, or to protect public health or morals or the rights and freedoms of others.
3. The provisions of this article do not bar the imposition of legal restrictions, including even deprivation of the exercise of the right of association, on members of the armed forces and the police.

Article 17. Rights of the Family

1. The family is the natural and fundamental group unit of society and is entitled to protection by society and the state.

2. The right of men and women of marriageable age to marry and to raise a family shall be recognized, if they meet the conditions required by domestic laws, insofar as such conditions do not affect the principle of nondiscrimination established in this Convention.
3. No marriage shall be entered into without the free and full consent of the intending spouses.
4. The States Parties shall take appropriate steps to ensure the equality of rights and the adequate balancing of responsibilities of the spouses as to marriage, during marriage, and in the event of its dissolution. In case of dissolution, provision shall be made for the necessary protection of any children solely on the basis of their own best interests.
5. The law shall recognize equal rights for children born out of wedlock and those born in wedlock.

Article 18. Right to a Name

Every person has the right to a given name and to the surnames of his parents or that of one of them. The law shall regulate the manner in which this right shall be ensured for all, by the use of assumed names if necessary.

Article 19. Rights of the Child

Every minor child has the right to the measures of protection required by his condition as a minor on the part of his family, society, and the state.

Article 20. Right to Nationality

1. Every person has the right to a nationality.
2. Every person has the right to the nationality of the state in whose territory he was born if he does not have the right to any other nationality.
3. No one shall be arbitrarily deprived of his nationality or of the right to change it.

Article 21. Right to Property

1. Everyone has the right to the use and enjoyment of his property. The law may subordinate such use and enjoyment to the interest of society.
2. No one shall be deprived of his property except upon payment of just compensation, for reasons of public utility or social interest, and in the cases and according to the forms established by law."
3. Usury and any other form of exploitation of man by man shall be prohibited by law.

Article 22. Freedom of Movement and Residence

1. Every person lawfully in the territory of a State Party has the right to move about in it, and to reside in it subject to the provisions of the law.
2. Every person has the right lo leave any country freely, including his own.
3. The exercise of the foregoing rights may be restricted only pursuant to a law to the extent necessary in a democratic society to prevent crime or to protect national security, public safety, public order, public morals, public health, or the rights or freedoms of others.
4. The exercise of the rights recognized in paragraph 1 may also be restricted by law in designated zones for reasons of public interest.
5. No one can be expelled from the territory of the state of which he is a national or be deprived of the right to enter it.
6. An alien lawfully in the territory of a State Party to this Convention may be expelled from it only pursuant to a decision reached in accordance with law.
7. Every person has the right to seek and be granted asylum in a foreign territory, in accordance with the legislation of the state and international conventions, in the event he is being pursued for political offenses or related common crimes.
8. In no case may an alien be deported or returned to a

country, regardless of whether or not it is his country of origin, if in that country his right to life or personal freedom is in danger of being violated because of his race, nationality, religion, social status, or political opinions.

9. The collective expulsion of aliens is prohibited.

Article 23. Right to Participate in Government

1. Every citizen shall enjoy the following rights and opportunities:

a. To take part in the conduct of public affairs, directly or through freely chosen representatives;
b. To vote and to be elected in genuine periodic elections, which shall be by universal and equal suffrage and by secret ballot that guarantees the free expression of the will of the voters; and
c. To have access, under general conditions of equality, to the public service of his country.

2. The law may regulate the exercise of the rights and opportunities referred to in the preceding paragraph only on the basis of age, nationality, residence, language, education, civil and mental capacity, or sentencing by a competent court in criminal proceedings.

Article 24. Right to Equal Protection

All persons are equal before the law. Consequently, they are entitled, without discrimination, to equal protection of the law.

Article 25. Right to Judicial Protection

1. Everyone has the right to simple and prompt recourse, or any other effective recourse, to a competent court or tribunal for protection against acts that violate his fundamental rights recognized by the constitution or laws of the state concerned or by this Convention, even though such violation may have been committed by persons acting in the course of their official duties.

2. The States Parties undertake:

a. To ensure that any person claiming such remedy shall have his rights determined by the competent authority provided for by the legal system of the state;
b. To develop the possibilities of judicial remedy; and
c. To ensure that the competent authorities shall enforce such remedies when granted.

CHAPTER III—ECONOMIC, SOCIAL, AND CULTURAL RIGHTS

Article 26. Progressive Development

The States Parties undertake to adopt measures, both internally and through international cooperation, especially those of an economic and technical nature, with a view to achieving progressively, by legislation or other appropriate means, the full realization of the rights implicit in the economic, social, educational, scientific, and cultural standards set forth in the Charter of the Organization of American States as amended by the Protocol of Buenos Aires.

CHAPTER IV—SUSPENSION OF GUARANTEES, INTERPRETATION, AND APPLICATION

Article 27. Suspension of Guarantees

1. In time of war, public danger, or other emergency that threatens the independence or security of a State Party, it may take measures derogating from its obligations under the present Convention to the extent and for the period of time strictly required by the exigencies of the situation, provided that such measures are not inconsistent with its other obligations under international law and do not involve discrimination on the ground of race, color, sex, language, religion, or social origin.

2. The foregoing provision does not authorize any suspension of the following articles: Article 3 (Right to Juridical Personality), Article 4 (Right to Life), Article 5 (Right to Humane Treatment), Article 6 (Freedom from Slavery), Article 9 (Freedom from *Ex Post Facto* Laws), Article 12 (Freedom of Conscience and Religion), Article 17 (Rights of the Family), Article 18 (Right to a

Name), Article 19 (Rights of the Child), Article 20 (Right to Nationality), and Article 23 (Right to Participate in Government), or of the judicial guarantees essential for the protection of such rights.

3. Any State Party availing itself of the right of suspension shall immediately inform the other States Parties, through the Secretary General of the Organization of American States, of the provisions the application of which it has suspended, the reasons that gave rise to the suspension, and the date set for the termination of such suspension.

Article 28. Federal Clause

1. Where a State Party is constituted as a federal state, the national government of such State Party shall implement all the provisions of the Convention over whose subject matter it exercises legislative and judicial jurisdiction.

2. With respect to the provisions over whose subject matter the constituent units of the federal state have jurisdiction, the national government shall immediately take suitable measures, in accordance with its constitution and its laws, to the end that the competent authorities of the constituent units may adopt appropriate provisions for the fulfillment of this Convention.

3. Whenever two or more States Parties agree to form a federation or other type of association, they shall take care that the resulting federal or other compact contains the provisions necessary for continuing and rendering effective the standards of this Convention in the new state that is organized.

Article 29. Restrictions Regarding Interpretation

No provision of this Convention shall be interpreted as:

a. Permitting any State Party, group, or person to suppress the enjoyment or exercise of the rights and freedoms recognized in this Convention or to restrict them to a greater extent than is provided for herein;
b. Restricting the enjoyment or exercise of any right or freedom recognized by virtue of the laws of any State Party or by virtue of another convention to which one of the said states is a party;

c. Precluding other rights or guarantees that are inherent in the human personality or derived from representative democracy as a form of government; or
d. Excluding or limiting the effect that the American Declaration of the Rights and Duties of Man and other international acts of the same nature may have.

Article 30. Scope of Restrictions

The restrictions that, pursuant to this Convention, may be placed on the enjoyment or exercise of the rights or freedoms recognized herein may not be applied except in accordance with laws enacted for reasons of general interest and in accordance with the purpose for which such restrictions have been established.

Article 31. Recognition of Other Rights

Other rights and freedoms recognized in accordance with the procedures established in Articles 76 and 77 may be included in the system of protection of this Convention.

CHAPTER V—PERSONAL RESPONSIBILITIES

Article 32. Relationship between Duties and Rights

1. Every person has responsibilities to his family, his community, and mankind.
2. The rights of each person are limited by the rights of others, by the security of all, and by the just demands of the general welfare, in a democratic society.

Appendix-8
International Covenant on Civil and Political Rights

Adopted and opened for signature, ratification and accession by General Assembly resolution 2200A (XXI) of 16 December 1966, entry into force 23 March 1976, in accordance with Article 49

Preamble

The States Parties to the present Covenant,

Considering that, in accordance with the principles proclaimed in the Charter of the United Nations, recognition of the inherent dignity and of the equal and inalienable rights of all members of the human family is the foundation of freedom, justice and peace in the world,

Recognizing that these rights derive from the inherent dignity of the human person,

Recognizing that, in accordance with the Universal Declaration of Human Rights, the ideal of free human beings enjoying civil and political freedom and freedom from fear and want can only be achieved if conditions are created whereby everyone may enjoy his civil and political rights, as well as his economic, social and cultural rights,

Considering the obligation of States under the Charter of the United Nations to promote universal respect for, and observance of, human rights and freedoms,

Realizing that the individual, having duties to other individuals and to the community to which he belongs, is under a responsibility to strive for the promotion and observance of the rights recognized in the present Covenant,

Agree upon the following articles:

PART I

Article 1

1. All peoples have the right of self-determination. By virtue of that right they freely determine their political status and freely pursue their economic, social and cultural development.

2. All peoples may, for their own ends, freely dispose of their natural wealth and resources without prejudice to any obligations arising out of international economic co-operation, based upon the principle of mutual benefit, and international law. In no case may a people be deprived of its own means of subsistence.

3. The States Parties to the present Covenant, including those having responsibility for the administration of Non-Self-Governing and Trust Territories, shall promote the realization of the right of self-determination, and shall respect that right, in conformity with the provisions of the Charter of the United Nations.

PART II

Article 2

1. Each State Party to the present Covenant undertakes to respect and to ensure to all individuals within its territory and subject to its jurisdiction the rights recognized in the present Covenant, without distinction of any kind, such as race, colour, sex, language, religion, political or other opinion, national or social origin, property, birth or other status.

2. Where not already provided for by existing legislative or other measures, each State Party to the present Covenant undertakes to take the necessary steps, in accordance with its constitutional processes and with the provisions of the present Covenant, to adopt such laws or other measures as may be necessary to give effect to the rights recognized in the present Covenant.

3. Each State Party to the present Covenant undertakes:

(a) To ensure that any person whose rights or freedoms as herein recognized are violated shall have an effective remedy, notwithstanding that the violation has been committed by persons acting in an official capacity;
(b) To ensure that any person claiming such a remedy shall have his right thereto determined by competent judicial, administrative or legislative authorities, or by any other competent authority provided for by the legal system of the State, and to develop the possibilities of judicial remedy;
(c) To ensure that the competent authorities shall enforce such remedies when granted.

Article 3

The States Parties to the present Covenant undertake to ensure the equal right of men and women to the enjoyment of all civil and political rights set forth in the present Covenant.

Article 4

1. In time of public emergency which threatens the life of the nation and the existence of which is officially proclaimed, the States Parties to the present Covenant may take measures derogating from their obligations under the present Covenant to the extent strictly required by the exigencies of the situation, provided that such measures are not inconsistent with their other obligations under international law and do not involve discrimination solely on the ground of race, colour, sex, language, religion or social origin.

2. No derogation from articles 6, 7, 8 (paragraphs I and 2), 11, 15, 16 and 18 may be made under this provision.

3. Any State Party to the present Covenant availing itself of the right of derogation shall immediately inform the other States Parties to the present Covenant, through the intermediary of the Secretary-General of the United Nations, of the provisions from which it has derogated and of the reasons by which it was actuated. A further communication shall be made, through the same intermediary, on the date on which it terminates such derogation.

Article 5

1. Nothing in the present Covenant may be interpreted as implying for any State, group or person any right to engage in any activity or perform any act aimed at the destruction of any of the rights and freedoms recognized herein or at their limitation to a greater extent than is provided for in the present Covenant.

2. There shall be no restriction upon or derogation from any of the fundamental human rights recognized or existing in any State Party to the present Covenant pursuant to law, conventions, regulations or custom on the pretext that the present Covenant does not recognize such rights or that it recognizes them to a lesser extent.

PART III

Article 6

1. Every human being has the inherent right to life. This right shall be protected by law. No one shall be arbitrarily deprived of his life.

2. In countries which have not abolished the death penalty, sentence of death may be imposed only for the most serious crimes in accordance with the law in force at the time of the commission of the crime and not contrary to the provisions of the present Covenant and to the Convention on the Prevention and Punishment of the Crime of Genocide. This penalty can only be carried out pursuant to a final judgement rendered by a competent court.

3. When deprivation of life constitutes the crime of genocide, it is understood that nothing in this article shall authorize any State Party to the present Covenant to derogate in any way from any obligation assumed under the provisions of the Convention on the Prevention and Punishment of the Crime of Genocide.

4. Anyone sentenced to death shall have the right to seek pardon or commutation of the sentence. Amnesty, pardon or commutation of the sentence of death may be granted in all cases.

5. Sentence of death shall not be imposed for crimes committed by persons below eighteen years of age and shall not be carried out on pregnant women.

6. Nothing in this article shall be invoked to delay or to prevent the abolition of capital punishment by any State Party to the present Covenant.

Article 7

No one shall be subjected to torture or to cruel, inhuman or degrading treatment or punishment. In particular, no one shall be subjected without his free consent to medical or scientific experimentation.

Article 8

1. No one shall be held in slavery; slavery and the slave-trade in all their forms shall be prohibited.
2. No one shall be held in servitude.
3.
   (a) No one shall be required to perform forced or compulsory labour;
   (b) Paragraph 3(a) shall not be held to preclude, in countries where imprisonment with hard labour may be imposed as a punishment for a crime, the performance of hard labour in pursuance of a sentence to such punishment by a competent court;
   (c) For the purpose of this paragraph the term "forced or compulsory labour" shall not include:
      (i) Any work or service, not referred to in subparagraph (b), normally required of a person who is under detention in consequence of a lawful order of a court, or of a person during conditional release from such detention;
      (ii) Any service of a military character and, in countries where conscientious objection is recognized, any national service required by law of conscientious objectors;
      (iii) Any service exacted in cases of emergency or calamity threatening the life or well-being of the community;
      (iv) Any work or service which forms part of normal civil obligations.

Article 9

1. Everyone has the right to liberty and security of person. No one shall be subjected to arbitrary arrest or detention. No one shall be deprived of his liberty except on such grounds and in accordance with such procedure as are established by law.

2. Anyone who is arrested shall be informed, at the time of arrest, of the reasons for his arrest and shall be promptly informed of any charges against him.

3. Anyone arrested or detained on a criminal charge shall be brought promptly before a judge or other officer authorized by law to exercise judicial power and shall be entitled to trial within a reasonable time or to release. It shall not be the general rule that persons awaiting trial shall be detained in custody, but release may be subject to guarantees to appear for trial, at any other stage of the judicial proceedings, and, should occasion arise, for execution of the judgement.

4. Anyone who is deprived of his liberty by arrest or detention shall be entitled to take proceedings before a court, in order the that court may decide without delay on the lawfulness of his detention and order his release if the detention is not lawful.

5. Anyone who has been the victim of unlawful arrest or detention shall have an enforceable right to compensation.

Article 10

1. All persons deprived of their liberty shall be treated with humanity and with respect for the inherent dignity of the human person.

2.

(a) Accused persons shall, save in exceptional circumstances, be segregated from convicted persons and shall be subject to separate treatment appropriate to their status as unconvicted persons;

(b) Accused juvenile persons shall be separated from adults and brought as speedily as possible for adjudication.

3. The penitentiary system shall comprise treatment of prisoners the essential aim of which shall be their reformation and social rehabilitation. Juvenile offenders shall be segregated

from adults and be accorded treatment appropriate to their age and legal status.

Article 11

No one shall be imprisoned merely on the ground of inability to fulfil a contractual obligation.

Article 12

1. Everyone lawfully within the territory of a State shall, within that territory, have the right to liberty of movement and freedom to choose his residence.

2. Everyone shall be free to leave any country, including his own.

3. The above-mentioned rights shall not be subject to any restrictions except those which are provided by law, are necessary to protect national security, public order (ordre public), public health or morals or the rights and freedoms of others, and are consistent with the other rights recognized in the present Covenant.

4. No one shall be arbitrarily deprived of the right to enter his own country.

Article 13

An alien lawfully in the territory of a State Party to the present Covenant may be expelled therefrom only in pursuance of a decision reached in accordance with law and shall, except where compelling reasons of national security otherwise require, be allowed to submit the reasons against his expulsion and to have his case reviewed by, and be represented for the purpose before, the competent authority or a person or persons especially designated by the competent authority.

Article 14

1. All persons shall be equal before the courts and tribunals. In the determination of any criminal charge against him, or of his rights and obligations in a suit at law, everyone shall be entitled to a fair and public hearing by a competent, independent and

impartial tribunal established by law. The press and the public may be excluded from all or part of a trial for reasons of morals, public order (ordre public) or national security in a democratic society, or when the interest of the private lives of the parties so requires, or to the extent strictly necessary in the opinion of the court in special circumstances where publicity would prejudice the interests of justice; but any judgement rendered in a criminal case or in a suit at law shall be made public except where the interest of juvenile persons otherwise requires or the proceedings concern matrimonial disputes or the guardianship of children.

2. Everyone charged with a criminal offence shall have the right to be presumed innocent until proved guilty according to law.

3. In the determination of any criminal charge against him, everyone shall be entitled to the following minimum guarantees, in full equality:

(a) To be informed promptly and in detail in a language which he understands of the nature and cause of the charge against him;
(b) To have adequate time and facilities for the preparation of his defence and to communicate with counsel of his own choosing;
(c) To be tried without undue delay;
(d) To be tried in his presence, and to defend himself in person or through legal assistance of his own choosing; to be informed, if he does not have legal assistance, of this right; and to have legal assistance assigned to him, in any case where the interests of justice so require, and without payment by him in any such case if he does not have sufficient means to pay for it;
(e) To examine, or have examined, the witnesses against him and to obtain the attendance and examination of witnesses on his behalf under the same conditions as witnesses against him;
(f) To have the free assistance of an interpreter if he cannot understand or speak the language used in court;
(g) Not to be compelled to testify against himself or to confess guilt.

4. In the case of juvenile persons, the procedure shall be such as will take account of their age and the desirability of promoting their rehabilitation.

5. Everyone convicted of a crime shall have the right to his conviction and sentence being reviewed by a higher tribunal according to law.

6. When a person has by a final decision been convicted of a criminal offence and when subsequently his conviction has been reversed or he has been pardoned on the ground that a new or newly discovered fact shows conclusively that there has been a miscarriage of justice, the person who has suffered punishment as a result of such conviction shall be compensated according to law, unless it is proved that the non-disclosure of the unknown fact in time is wholly or partly attributable to him.

7. No one shall be liable to be tried or punished again for an offence for which he has already been finally convicted or acquitted in accordance with the law and penal procedure of each country.

Article 15

1. No one shall be held guilty of any criminal offence on account of any act or omission which did not constitute a criminal offence, under national or international law, at the time when it was committed. Nor shall a heavier penalty be imposed than the one that was applicable at the time when the criminal offence was committed. If, subsequent to the commission of the offence, provision is made by law for the imposition of the lighter penalty, the offender shall benefit thereby.

2. Nothing in this article shall prejudice the trial and punishment of any person for any act or omission which, at the time when it was committed, was criminal according to the general principles of law recognized by the community of nations.

Article 16

Everyone shall have the right to recognition everywhere as a person before the law.

Article 17

1. No one shall be subjected to arbitrary or unlawful interference with his privacy, family, home or correspondence, nor to unlawful attacks on his honour and reputation.
2. Everyone has the right to the protection of the law against such interference or attacks.

Article 18

1. Everyone shall have the right to freedom of thought, conscience and religion. This right shall include freedom to have or to adopt a religion or belief of his choice, and freedom, either individually or in community with others and in public or private, to manifest his religion or belief in worship, observance, practice and teaching.

2. No one shall be subject to coercion which would impair his freedom to have or to adopt a religion or belief of his choice.

3. Freedom to manifest one's religion or beliefs may be subject only to such limitations as are prescribed by law and are necessary to protect public safety, order, health, or morals or the fundamental rights and freedoms of others.

4. The States Parties to the present Covenant undertake to have respect for the liberty of parents and, when applicable, legal guardians to ensure the religious and moral education of their children in conformity with their own convictions.

Article 19

1. Everyone shall have the right to hold opinions without interference.

2. Everyone shall have the right to freedom of expression; this right shall include freedom to seek, receive and impart information and ideas of all kinds, regardless of frontiers, either orally, in writing or in print, in the form of art, or through any other media of his choice.

3. The exercise of the rights provided for in paragraph 2 of this article carries with it special duties and responsibilities. It may therefore be subject to certain restrictions, but these shall only be such as are provided by law and are necessary:

(a) For respect of the rights or reputations of others;
(b) For the protection of national security or of public order (ordre public), or of public health or morals.

Article 20

1. Any propaganda for war shall be prohibited by law.
2. Any advocacy of national, racial or religious hatred that constitutes incitement to discrimination, hostility or violence shall be prohibited by law.

Article 21

The right of peaceful assembly shall be recognized. No restrictions may be placed on the exercise of this right other than those imposed in conformity with the law and which are necessary in a democratic society in the interests of national security or public safety, public order (ordre public), the protection of public health or morals or the protection of the rights and freedoms of others.

Article 22

1. Everyone shall have the right to freedom of association with others, including the right to form and join trade unions for the protection of his interests.

2. No restrictions may be placed on the exercise of this right other than those which are prescribed by law and which are necessary in a democratic society in the interests of national security or public safety, public order (ordre public), the protection of public health or morals or the protection of the rights and freedoms of others. This article shall not prevent the imposition of lawful restrictions on members of the armed forces and of the police in their exercise of this right.

3. Nothing in this article shall authorize States Parties to the International Labour Organisation Convention of 1948 concerning Freedom of Association and Protection of the Right to Organize to take legislative measures which would prejudice, or to apply the law in such a manner as to prejudice, the guarantees provided for in that Convention.

Article 23

1. The family is the natural and fundamental group unit of society and is entitled to protection by society and the State.

2. The right of men and women of marriageable age to marry and to found a family shall be recognized.

3. No marriage shall be entered into without the free and full consent of the intending spouses.

4. States Parties to the present Covenant shall take appropriate steps to ensure equality of rights and responsibilities of spouses as to marriage, during marriage and at its dissolution. In the case of dissolution, provision shall be made for the necessary protection of any children.

Article 24

1. Every child shall have, without any discrimination as to race, colour, sex, language, religion, national or social origin, property or birth, the right to such measures of protection as are required by his status as a minor, on the part of his family, society and the State.

2. Every child shall be registered immediately after birth and shall have a name.

3. Every child has the right to acquire a nationality.

Article 25

Every citizen shall have the right and the opportunity, without any of the distinctions mentioned in article 2 and without unreasonable restrictions:

(a) To take part in the conduct of public affairs, directly or through freely chosen representatives;
(b) To vote and to be elected at genuine periodic elections which shall be by universal and equal suffrage and shall be held by secret ballot, guaranteeing the free expression of the will of the electors;
(c) To have access, on general terms of equality, to public service in his country.

Article 26

All persons are equal before the law and are entitled without any discrimination to the equal protection of the law. In this respect, the law shall prohibit any discrimination and guarantee to all persons equal and effective protection against discrimination on any ground such as race, colour, sex, language, religion, political or other opinion, national or social origin, property, birth or other status.

Article 27

In those States in which ethnic, religious or linguistic minorities exist, persons belonging to such minorities shall not be denied the right, in community with the other members of their group, to enjoy their own culture, to profess and practise their own religion, or to use their own language.

Appendix-9

International Covenant on Economic, Social and Cultural Rights

Adopted and opened for signature, ratification and accession by General Assembly resolution 2200A (XXI) of 16 December 1966 entry into force 3 January 1976, in accordance with article 27

Preamble

The States Parties to the present Covenant,

Considering that, in accordance with the principles proclaimed in the Charter of the United Nations, recognition of the inherent dignity and of the equal and inalienable rights of all members of the human family is the foundation of freedom, justice and peace in the world,

Recognizing that these rights derive from the inherent dignity of the human person,

Recognizing that, in accordance with the Universal Declaration of Human Rights, the ideal of free human beings enjoying freedom from fear and want can only be achieved if conditions are created whereby everyone may enjoy his economic, social and cultural rights, as well as his civil and political rights,

Considering the obligation of States under the Charter of the United Nations to promote universal respect for, and observance of, human rights and freedoms,

Realizing that the individual, having duties to other individuals and to the community to which he belongs, is under a responsibility to strive for the promotion and observance of the rights recognized in the present Covenant,

Agree upon the following articles:

PART I

Article 1

1. All peoples have the right of self-determination. By virtue of that right they freely determine their political status and freely pursue their economic, social and cultural development.

2. All peoples may, for their own ends, freely dispose of their natural wealth and resources without prejudice to any obligations arising out of international economic co-operation, based upon the principle of mutual benefit, and international law. In no case may a people be deprived of its own means of subsistence.

3. The States Parties to the present Covenant, including those having responsibility for the administration of Non-Self-Governing and Trust Territories, shall promote the realization of the right of self-determination, and shall respect that right, in conformity with the provisions of the Charter of the United Nations.

PART II

Article 2

1. Each State Party to the present Covenant undertakes to take steps, individually and through international assistance and co-operation, especially economic and technical, to the maximum of its available resources, with a view to achieving progressively the full realization of the rights recognized in the present Covenant by all appropriate means, including particularly the adoption of legislative measures.

2. The States Parties to the present Covenant undertake to guarantee that the rights enunciated in the present Covenant will be exercised without discrimination of any kind as to race, colour, sex, language, religion, political or other opinion, national or social origin, property, birth or other status.

3. Developing countries, with due regard to human rights and their national economy, may determine to what extent they would guarantee the economic rights recognized in the present Covenant to non-nationals.

Article 3

The States Parties to the present Covenant undertake to ensure the equal right of men and women to the enjoyment of all economic, social and cultural rights set forth in the present Covenant.

Article 4

The States Parties to the present Covenant recognize that, in the enjoyment of those rights provided by the State in conformity with the present Covenant, the State may subject such rights only to such limitations as are determined by law only in so far as this may be compatible with the nature of these rights and solely for the purpose of promoting the general welfare in a democratic society.

Article 5

1. Nothing in the present Covenant may be interpreted as implying for any State, group or person any right to engage in any activity or to perform any act aimed at the destruction of any of the rights or freedoms recognized herein, or at their limitation to a greater extent than is provided for in the present Covenant.

2. No restriction upon or derogation from any of the fundamental human rights recognized or existing in any country in virtue of law, conventions, regulations or custom shall be admitted on the pretext that the present Covenant does not recognize such rights or that it recognizes them to a lesser extent.

PART III

Article 6

1. The States Parties to the present Covenant recognize the right to work, which includes the right of everyone to the opportunity to gain his living by work which he freely chooses or accepts, and will take appropriate steps to safeguard this right.

2. The steps to be taken by a State Party to the present Covenant to achieve the full realization of this right shall include technical and vocational guidance and training programmes, policies and techniques to achieve steady economic, social and cultural development and full and productive employment under conditions safeguarding fundamental political and economic freedoms to the individual.

Article 7

The States Parties to the present Covenant recognize the right of everyone to the enjoyment of just and favourable conditions of work which ensure, in particular:

(a) Remuneration which provides all workers, as a minimum, with:
   (i) Fair wages and equal remuneration for work of equal value without distinction of any kind, in particular women being guaranteed conditions of work not inferior to those enjoyed by men, with equal pay for equal work;
   (ii) A decent living for themselves and their families in accordance with the provisions of the present Covenant;

(b) Safe and healthy working conditions;

(c) Equal opportunity for everyone to be promoted in his employment to an appropriate higher level, subject to no considerations other than those of seniority and competence;

(d) Rest, leisure and reasonable limitation of working hours and periodic holidays with pay, as well as remuneration for public holidays

Article 8

1. The States Parties to the present Covenant undertake to ensure:
   (a) The right of everyone to form trade unions and join the trade union of his choice, subject only to the rules of the organization concerned, for the promotion and protection of his economic and social

interests. No restrictions may be placed on the exercise of this right other than those prescribed by law and which are necessary in a democratic society in the interests of national security or public order or for the protection of the rights and freedoms of others;

(b) The right of trade unions to establish national federations or confederations and the right of the latter to form or join international trade-union organizations;

(c) The right of trade unions to function freely subject to no limitations other than those prescribed by law and which are necessary in a democratic society in the interests of national security or public order or for the protection of the rights and freedoms of others;

(d) The right to strike, provided that it is exercised in conformity with the laws of the particular country.

2. This article shall not prevent the imposition of lawful restrictions on the exercise of these rights by members of the armed forces or of the police or of the administration of the State.
3. Nothing in this article shall authorize States Parties to the International Labour Organisation Convention of 1948 concerning Freedom of Association and Protection of the Right to Organize to take legislative measures which would prejudice, or apply the law in such a manner as would prejudice, the guarantees provided for in that Convention.

Article 9

The States Parties to the present Covenant recognize the right of everyone to social security, including social insurance.

Article 10

The States Parties to the present Covenant recognize that:

1. The widest possible protection and assistance should be accorded to the family, which is the natural and

fundamental group unit of society, particularly for its establishment and while it is responsible for the care and education of dependent children. Marriage must be entered into with the free consent of the intending spouses.

2. Special protection should be accorded to mothers during a reasonable period before and after childbirth. During such period working mothers should be accorded paid leave or leave with adequate social security benefits.
3. Special measures of protection and assistance should be taken on behalf of all children and young persons without any discrimination for reasons of parentage or other conditions. Children and young persons should be protected from economic and social exploitation. Their employment in work harmful to their morals or health or dangerous to life or likely to hamper their normal development should be punishable by law. States should also set age limits below which the paid employment of child labour should be prohibited and punishable by law.

Article 11

1. The States Parties to the present Covenant recognize the right of everyone to an adequate standard of living for himself and his family, including adequate food, clothing and housing, and to the continuous improvement of living conditions. The States Parties will take appropriate steps to ensure the realization of this right, recognizing to this effect the essential importance of international co-operation based on free consent.

2. The States Parties to the present Covenant, recognizing the fundamental right of everyone to be free from hunger, shall take, individually and through international co-operation, the measures, including specific programmes, which are needed:

(a) To improve methods of production, conservation and distribution of food by making full use of technical and scientific knowledge, by disseminating knowledge of the principles of nutrition and by developing or reforming agrarian systems in such a way as to achieve the most efficient development and utilization of natural resources;

(b) Taking into account the problems of both food-importing and food-exporting countries, to ensure an equitable distribution of world food supplies in relation to need.

Article 12

1. The States Parties to the present Covenant recognize the right of everyone to the enjoyment of the highest attainable standard of physical and mental health.

2. The steps to be taken by the States Parties to the present Covenant to achieve the full realization of this right shall include those necessary for:

(a) The provision for the reduction of the stillbirth-rate and of infant mortality and for the healthy development of the child;
(b) The improvement of all aspects of environmental and industrial hygiene;
(c) The prevention, treatment and control of epidemic, endemic, occupational and other diseases;
(d) The creation of conditions which would assure to all medical service and medical attention in the event of sickness.

Article 13

1. The States Parties to the present Covenant recognize the right of everyone to education. They agree that education shall be directed to the full development of the human personality and the sense of its dignity, and shall strengthen the respect for human rights and fundamental freedoms. They further agree that education shall enable all persons to participate effectively in a free society, promote understanding, tolerance and friendship among all nations and all racial, ethnic or religious groups, and further the activities of the United Nations for the maintenance of peace.

2. The States Parties to the present Covenant recognize that,

with a view to achieving the full realization of this right:

(a) Primary education shall be compulsory and available free to all;
(b) Secondary education in its different forms, including technical and vocational secondary education, shall be made generally available and accessible to all by every appropriate means, and in particular by the progressive introduction of free education;
(c) Higher education shall be made equally accessible to all, on the basis of capacity, by every appropriate means, and in particular by the progressive introduction of free education;
(d) Fundamental education shall be encouraged or intensified as far as possible for those persons who have not received or completed the whole period of their primary education;
(e) The development of a system of schools at all levels shall be actively pursued, an adequate fellowship system shall be established, and the material conditions of teaching staff shall be continuously improved.

3. The States Parties to the present Covenant undertake to have respect for the liberty of parents and, when applicable, legal guardians to choose for their children schools, other than those established by the public authorities, which conform to such minimum educational standards as may be laid down or approved by the State and to ensure the religious and moral education of their children in conformity with their own convictions.

4. No part of this article shall be construed so as to interfere with the liberty of individuals and bodies to establish and direct educational institutions, subject always to the observance of the principles set forth in paragraph I of this article and to the requirement that the education given in such institutions shall conform to such minimum standards as may be laid down by the State.

Article 14

Each State Party to the present Covenant which, at the time of becoming a Party, has not been able to secure in its metropolitan territory or other territories under its jurisdiction compulsory primary education, free of charge, undertakes, within two years, to work out and adopt a detailed plan of action for the progressive implementation, within a reasonable number of years, to be fixed in the plan, of the principle of compulsory education free of charge for all.

Article 15

1. The States Parties to the present Covenant recognize the right of everyone:
   (a) To take part in cultural life;
   (b) To enjoy the benefits of scientific progress and its applications;
   (c) To benefit from the protection of the moral and material interests resulting from any scientific, literary or artistic production of which he is the author.
2. The steps to be taken by the States Parties to the present Covenant to achieve the full realization of this right shall include those necessary for the conservation, the development and the diffusion of science and culture.
3. The States Parties to the present Covenant undertake to respect the freedom indispensable for scientific research and creative activity.
4. The States Parties to the present Covenant recognize the benefits to be derived from the encouragement and development of international contacts and co-operation in the scientific and cultural fields.

Bibliography

Authoritative and authentic books authored by Dr. James Vadackumchery

Police Criminology and Crimes, *(ISBN: 81-7835-094-7)* Kalpaz Publications, Delhi, 2002.

Society, Police and Crimes: Tasks and Challenges, *(ISBN: 81-7341-266-0),* Indian Publishers' Distributors, Delhi, 2002.

Policing the Police: A Nation's Cry, *(ISBN:81-7479-060-81),* Kaveri Books, Delhi, 2003.

Indian Police and Nexus Crime, *(ISBN: 81-7835-037-8),* Kalpaz Publications, Delhi, 2002.

Crime and Society: Current Issues and Trends, *(ISBN: 81-7648-024-X),* A.P.H. Publishing Corporation, Delhi, 1999.

Crime, Police and Correction, *(ISBN: 81-7024-939-2),* A.P.H. Publishing Corporation, Delhi, 1998.

Indian Police and Miscarriage of Justice, *(ISBN: 81-7024-792-6),* A.P.H. Publishing Corporation, Delhi, 1997.

Police, Victim and Victim Justice, *(ISBN: 81-7479-043-8),* Kaveri Books. Delhi, 2001.

Police, Women and Gender Justice, *(ISBN: 81-7648-137-8),* A.P.H. Publishing Corporation, Delhi, 2000.

The Police and Delinquency in India, *(ISBN: 81-7024-725-X),* A.P.H. Publishing Corporation, Delhi, 1996.

Misguiding Philosophies and Millennium Police, *(ISBN: 81-7341-278-2),* Indian Publishers' Distributors, Delhi, 2003.

Sociology of Policing India: 2000 and Beyond, *(ISBN: 81-7341-279-0),* Indian Publishers' Distributors, Delhi, 2003.

Wounded Justice and the Story of Indian Police, *(ISBN: 81-7479-045-4),* Kaveri Books, Delhi, 2001.

Indian Police and Equal Justice Under Law, *(ISBN: 81-7648-066-5),* A.P.H. Publishing Corporation, Delhi, 1999.

The Police, the Court and Injustice, *(ISBN: 81-7024-806-X),* A.P.H. Publishing Corporation, Delhi, 1997.

Human Behaviour and Law Enforcement, *(ISBN: 81-7024-688-1),* Ashish Publishing House, Delhi, 1995.

Crime, Law and Police Science, *(ISBN: 81-7022-995-2),* (Second edition), Concept Publishing Company, Delhi, 2003.

Police Morality, *(ISBN: 81-7835-038-6),* Kalpaz Publications, Delhi, 2001.

Policing the Largest Democracy: 50 Years and After, *(ISBN: 81-7024-979-1),* A.P.H. Publishing Corporation, Delhi, 1998.

Human Rights and the Police in India, *(ISBN: 81-7024-722-5),* A.P.H. Publishing Corporation, Delhi, 1996.

Police Enforcement Crimes and Injustice, *(ISBN: 81-212-0471-5),* Gyan Publishing House, Delhi, 2001.

Departmental Inquiries and Injustice, *(ISBN: 81-7024-899-X),* A.P.H. Publishing Corporation, Delhi, 1997.

Indian Police 2001: What Went Wrong Here? *(ISBN: 81-7024-967-8),* A.P.H. Publishing Corporation, Delhi, 1998.

Police Leadership: The Inside Story, *(ISBN: 81-7648-120-3),* A.P.H. Publishing Corporation, Delhi, 1999.

National Police Commission: Issues for Rethinking, *(ISBN: 81-7024-826-4),* A.P.H. Publishing Corporation, Delhi, 1998.

The Police, The Accused and Criminal Injustice, *(ISBN: 91-7024-806-X),* A.P.H. Publishing Corporation, Delhi, 1997.

Management Thoughts on Police Administration, *(ISBN: 81-7024-914-7),* A.P.H. Publishing Corporation, Delhi, 1998.

Police Interrogation: DOs which the Police do not DO, *(ISBN: 81-7024-974-0),* A.P.H. Publishing Corporation, Delhi, 1998.

Why I am not a Policeman, *(ISBN: 81-7479-042-X),* Kaveri Books, Delhi, 2001.

Criminology and Penology, Kairali Books International, Trivandrum, 1983.

Bankers' Safety: Methods and Techniques, *(ISBN: 81-7022-937-5),* (Second edition), Concept Publishing Company, Delhi, 2002.

Professional Police Witness Interviewing, *(ISBN: 81-7648-061-4),* A.P.H. Publishing Corporation, Delhi, 1999.

Human Relations in Banking: How to get along better with people?, Santha Publishing House, Cochin, 1988.

Public Relations at the Cutting Edge Level: Case-study materials, National, Delhi, 1985

Human Rights Friendly Police: A Myth or Reality?, *(ISBN: 81-7648-150-5),* A.P.H. Publishing Corporation, Delhi, 2000.

Police and Human Rights,(ed.), Kerala Police Officers' Association, Thiruvananthapuram, 1994.

Police and the Society, Kairali Books International, Trivandrum, 1985.

Human Values and Police Behaviour, Bureau of Police Research and Development, Ministry of Home Affairs, Government of India, 2000.

Child Labour (Malayalam), State Literacy Mission, Thiruvananthapuram, 2000.

Juvenile Delinquency (Malayalam), State Literacy Mission, Thiruvananthapuram, 2000.

United Nations and Indian Mysticism: Parallels on Human Rights and Police, *(ISBN: 81-7022-664-2),* Concept Publishing Company, Delhi, 2002.

India's Supreme Court and Police: Consensus and Conflicts, *(ISBN: 81-7341-301-0),* Indian Publishers' Distributors, Delhi, 2003.

Road Users' Guide (Malayalam), Assistant Motor Vehicle Inspectors' Association, Ernakulam, 1997.

Values and God's Commandments, (Malayalam) Catechetical Centre, Thalassery, 1995.

Acquittals in Administration of Justice, Ph.D. Thesis, Kerala University, (mimeo), Thiruvananthapuram, 1983.

Activism, Accountability and Justice *(ISBN: 81-7341-4324-X),* Indian Publishers' Distributors, Delhi, 2004.

The Police, The People and Criminal Justice, *(ISBN: 81-7024-862-9),* A.P.H. Publishing Corporation, Delhi, 1999.

Police and the People (Translation of the title: Public Relations at the Cutting Edge Level: Case-study materials by Prof. C.K. Muhammed Ummer), The State Institute of Language, Kerala, Thiruvananthapuram, 2000.

Third Millennium Police: Take off Trends in India, *(ISBN: 81-7648-062-2),* A.P.H. Publishing Corporation, Delhi, 1999.

The Justice Less Administered, *(ISBN: 81-7341-380-0),* Indian Publishers' Distributors, Delhi, 2005.

Goodbye, Police: Memoirs of a Criminologist, *(ISBN: 81-7341-390-8),* Indian Publishers' Distributors, Delhi, 2005.

Judiciary and Juvinile Justice, *(ISBN: 81-7341-389-4),* Indian Publishers' Distributors, Delhi, 2005.

The Unseen Phases of Crimes, (Malayalam), *(ISBN: 81-909360-1-8)*, H&C Publishing House, Trissur 2009.

The Complete Reference: Methodology of Research in Criminology Law Justice and Correction (Vol. I), *(ISBN: 81-7341-414-8)*, Indian Publishers' Distributors, Delhi, 2007.

The Complete Reference: Methodology of Research in Criminology Law Justice and Correction (Vol. II), *(ISBN: 81-7341-448-0)*, Indian Publishers' Distributors, Delhi, 2010.

The Complete Reference: Methodology of Research in Criminology Law Justice and Correction (Vol. III), *(ISBN: 81-7341-449-7)*, Indian Publishers' Distributors, Delhi, 2010.

United Nations and Prison Justice: The Complete Revision of the Standard Minimum Rules for the Treatment of Prisoners, (ISBN: 978-818-069-9610), Concept Publishing Company (Pvt.) Ltd., New Delhi, 2014.

Contemporary Indian Criminology (*ISBN: 978-93-5125-100-2*), Concept Publishing Company (Pvt.) Ltd., New Delhi, 2015.

Management Thoughts for Justice Administration, (*ISBN: 13-978-81-7268-233-0 (HB)*), Logos Press, New Delhi, 2013.

U.N. Universal Declaration of Human Rights and Criminal Justice: The Total Revision (*ISBN: 13-978-81-8069-912-2*) Concept Publishing Company (Pvt.) Ltd., New Delhi, 2012.

Kuttakrithyangalile Kazhukanmar, (Malayalam) (*ISBN: 978-81-300-1598-9*), Poorna Publications, Kozhikode, 2014.

Kolayalikalude Pinnampuram, (Malayalam) (*ISBN: 81-7705-321-0*) Prabhath Book House, Thiruvananthapuram, 2015.

Kuttakrithyangalude Baliyadukal, (Malayalam) Poorna Publications, Kozhikode [To be released soon].

Singapooril Ninnoru Kuttapathram, (Malayalam) Prabhath Book House, Thiruvananthapuram, 2017.

Human Rights: A Fair Trial of United Nations (Vol. I) Concept Publishing Company (Pvt.) Ltd., New Delhi, 2018.

Human Rights: A Fair Trial of United Nations (Vol. II) Concept Publishing Company (Pvt.) Ltd., New Delhi, 2018.

Advanced Criminology or The WHY of Crimes, Concept Publishing Company (Pvt.) Ltd., New Delhi, 2018.

Advanced Criminology: The HOW of Crime Control and Reduction (Under Publication).

Index

Equal remuneration, 26, 35, 156–58, 160, 162, 195, 197, 244, 266, 305

Ethnic conflict, 33, 187, 206, 261, 270

Neo-colonialism, 34, 228, 262
Pre-trial detention, 17, 55